Home-Cooking Sampler

Home-Cooking Sampler

FAMILY FAVORITES FROM

A TO Z

Peggy K. Glass

PRENTICE HALL PRESS

New York   London   Toronto   Sydney   Tokyo

Prentice Hall Press
Gulf + Western Building
One Gulf + Western Plaza
New York, New York 10023

Copyright © 1989 by Peggy K. Glass

PRENTICE HALL PRESS and colophon are registered
trademarks of Simon & Schuster Inc.

Library of Congress Cataloging-in-Publication Data

Glass, Peggy K.
Home-cooking sampler: family favorites from A to Z/Peggy K.
Glass. —1st ed.
p.   cm.
Includes index.
ISBN 0-13-301920-9: $19.95
1. Cookery, American.   I. Title.
TX715.G55415 1988
641.5973—dc19   88-7571
                                  CIP
Designed by J. C. Suarès, Laurence Alexander, and Virginia Pope-Boehling

Manufactured in the United States of America

10 9 8 7 6 5 4 3 2 1

First Edition

To my children,
Adam, Rebecca, and Noah,
with love

Acknowledgments

~~~~~~~~~~~~~~~~~~~~

I've loved remembering events, places, and people through food. A book like *Home-Cooking Sampler* is built on those happy memories and good times. For that, I'm grateful to my parents, Jane and Burton Kohn, and to my family and many Indianapolis friends, some mentioned in the book and others just in my heart.

Over the years my friends have shared stories about legendary stuffed cabbages, custards gone to ruin, and the rice puddings of their childhoods. And they've shared their family favorites: Susan's pecan pie, Gail's baked beans and lasagna, and Linda's breads. I've taxed my friendships with Cindy and Deborah debating the choice of melted chocolate or cocoa in cakes, ground beef or lamb in shepherd's pie, Manhattan red or New England white clam chowder, baking powder versus baking soda leavening, and the merits of pastry bags. In the process of testing recipes for the book, my students, neighbors, and my children's teachers and soccer teams have been the recipients of many dubious treasures. My family has eaten and critiqued more chocolate cakes, barbequed spareribs, carrot cakes, and fried chicken than they'd ever dreamed of or hoped for. When at last they hollered "enough chocolate cake!" I knew it was time to wrap up the book.

Authors need daily encouragement and support. I'm indebted to my husband, Len, for many things: for his pride in my work; for his clarity and kindness in reading the manuscript; and for his unending patience and good humor. Many thanks to my sister Laurie Kohn Steele and my friend Lorie Hamermesh for their love and generosity; and to Donna and Laurie and all my friends in Newton who've tasted my failures as well as successes and have forgiven me both.

The book exists in part because of Madeleine Kamman's teaching, which helped me understand and love the creation of good food.

My thanks to Judith Weber, who took a chance, and directed me through the literary process with wisdom and sensitivity; to Toula Polygalaktos and Marilyn Abraham, who filled the void with their supportive collaboration; and to Susan Friedland, whose experience and professional rigor made me think long and hard to make the book better and still mine.

—Peggy K. Glass

Contents

x

R

S

T

Introduction

~~~~~~~~~~~~~~~~~~~~~

For many years, I've been busy at home writing food magazine articles; running my own cooking school; teaching; and raising children, goats, bees, a dog, and a garden. Family life and cooking are important, satisfying, and closely related parts of my life. Family food is at the heart of home. The activities in the kitchen produce more than food. The wonderful aromas, shared activity, and tastes bring back happy memories for me and make new ones that will last a lifetime for my children. They share the fun of creation, develop a broader taste and appreciation of food, and take pride in their ability to master even simple tasks like husking corn, kneading bread, whipping cream, and assembling pizza.

In my cooking classes, many of my students wanted to know what I made for my family every day. The pâtés, butter sauces, and French pastries were fine for "wowing" their guests, but they were especially interested in foods that would please their families on a daily basis. For family gatherings, traditional holidays, or children's tastes, they wanted the joy, simplicity, and predictability of home cooking.

Home-Cooking Sampler developed as a way of preserving and sharing our family favorites, but I also saw the book as a teaching tool to update classic recipes. I've tried to clarify and explain important techniques, to alert the cook to critical steps, and to discuss the importance of quality ingredients because I believe that with an understanding of cooking techniques and ingredients, a basic recipe can be embellished or changed by varying seasonal ingredients and accommodating family preferences.

Home-Cooking Sampler is meant to be a browsing book as well as a practical collection of favorites. The recipes and text are listed alphabetically by preparation and by how we know the dish: Fried Chicken, Baked Alaska, Grilled Cheese, Mashed Potatoes, Corned Beef Hash, Caesar Salad. There is an index by specific food categories (Apples, Breads, Cakes, Chicken, Potatoes, Salads). For practical cooking purposes, you might find it more useful to refer to the index for particular recipes. The alphabetic sampler seems a friendly and easy-to-use format, in keeping with familiar and traditional recipes. While looking through the book, I hope the recipes and stories will conjure up happy memories and be an impetus for you to treat family and friends to the best food . . . homemade.

A NOTE ON INGREDIENTS AND TECHNIQUES

Flour

All-purpose flour is used throughout the book unless otherwise stated.

For baking bread, read the panel on the side of all-purpose flours to find one with 11 or 12 grams of protein per cup of flour. It's the gluten protein working with the yeast that provides the elasticity and aeration for great bread.

In pastry and cake baking, look for an all-purpose flour with 9 to 11 grams of protein per cup. To make cake flour from all-purpose flour, take out 2 tablespoons of flour per cup and substitute 2 tablespoons cornstarch.

Before measuring flour, aerate it by stirring it with a spoon to fluff it up.

Fats

Unsalted butter is specified for all baking and pastry recipes because of its superior taste. In all other recipes, salted butter or unsalted butter may be used unless otherwise suggested. Salted butter is specified in recipes where browning is desirable (e.g., Chicken Almondine). Store butter well wrapped to prevent off-tastes from other foods. Freeze butter to keep it fresh longer.

Emulsified solid vegetable shortening has a role in improving the texture of pie crusts, cakes, and frostings. In pie crusts, butter combined with shortening produces a crust that has the butter flavor but also a lighter, flakier texture. Shortening gives cakes and frostings a light texture, but little taste.

Oil produces moist cakes that keep well but are denser in texture. The burning point of oil is higher than that of butter, so for sautéing, oil or a combination of butter (for flavor) and oil (for stability) is often used. Oil is used in dishes that may be served chilled (e.g., Eggplant Relish, Stuffed Peppers) since it doesn't congeal.

Yeast

Yeast is a living organism that feeds on sugar and produces carbon dioxide bubbles and alcohol. The carbon dioxide bubbles are trapped in the gluten protein strands and cause the dough to rise. The alcohol is burned off when the bread bakes. In wine making, the alcohol remains.

Newly developed strains of yeast can make dough rise in half the time, which is a help if you aren't good at planning ahead.

Yeast loves the elastic gluten protein of wheat flour. In the presence of water, the yeast aerates and raises the dough. So, when buying flour to make yeast bread, look on the side panels of the flour packages and compare. Buy a flour that has a high percentage of protein (gluten) per cup, or one that says "bread flour" or "hard winter wheat."

Yeast is slowed down by cold, by salt, by very rich (butter) or very sweet (sugar) coffee cake dough, and by heavier flours (whole wheat), or those with weak gluten protein (rye). Whole wheat and rye breads are usually mixed with white flour for a lighter loaf.

Yeast is killed either by mixing it with liquids that are too hot or, eventually, by hot ovens. Anxious children are relieved to know they aren't eating a living thing!

Proofing the yeast simply means making sure it's alive. When you add active dry yeast to warm water or liquid (105 to 115 degrees) and give it a pinch of sugar to feed on, it will spring to life from the cold of the refrigerator where it should be stored, and it will begin to bubble and increase in size in just a few minutes. You'll know your bread will rise nicely when you've seen this activity. If the yeast does nothing, don't proceed or your efforts will be futile. Use a newer, fresher batch of yeast. The envelope or jar should be dated.

For a light loaf of bread, knead the dough until smooth but not sticky. Don't add so much flour that the dough becomes dry and unyielding. Greasing your hands may help prevent the dough from sticking to them.

Most recipe suggestions for getting the dough to "rise until double" don't work for me. I bake bread on a rainy day and there's no sunny window; when the heater's not in use, there's no warm register to rest the pans on; my pilotless ignition stovetop and electric oven provide no source of warmth. I get the dough to rise quickly by putting the towel-draped bowl of dough over a small bowl or saucepan with a few inches of hot water. The warm steam rises to warm the dough just enough to activate the yeast but not enough to kill it. The first rising takes about an hour and the second about 30 minutes with regular active dry yeast.

Broth and Stock

For sauces, soups, and stews, there is nothing better than homemade stock with its protein-rich, natural-gelatin goodness. A good stock is made with meaty bones, water, wine, aromatics, and just a pinch of salt. A long slow cooking extracts the gelatin protein from the bones and cartilage. Unfortunately, rich stocks aren't always tucked away in the freezer, so canned broth must be substituted. Most canned broths are overwhelmed with salt and need to be diluted by half with water when used in place of stock.

In recipes where it is preferred, stock is listed as the first ingredient with an alternative canned broth and water measurement following.

Cream

Heavy cream can be boiled and reduced by nearly half to make a thickened sauce before it "breaks." Even added as an enrichment to an acid base, cream has enough butterfat to prevent the soup or sauce from curdling. Sour cream can also be boiled in a sauce with no problem.

When a recipe calls for heavy cream or sour cream, do not substitute less rich cream (light cream or half-and-half), milk, buttermilk, or yogurt without understanding that without a starch stabilizer like flour the sauce or soup will curdle if boiled. The sauce or soup may be heated but not to the boiling point.

If you've ever over whipped cream to the point of butter, stir in a little extra fluid cream and the whipped cream will loosen up.

Baking Tips

Opening the oven door causes a big heat loss and drop in temperature so that the heating element goes on immediately to compensate. Consequently, cookies, biscuits, or any small pastries that bake for a short time often overbrown on the bottom. In these recipes, I preheat the oven 25 degrees higher than the baking temperature and immediately reduce the temperature by 25 degrees when I put the cookies, biscuits, or pastries in the oven. Glass-windowed ovens were a brilliant idea for those eager to check the progress of their baking.

Bake on the lower racks of the oven for good bottom browning (pies and tarts), and on the middle or upper racks for better top browning (casseroles, cakes, cookies).

In baking, most pans and baking sheets are greased with shortening since the taste doesn't come through and the burning point of shortening is higher than that of butter. Dust cake pans lightly with flour on the bottom, shake to cover evenly, and turn the pan over to shake out any excess flour.

Baking Cakes

If using glass baking pans, reduce the oven temperature by 25 degrees. Like consistencies and temperatures combine and mix best in batters.

Bring eggs and liquid to room temperature before mixing so the eggs beat up lighter and the liquid won't break down the emulsified and thickened batter.

In most recipes, the time to beat the batter is when you're creaming the butter, sugar, and eggs. When adding dry ingredients, add them on low speed and mix until combined. Overbeaten cakes tend to develop holes.

Cakes are finished baking when they begin to pull away from the sides of the pan, when they're a nice golden color, when a toothpick inserted in the center comes out clean, when the center of the cake springs back if gently pressed, and sometimes, when the cake sounds quiet, letting you know that enough water has evaporated from the batter.

Frosting protects cakes from the air and from drying out. Once the cake has been cut, cover the cut surface with a piece of wax paper or plastic wrap to keep the cake fresh.

Baking Pies

Chilling pie dough is important for a tender crust. Gluten, the elastic property of flour protein, develops when water is added to the dough. Overworking the dough will develop the gluten in flour, so use a gentle hand or a restrained processor. A pie crust that uses sour cream or butter or egg yolks to hold it together will be more tender than one bound with water. Refrigerating the dough and letting it rest will relax the gluten, making it easier to roll out and less likely to shrink when prebaked in the oven.

Reheat pies and crisp the bottom crust by placing on the bottom rack of a preheated 400-degree oven. Cover the top loosely with foil and bake 10 to 15 minutes.

For warming frozen pastries, place the cookies or rolls or biscuits on a baking sheet. Place in a *cold* oven and set to bake at 300 degrees. In 10 to 15 minutes, they'll be warm and fresh.

Angel Food

The food of angels, light as a cloud: *my* memories are of inverted angel food cake pans on glass Coke bottles. The glass bottles seem nearly extinct, but my love of angel food cakes goes on, especially when I have a number of frozen egg whites left over from sauces and custards. My children sometimes call this a marshmallow cake—sweet, light, and springy. It works well as a base for strawberry shortcake since it soaks up the sweetened strawberry juice.

Remember *not* to grease the angel food cake pan or the cake will have an impossible time clinging to the slippery walls. Egg whites won't whip to a glossy meringue if there's a speck of fat or egg yolk, so be sure to wash and dry the mixing bowl to eliminate any grease, and be careful in separating the eggs.

Serves 10

1 cup minus 2 tablespoons (⅞ cup) flour

½ cup confectioners' sugar

1½ cups egg whites (approximately 12), at room temperature

1 teaspoon cream of tartar

½ teaspoon salt

1 tablespoon water

1 teaspoon vanilla extract

1 cup superfine granulated sugar

2 drops almond extract (optional)

continued on next page

- Prepare a 10-inch angel food cake pan with a removable bottom by washing and drying well. Preheat the oven to 350 degrees.
- Sift the flour and confectioners' sugar together six times.
- Wash and dry a mixing bowl. Add the egg whites and beat on high speed until foamy. Add the cream of tartar and salt and continue beating on high speed until stiff. Beat in the water and vanilla. Gradually add the superfine sugar, a few tablespoons at a time, until the meringue is glossy and very thick. Add the almond flavoring.
- In four parts, carefully and gently fold in the sifted flour-sugar mixture until no flour is visible, deflating the mixture as little as possible.
- Spread the batter in the clean, dry cake pan and bake in the lower half of the oven until browned, and the center of the cake is springy, about 45 minutes. Invert the cake pan over a bottle and leave it hanging for an hour before running a knife around the edge and removing the cake from the pan. This cake is difficult to cut because it's so springy. It requires an old-fashioned angel food cake cutter with long prongs, or at least a serrated knife.

2

Variation: To make Chocolate Angel Food, reduce the amount of flour to ¾ cup and sift the flour with the confectioners' sugar and ¼ cup unsweetened cocoa.

Apple Butter

Apple butter takes applesauce a few steps further. It's cooked longer, enriched with spices and the added piquancy of cider vinegar. This flavorful, thick fruit butter is a perfect topping for corn bread or buttered raisin bread toast. The creamy texture of cooked Macintosh apples works well for apple butter.

Makes three 8-ounce jars

2 pounds (4 to 6) tart apples (Macintosh), cut into eighths
¾ cup water
¼ cup cider vinegar

1½ cups sugar, or to taste
1½ teaspoons cinnamon
¼ teaspoon ground cloves
¼ teaspoon ground allspice

- In a stainless steel or enamel saucepan, combine the apples, water, and vinegar. Cover and simmer until soft, about 15 to 20 minutes.
- Put the apple mixture through a food mill and add approximately 1½ cups sugar (¼ to ½ cup sugar for each cup of puree, according to taste). Stir in the spices.
- Return the mixture to the saucepan. Simmer over low heat until the mixture becomes darker and nearly thick enough to stand in soft peaks. Stir often to prevent burning on the bottom. Transfer to sterilized jars and seal immediately. Cool and refrigerate.

3

Apple Crisp

Crisps are similar to fruit buckles, brown Bettys, cobblers, and pandowdies. They're all sweetened fruit desserts baked with various pastry tops: biscuits, cookie dough, bread-crumb streusel, pie dough, cake batter, and so on. These desserts are faster and safer if you're not sure of your pie crust skills.

French apple crumb pie without a bottom crust might be another way of describing apple crisp. The "crisp" comes from a crunchy streusel topping textured with oatmeal or nuts. Apple crisp is nearly always served à la mode.

Serves 10 to 12

4

2½ pounds (7 to 8) baking apples (Golden Delicious, Cortland, Rome), peeled, cored, and sliced (8 cups sliced apples)
½ cup granulated sugar

1 tablespoon lemon juice
1 teaspoon cinnamon
Pinch of ground allspice
Grating of nutmeg
Pinch of salt

For the topping

1½ cups flour
¾ cup rolled oats or finely chopped nuts

1 cup brown sugar
12 tablespoons unsalted butter
Vanilla ice cream or whipped cream

- Generously grease a 9-by-13-inch or 8-by-12-inch baking pan with butter. Preheat the oven to 375 degrees.
- Combine the apples, sugar, lemon juice, and spices. Spread in the bottom of the prepared pan.
- To make the topping, combine the flour, oats, and brown sugar. Work in the butter with a pastry blender until the mixture is crumbly. Spread evenly over the apples and press down gently.
- Bake until the apples are tender and the top is golden, about 50 minutes. Serve slightly warm with a scoop of vanilla ice cream or whipped cream.

Apple Pies

Every family must have its heirloom apple pie recipe: with brown sugar or white; cinnamon or lemon; double crusted or single; served with cheddar cheese or ice cream. As a judge in a local apple pie contest (just as filling as the chili contest I judged, but no indigestion!), I can attest to the popularity and variety of apple pies.

As simple as it seems, a *good* apple pie isn't so easy to make. Success depends upon the *crust*—flaky, tender, and well-browned even on the bottom—and, equally important, the variety of *apple*—one that bakes to tenderness but doesn't turn to applesauce. The *thickener,* whether flour, cornstarch, or tapioca, should bind the juices adequately but not be gummy. As I said, not so easy.

Here are three apple pies that are beloved family traditions: one with a precooked apple filling flavored and colored with cinnamon "red-hot" candies; one with a simple apple-cinnamon caramel filling enclosed in a light, flaky double crust; and one, similar to apple crisp, with a streusel topping—my daughter's favorite Dutch apple pie. It's hard to decide which one to make.

Red Hot Apple Pie

The apples, precooked to guarantee a soft and tender filling, are lightly colored with the red candies, which give a spicy cinnamon taste. The double crust can be decorated with apple cutouts for an impressive finish.

Makes one 10-inch pie

For the pastry

3 cups flour

4 tablespoons sugar

½ teaspoon salt

8 tablespoons unsalted butter, chilled

½ cup solid vegetable shortening

2 egg yolks

4 tablespoons cold water (approximately)

For the filling

2¼ pounds (about 6) baking apples (Golden Delicious, Cortland, Rome), peeled, cored, and sliced (6 cups sliced apples)

⅓ cup water

1 cup sugar

3½ tablespoons cornstarch

½ teaspoon salt

3 tablespoons unsalted butter

¼ cup "red-hot" candies

▪ Lightly grease a 10-inch pie plate with shortening.

▪ To make the pastry, in a bowl or food processor combine the flour, sugar, and salt. Cut in the butter and shortening until the mixture resembles meal. Mix the yolks and water together. Add to the bowl, tossing lightly with a fork until the mixture nearly sticks together to form a dough. Or, with the motor running, add the yolks and water through the feed tube and process until the dough just begins to form a mass—don't let it form a ball of dough.

▪ Turn the dough out onto a flat surface and gently knead it a few times until it is more homogenous and forms a ball. Divide the dough (⅔ and ⅓) and form into two discs. Wrap each in plastic wrap and refrigerate at least 30 minutes to firm the dough and relax the gluten so the dough will be less likely to stick and shrink back as you roll it.

▪ Roll the larger disc of dough into a 14-inch circle to fit the pie plate. I find it easiest to roll up the dough on the rolling pin and unroll it over the pie plate to transfer it, or, alternatively, to fold it loosely in quarters, put the point in the center of the pie plate and unfold it. Either way, be decisive and positive and make the dough think you know what you're doing. Without stretching the dough, gently press it into the sides of the pan. Leaving a ¾-inch overhang, trim around the edge with a scissors and add the excess dough to the remaining disc of dough. Refrigerate the bottom crust while you make the filling.

▪ To make the filling, combine the apples and water in a large saucepan. Cook, uncovered, over medium heat, stirring gently, until the apples are soft and tender but not mushy, about 5 to 8 minutes. Combine the sugar, cornstarch, and salt, and gently blend into the apples. Add the butter and continue to cook until thickened, about 5 minutes. Stir in the "red-hot" candies and cool.

▪ Preheat the oven to 425 degrees.

▪ Spoon the apples into the chilled pie shell. Brush the edge with water. Roll out the remaining dough to fit the top. Lay it over the apples and press the edges together gently to seal. Trim the top dough to match the bottom and crimp the dough to form a decorative edge. Cut vent holes and decorate the top with leftover dough cutouts of apples or leaves. For a nice color, brush the top and edges with just a little milk and sprinkle with sugar.

▪ Place on a baking sheet. Bake 15 minutes on the lowest rack of the oven. Reduce the heat to 350 degrees and continue to bake until golden brown, about 30 to 40 minutes. Serve warm or at room temperature.

Apple Pie—Sweet and Simple

This is the quintessential all-American apple pie for those who are equally partial to the crust and the filling. The apples are tossed with a caramel sauce before baking in the double crust. Initially high bottom heat guarantees a nicely browned bottom crust.

Makes one 9-inch pie

For the crust

2 cups flour

1 tablespoon sugar

¾ teaspoon salt

⅔ cup solid vegetable shortening

7 tablespoons cold water

For the filling

2 pounds (about 5) baking apples (Golden Delicious, Cortland, Rome), peeled, cored, and sliced (5 cups sliced apples)

2 tablespoons cornstarch

1 teaspoon cinnamon

Grating of fresh nutmeg

¾ cup sugar

¼ cup apple juice or cider

¼ cup heavy cream

2 tablespoons unsalted butter

¼ teaspoon salt

⅓ cup chopped walnuts or pecans (optional)

Milk and sugar to glaze the top

- To make the crust, in a bowl or food processor combine the flour, sugar, and salt. Cut in the shortening until it resembles meal. Add the water to the bowl gradually, tossing gently with a fork until it nearly sticks together to form a dough. Or add the water all at once through the feed tube with the motor running and process only until the dough begins to form a mass.
- Turn the dough out on a floured flat surface and knead gently a few times to form it into a ball. Form into 2 discs (one ⅔ and the other ⅓ of the dough) for the top and bottom crusts, wrap each in plastic wrap, and refrigerate for at least 30 minutes to chill the dough.
- Lightly grease a 9-inch pie plate with shortening. Preheat the oven to 425 degrees.

▪ On a lightly floured surface, roll out the bottom crust to a 13-inch circle. Carefully transfer it to the prepared pie plate and gently press it into the bottom and sides without stretching it. Allowing a ¾-inch overhang, trim the edges of the dough with scissors. Use any trimmings for the top crust. Chill the bottom crust while making the filling.

▪ To make the filling, toss the apples with the cornstarch, cinnamon, and nutmeg until well mixed.

▪ In a large saucepan, combine the sugar, apple juice, cream, butter, and salt. Bring to a boil and cook until thickened and lightly colored, about 5 minutes.

▪ Cool 5 minutes and combine the sugar mixture with the apples and nuts. Spoon the filling into the chilled pie shell.

▪ Roll out the top crust on a floured surface and carefully place it over the apples. Press the edges of the dough together to seal and trim the top crust to match the bottom. Crimp the edges and make a decorative border. Cut a few vent holes in the top. Brush lightly with milk and sprinkle lightly with about a tablespoon of sugar.

▪ Place the pie plate on a heavy cookie sheet (to catch any overflow) and bake on the bottom shelf of the oven for 10 minutes. Reduce the temperature to 375 degrees and continue to bake until the crust is golden and the apples are tender, about 45 minutes.

Apple Crumb Pie

With only a bottom crust, this is for pie-lovers partial to sweet apple fillings topped with a thick layer of crunchy cinnamon, brown sugar, and oat streusel. Apple cider and rolled oats give the crust a unique taste and texture.

Makes one 9-inch pie

For the crust

1¼ cups flour
¼ cup rolled oats, quick or old fashioned
1 tablespoon sugar
¼ teaspoon salt

3 tablespoons unsalted butter
3 tablespoons solid vegetable shortening
3 to 4 tablespoons cold apple cider or apple juice

For the filling

2 pounds (about 5) baking apples (Golden Delicious, Cortland, Rome), peeled, cored, and sliced (5 cups sliced apples)

½ cup granulated sugar
3 tablespoons flour
1 teaspoon cinnamon

For the streusel topping

8 tablespoons butter, melted
¾ cup brown sugar
1½ cups flour
¼ cup rolled oats
½ teaspoon cinnamon
Pinch of nutmeg

Pinch of allspice
Pinch of salt

Vanilla ice cream

- To make the crust, in a bowl or food processor combine the flour, oats, sugar, and salt. Cut in the butter and shortening until it resembles meal. Add the cider gradually to the bowl, tossing gently with a fork until the mixture nearly sticks together to form a dough. Or add the cider all at once through the feed tube with the motor running and process until the dough *begins* to form a ball.
- Turn the dough out onto a floured flat surface and knead gently a few times until the dough forms a ball. Press into a disc, wrap it in plastic wrap, and refrigerate while making the filling.
- Lightly grease a 9-inch pie plate with shortening. Preheat the oven to 425 degrees.
- On a lightly floured surface, roll out the chilled dough to a 13-inch circle. Carefully transfer the dough to the prepared pie plate and press gently into the bottom and sides without stretching the dough. Trim the dough, leaving a 1-inch overhang. Turn the edge under and crimp to make a decorative border. Chill in the refrigerator while you make the filling.
- To make the filling, combine the apples, sugar, flour, and cinnamon, mix well, and put the filling in the pie shell.
- To make the streusel topping, rub together the melted butter, brown sugar, flour, oats, spices, and salt. Crumble over the apples and press down gently.
- Place the pie pan on a heavy baking sheet (in case of overflow) and bake on the bottom shelf of the oven for 10 minutes. Reduce the oven temperature to 350 degrees and continue baking until the top is golden, the filling is bubbly, and the apples are tender (poke carefully with a paring knife), about 40 to 45 minutes. Serve the pie slightly warm, à la mode!

Applesauce

Here's where that old-fashioned invention, the food mill, is indispensable. Every kitchen needs a food mill if only to make applesauce, a food even young children can master and we all enjoy eating. The coring and peeling step is eliminated, which means you can make quarts of applesauce at the fall harvest with little effort. Frozen in plastic containers, this autumn bounty can become a spring luxury.

Every variety of apple has a distinctive taste and texture, and each cooks differently. For baking, I stick with Golden Delicious since they're available year-round and hold their shape well. In apple season, I look for Cortlands, Baldwins, Gravensteins, or Rome Beauties. For applesauce, the Macintosh produces a creamy texture, and a combination of varieties produces a great taste. For any food as simple as applesauce, the more flavorful the ingredients, the more delicious the final result. So, start with apples that taste good and you can't miss. You may find sugar unnecessary.

Makes about 1 quart

2 pounds (4 to 6 large) apples, cut in eighths
¾ cup water
Squeeze of lemon juice
Pinch of salt

Approximately 1½ cups sugar (¼ to ½ cup sugar per cup of purée, according to taste)
1 teaspoon cinnamon (optional)

- Combine the apples, water, lemon juice, and salt in a saucepan. Cover and simmer on low heat, stirring a few times, about 15 to 20 minutes. The apples should be very soft.
- Put the apples through the food mill and return to the pan. Add the sugar in parts, tasting to check for sweetness, and stir to dissolve. You can simmer to a thicker consistency or add water for a thinner consistency.

Applesauce Cake

Here's a moist spice cake that makes great snacks as a simple sliced loaf cake or, as a special treat, baked as a layer cake and topped with a cream cheese frosting or whipped cream. If you use pear sauce (the food mill again!) and ginger instead of applesauce and cinnamon, you'll have a totally new cake.

Serves 8 to 10

8 tablespoons unsalted butter, softened

1 cup sugar

1 egg, at room temperature

2 cups flour

1 teaspoon baking soda

1 teaspoon double-acting baking powder

1 teaspoon cinnamon

½ teaspoon salt

¼ teaspoon ground allspice

1¼ cups applesauce, at room temperature

1 cup chopped pitted dates or raisins or pitted prunes

1 cup coarsely chopped walnuts

A

13

- Grease well and lightly flour one 5- by 9- inch loaf pan or a 9-by-13-inch cake pan. Preheat the oven to 350 degrees.
- Cream the butter and add the sugar gradually, beating until light. Add the egg and beat until pale and frothy.
- Sift together the flour, baking soda, baking powder, cinnamon, salt, and allspice.
- Alternately add the dry ingredients and the applesauce to the butter-egg mixture. Mix just until the batter is thoroughly combined. Fold in the dates and the nuts.
- Spread the batter evenly in the prepared pan and bake on the middle rack of the oven until the cake tests done, 60 to 70 minutes for the loaf pan or 35 to 40 minutes for the layer cake. The center should be springy, the cake should begin to pull away from the sides of the pan, and a toothpick inserted in the center should come out clean.
- Cool the loaf for 15 minutes before turning out on a wire rack to cool completely. For the layer cake, cool completely before frosting or serve warm with whipped cream.

continued on next page

Note: For a cream cheese frosting: Beat 3 ounces cream cheese, 2 tablespoons unsalted butter, 1½ cups confectioners' sugar, and a pinch of salt until smooth.

Artichokes

14

My mother's boundless curiosity and interest in the world expanded the horizons of my Indiana childhood. She introduced us to the exotic pleasures of unknown foods and the places they came from, and made food an adventure. Artichokes, while not classic in every home, were a favorite in ours when dipped in butter.

My adult interest in artichokes was fueled by the fried artichoke hearts in Castroville, California, and the beautiful fields of artichokes between Castroville and San Francisco. And then, artichokes were the teething vegetables of our three children. They soon became children's school snacks with a drizzle of vinaigrette, and our favorite picnic food stuffed with a seafood or pasta salad. We still enjoy artichokes for dinner, usually cold with a creamy herbed vinaigrette or homemade mayonnaise.

Artichokes don't ever turn a beautiful green color, but their taste more than makes up for that. Aromatics, vinegar, and a bit of oil in the cooking water give artichokes so much flavor that you can eat them without any dipping sauce at all.

Serves 4

4 large firm artichokes
2 quarts water
½ cup white vinegar
¼ cup olive oil or vegetable oil
1 clove garlic, peeled

A few celery tops
1 tablespoon salt
2 whole cloves
5 whole peppercorns

- Soak the artichokes in water and scrub them until clean. Cut off the stem and ¾ inch from the top. Trim the tips of the leaves.
- Put the 2 quarts water and remaining ingredients in a stainless-steel pot large enough to hold the artichokes. Bring to a boil and add the trimmed artichokes.
- Return to a boil, cover, and boil the artichokes until a leaf can be pulled out without resistance, about 30 to 35 minutes. Taste to check for tenderness.
- Drain the artichokes, turning them upside down and squeezing out some of the excess water. Cool on a wire rack until cool enough to handle.
- Gently spread out the leaves and pull out the very center leaves in a clump to expose the choke. Remove the hairy, fibrous choke with a grapefruit spoon, being careful not to scoop out the delicious heart as well.
- Insert the center leaves upside down and serve warm with butter, or cool with a sauce, Mayonnaise (see page 174), or Vinaigrette (see page 288). Or serve cold, filled with a seafood, chicken, or pasta salad.

15

B.L.T. Sandwich

Bacon Lettuce and Tomato Sandwiches aren't done until the M for Mayonnaise is added. White bread is traditional, but the debate rages about plain or toasted. And a few slices of ripe avocado won't hurt.

Makes 1 sandwich

2 slices of quality bread, plain or toasted

1 to 2 tablespoons Mayonnaise (see page 174)

2 lettuce leaves, washed and dried

4 slices of bacon, cooked until crisp

3 thin slices from a garden tomato

3 thin slices from a ripe and peeled avocado (optional)

- Spread the bread or toast with half the mayonnaise. Lay a slice of lettuce over the mayonnaise. Layer on the bacon, tomato slices, avocado, and another lettuce leaf.
- Spread the second slice of bread or toast with the remaining mayonnaise and place, mayonnaise side down, onto the lettuce. Cut the sandwich in half on the diagonal and serve.

Bagels

Everyone knows that bagels are more than hard doughnuts when Burger King puts them on their breakfast menu. The combination of chewy *and* crusty is a bagel's charm, and it comes from the combination of boiling *and* baking. It's a real event when I announce to children that I've made yeast dough for bagels. They're fun to make and especially good hot from the oven.

Makes 12 bagels

1½ cups warm water

Pinch of sugar

2 ¼-ounce envelopes (2 scant table-spoons) active dry yeast

4½ to 5 cups flour

1 tablespoon sugar

1 tablespoon salt

4 tablespoons vegetable or corn oil

1 tablespoon sugar

1 tablespoon salt

Egg wash (1 egg beaten with 1 table-spoon milk)

Poppy seeds, caraway seeds, sesame seeds, or coarse salt

- In a small bowl, mix ½ cup of the water and pinch of sugar; sprinkle the yeast over the warm water. Let the yeast proof until bubbly, about 10 minutes, to be sure it's active.
- In a mixing bowl, combine 3 cups of the flour, and 1 tablespoon each of sugar and salt.
- Add the proofed yeast, remaining water, and 2 tablespoons of the oil to the flour and stir vigorously. Stir in another cup of flour and turn the dough out onto a floured surface. Gradually knead in enough additional flour until the dough is smooth and elastic and no longer sticky.
- Add the remaining oil to a clean bowl and add the dough, turning to coat all sides of the dough. Cover with a towel and let the dough rise until doubled in bulk, about 1 hour.
- Punch the dough down and divide into 12 equal pieces. Form each piece into a smooth round ball of dough and poke a 1½-inch hole in the center of each with your finger. Set aside and let the bagels rise until puffy, about 15 minutes.

- Lightly grease 2 baking sheets with shortening. Preheat the oven to 400 degrees.
- Add 1 tablespoon each of salt and sugar to a large, wide pan with 1½ inches of water in it. Bring to a boil and add just 4 bagels at a time (they will expand). Simmer for 3 minutes; turn and simmer for 2 minutes; turn and simmer for 1 minute more. Drain the bagels on a clean dish towel and arrange on the prepared baking sheet. Continue simmering the remaining bagels until all 12 are done.
- Brush the tops of the bagels lightly with some egg wash, trying not to let it drip down onto the baking sheet. Sprinkle the bagels with seeds or salt.
- Bake in the upper half of the oven for 10 minutes. Reduce the oven temperature to 375 degrees and continue baking until lightly browned, about 15 to 20 minutes. Cool on a wire rack.
- Slice and serve with butter or cream cheese.

B

Baked Alaska

Baked Alaska, that contradiction of cake, ice cream, and *baked* meringue, has always seemed as spectacular and daring a finale as fireworks on the Fourth of July! If you don't have a freezer that keeps ice cream very firm and frozen, don't attempt it. The success is in the dramatic presentation, so making the cake from scratch isn't necessary. A good butter poundcake or one square chocolate cake layer make a fine base for the ice cream. Assemble ahead of time on a foil-lined cookie sheet and freeze until serving time. Warmed liqueurs poured over the top and ignited are the fireworks finish if you can work quickly and really want a spectacular ending before the ice cream melts.

Serves 8

1 4-by-8 inch poundcake, *or* 1 8-inch square cake layer

3 tablespoons liqueur (optional)

1 quart ice cream, any flavor

4 egg whites

¼ teaspoon cream of tartar

½ cup sugar

½ teaspoon vanilla extract

3 tablespoons liqueur, warmed for flaming (optional)

- Line a baking sheet with foil. Cut the poundcake in half horizontally and lay side by side to make an 8-inch square, or place the cake layer on the foil. Brush with liqueur. Soften the ice cream just enough to spread it on the cake. Freeze until very firm.
- Preheat the oven to 450 degrees.
- Make a meringue by beating the egg whites until frothy. Add the cream of tartar and continue beating on high speed until soft peaks form. Gradually beat in the sugar and vanilla, and continue beating until stiff and glossy.
- Cover the ice cream and cake completely with the meringue.
- Bake until the meringue is lightly colored, about 4 to 5 minutes. Serve immediately, or warm the liqueur, pour it over the baked meringue, and carefully ignite it. When the flames die out, cut and serve.

Baked Apples

I first remember baked apples stuffed with brown sugar and raisins, wrapped in foil, and baked in the embers of an early winter fire. Nowadays apples are "baked" quickly in a microwave. That old way lacks precision but seems so much more romantic!

Serves 6

6 large baking apples (my mother-in-law says Rome Beauties are the best, but you could also use Cortlands or Golden Delicious)

½ cup brown sugar (approximately)

½ teaspoon cinnamon

¼ cup raisins (optional)

1 tablespoon unsalted butter

Water

Heavy cream (optional)

- Preheat the oven to 375 degrees.
- Core the apples from the bottom without going all the way through the apple. A melon baller or serrated grapefruit knife does a better job than an apple corer. Peel the skin about ⅓ of the way down from the opening. Pierce the remaining skin around the apple with a paring knife and arrange the apples in a shallow baking dish that holds them fairly snugly.
- Combine the sugar, cinnamon, and the raisins. Dot the tops with bits of butter. Add water to the dish to a depth of ½ inch. Cover loosely with foil and bake for 1 hour, or until the apples are soft but not falling apart. Baking time will vary with the apple type. From time to time, baste the apples with the pan juices, which will reduce and thicken as the apples bake.
- For microwave baking, add ½ cup of water to the dish. Cover the prepared apples with wax paper and microwave on high power for 15 to 20 minutes, turning the apples every 5 minutes to help them cook evenly. Baste the apples with the juices. You may reduce the juices in a saucepan over medium heat and spoon over the apples.
- Serve the apples with some of the reduced sauce, and a little heavy cream.

Baked Beans

Baked beans have always seemed the mandatory and best accompaniment to baked ham or hot dogs, and the perfect side dish along with coleslaw and potato salad for cold sliced turkey, ham, or chicken. There's no comparison between canned baked beans and homemade. The long, slow oven cooking melds the flavors of the salt pork and maple syrup and gives the beans a rich, thick, flavorful sauce. Baked beans are a true American delicacy that vary from region to region. New Englanders love the taste of maple syrup or molasses in their beans. Elsewhere, baked beans may be less sweet and flavored with ketchup.

Serves 8

1 pound small white dried beans (navy beans)
½ cup maple syrup or molasses
⅔ cup brown sugar
½ cup finely chopped onion
2 teaspoons dry mustard

1 teaspoon salt
½ teaspoon baking soda
¼ pound salt pork, scored and cut in chunks
Hot water, as needed

- Soak the beans overnight in water to cover by three times the depth of the beans.
- Preheat the oven to 275 degrees.
- Drain the beans and put them in a pot, adding more water to amply cover. Bring the water to a slow boil and simmer them, partially covered, until softened but not cooked through, about 30 minutes. Drain the beans well and transfer them to a 2-quart bean pot or heavy ovenproof casserole with a lid.
- Add the remaining ingredients and stir to mix. Add hot water to cover the beans by 1 inch. Partially cover the pot or casserole.
- Bake 5 to 6 hours, stirring occasionally and adding more water as needed to keep the beans moist.

Baked Ham

Mustard-coated or fruit glazed, baked hams are always top choice for family gatherings and buffet entertaining. They work well either warm with baked beans or scalloped potatoes, or sliced cold for sandwiches and served with coleslaw and potato salad.

Bourbon, brown sugar, mustard, and marmalade used to transform an ordinary ham into something special in my mother's kitchen. My job was to stick the cloves into the scored rind and hope that I wouldn't eat one at dinner.

Serves 12 to 14

1 12- to 14-pound precooked, smoked ham   About 20 whole cloves

For the glaze

1½ cups firmly packed brown sugar   1½ cups apple juice
1 tablespoon prepared mustard   ½ cup bourbon
6 tablespoons orange or ginger marmalade (approximately)   Orange slices for garnish

- Trim the ham of most excess fat. Score the ham by cutting ¼ inch through the rind with a sharp knife to make 1½-inch diamonds. Place on a rack in a roasting pan, fat side up. Stick cloves into the centers of the diamonds.
- Preheat the oven to 300 degrees.
- To make the glaze, combine the brown sugar and mustard. Add enough marmalade to make a thick paste. Spread the mixture over the top of the ham, being careful not to pull out the cloves.
- Pour the apple juice and bourbon into the roasing pan. Cover the ham loosely with foil.
- Bake the ham for 2 hours, basting occasionally with the juices after 1 hour. Remove from the oven.
- Increase the temperature to 450 degrees. Remove the foil and bake, basting often, until the glaze is browned and thickened, 15 to 20 minutes.
- Transfer the ham to a platter and garnish with orange slices. Cool the ham before cutting into thin slices, removing the cloves as you slice.

Banana Bread

Banana bread has become a family standard as a medium for peanut butter and honey sandwiches. It's my answer to a surplus of overripe bananas and hungry children. The bread freezes well, so you might double the recipe and freeze a loaf for emergency lunches or snacks.

Makes 1 loaf

2 cups flour

2½ teaspoons double-acting baking powder

½ teaspoon salt

½ cup solid vegetable shortening

1 cup sugar

2 eggs, at room temperature

Grated zest of one orange, or ½ teaspoon vanilla extract

2 medium ripe bananas, mashed to make 1 cup

¼ cup currants (optional)

- Grease well and lightly flour a 5-by-9-inch loaf pan. Preheat the oven to 350 degrees.
- Sift the flour, baking powder, and salt; set aside.
- Cream the shortening and sugar until light and fluffy. Add the eggs one at a time and beat until light, scraping the bowl a few times. Add the orange zest or vanilla and the mashed banana a bit at a time, beating until the mixture is smooth. (It will look terrible!) Add the currants.
- On low speed, add the sifted dry ingredients to the banana mixture a little at a time and beat just until the batter is thoroughly mixed. Transfer to the prepared pan.
- Bake in the middle of the oven until the bread is golden, begins to pull away from the sides of the pan, and a toothpick inserted in the center comes out clean, about 60 to 70 minutes. Cool 15 minutes before running a knife around the edge of the pan and turning the bread onto a wire rack to cool completely.

BARBEQUE SAUCES

For marinating, basting, or adding zip to sauces, nothing is quite as good as homemade barbeque sauce. Making your own is easy and gives you the chance to add your personal touch and adjust the spiciness to your taste.

Barbeque sauces are based on a combination of *tart, sweet,* and *savory.* The tart ingredient is usually vinegar, the sweet can be ketchup or fruit jam, and the savory is either Worcestershire or soy sauce. These sauces can be made in *minutes.* The only easier barbeque sauce is one that my children can make in 10 *seconds* by combining the untouched Chinese take-out condiments (hot mustard, sweet dipping sauce, hoisin and soy sauces) in a jar!

It's a good idea to precook ribs to eliminate some of the fat. Boiling the ribs in water is the least satisfactory method since the meat falls off the bone and the texture of the meat is lost. Try marinating the ribs in sauce and baking slowly for almost an hour before grilling and basting with more sauce. Meats that need tenderizing can be simmered in a flavorful broth, then grilled and basted with sauce. Chicken can be marinated in sauce and then grilled or baked in the oven until the skin is dark and the sauce is caramelized and thick (that requires lots of turning and basting). The white meat of chicken requires much less grilling or baking time than dark. When pressed, the chicken should neither be squishy nor hard, but just firm. For oven baking, be sure to use foil on the bottom of pans to make the clean up easier, or, even better, use disposable foil pans.

These 10-minute sauces are super on beef, chicken, or ribs. They make enough for at least 4 pounds of ribs or 2 whole chickens. Bake ribs or chicken pieces in a 350 degree oven until tender and glazed, about 1½ hours, basting and turning four or five times.

Spicy Tomato Barbeque Sauce

Makes approximately 2 cups

½ cup chopped onion

1 cup ketchup (see page 155)

¼ cup brown sugar

¼ cup cider vinegar

2 tablespoons Worcestershire sauce

2 tablespoons vegetable oil

1 tablespoon chili powder, or to taste

1 teaspoon dry mustard

½ teaspoon black pepper

Tabasco to taste

- Combine all the ingredients in a saucepan and simmer about 4 minutes.

Oriental Fruit Barbeque Sauce

Makes approximately 2 cups

¾ cup apricot jam

¼ cup ketchup (see page 155) or hoisin sauce.

¼ cup soy sauce

¼ cup rice wine or cider vinegar

¼ cup brown sugar

2 tablespoons vegetable oil

1 teaspoon roasted sesame oil (optional)

1 tablespoon grated peeled gingerroot

1 clove garlic, peeled and minced

- Combine all the ingredients in a saucepan and simmer about 4 minutes.

Barley-Mushroom Casserole

This is a winter, stick-to-your-ribs dish that's great by itself or matched with pot roast or chicken or lamb stew. Not as quick-cooking as rice or bulgar wheat but just as delicious, barley shouldn't be forgotten in our contemporary hurry.

This casserole uses pilaf and risotto techniques. The barley is sautéed in butter to coat the grains and prevent them from sticking together. Onions and mushrooms are added for flavor and texture. The liquid is added in parts as it is absorded.

Serves 8

6 tablespoons butter

½ pound mushrooms, sliced (about 2½ cups)

1 large onion, finely chopped

1½ cups barley

4 cups chicken stock *or* 3 cups chicken or beef broth and 1 cup water (approximately)

Freshly ground black pepper

Salt (if using stock)

- Preheat the oven to 350 degrees.
- In a heavy ovenproof casserole, melt 3 tablespoons of the butter and sauté the mushrooms over medium heat until they begin to give off their juices. Remove the mushrooms to a bowl and reserve.
- In the same casserole, melt the remaining 3 tablespoons butter and sauté the onions over low heat until soft but not colored, about 5 minutes. Add the barley and continue to sauté for 5 minutes more, stirring frequently.
- Heat 2 cups of the stock and stir into the hot barley. Add the reserved mushrooms and mix well. Cover and bake for 30 minutes.
- Stir in 2 more cups of hot stock and bake another 30 minutes.
- Bake another 30 minutes, adding water if too dry.
- Season with pepper and salt, if needed, before serving.

Barley-Vegetable Soup

This fall and winter standby is usually served in large mugs on chilly days. With salad and a homemade bread, it's a substantial and warming lunch or dinner. Barley adds heartiness to this simple vegetable soup, which is enriched with meaty bones.

Serves 6 to 8

2 tablespoons butter
½ cup chopped onions
½ cup chopped celery
½ cup chopped carrots
½ pound mushrooms, sliced (2½ cups)
1 pound meaty soup bones (lamb neck, beef shin bones)
½ teaspoon dried thyme *or* a few sprigs of fresh thyme
2 tablespoons flour

2 cups peeled, seeded, and chopped tomatoes *or* 1 1-pound can peeled tomatoes, drained and chopped (optional)
4 cups chicken or beef broth
2 cups water
¼ cup barley
½ cup finely chopped parsley
Salt and freshly ground black pepper to taste

- In a large heavy pot, melt the butter. Add the onions, celery, and carrots. Sauté over low heat for 5 minutes, stirring to prevent the vegetables from coloring. Add the mushrooms and sauté a few minutes more. Add the meat bones and cook an additional 5 minutes, stirring often. Add the thyme, flour, and tomatoes. Stir well. Add the broth and water and bring to a boil. Stir in the barley.
- Simmer, covered, until the vegetables and barley are tender, about 1½ hours. Remove the meat bones and add any meat from the bones to the soup. Remove the sprigs of thyme and skim the fat from the soup if necessary. Stir in the parsley and season with salt and pepper.

Bean Salad

Bean salad can be made by cooking dried beans, but part of the joy of this summer standard is it's speed and ease. Canned beans are wonderful with a good mustardy vinaigrette and a few additions that can make this a one-dish lunch.

Serves 6

1 1-pound can garbanzo beans

1 1-pound can small white beans

1 1-pound can red kidney or black beans

½ pound small green beans cooked al dente, drained, plunged into ice water, and drained again; or use 1 10-ounce package frozen French-cut green beans, broken up in boiling water and drained

3 stalks celery, thinly sliced

¼ cup chopped red onion

¼ cup finely chopped parsley

Hard-boiled eggs or cherry tomatoes for garnish

For the dressing

3 tablespoons red wine vinegar

2 tablespoons Dijon mustard

1 clove garlic, pressed

½ teaspoon salt

Freshly ground black pepper

½ teaspoon cumin or oregano

½ cup vegetable oil, *or* a combination of olive oil and vegetable oil

• Drain the canned beans and run them under hot water to warm. Drain well in a colander. Combine all the salad ingredients, except the parsley and eggs, in a large bowl.

• In a bowl or food processor, whisk together or process the vinegar, mustard, garlic, salt, pepper, and spice. Add the oil very slowly, whisking constantly, or process, slowly adding the oil through the feed tube while the motor is running. The vinaigrette will thicken.

continued on next page

- Pour half the dressing over the salad ingredients and toss well, adding more as needed to coat the beans.
- To retain its green color, add the parsley just before serving. Toss well.
- Serve the salad on a platter and garnish with sliced or halved eggs or tomatoes.

Variations

Artichoke hearts, cooked, or, if canned, drained and soaked in water to eliminate the canned taste, and squeezed to drain.

Hearts of palm, drained, soaked, and drained well, then thinly sliced.

Black or green pitted olives.

For a one-dish lunch, 3 cups julienned ham or smoked turkey.

B

Beef and Rice "Good Stuff"

Ever since I was a beginning cook, when my only heat source was an electric frying pan and every penny counted, Beef and Rice "Good Stuff" has been a staple of life. This one-dish meal got its name because it consisted of basic ingredients simply cooked, and it was *good!* Even today, for a fast dinner that everyone likes, this Good Stuff does the trick, accompanied by a green salad and followed by a gooey dessert.

Serves 6 to 8

1½ pounds lean ground beef

1 medium onion, finely chopped

2 cloves garlic, minced

1 small green pepper, finely chopped

⅓ pound mushrooms, chopped

1 tablespoon Worcestershire sauce

3 tomatoes, peeled, seeded, and chopped, *or* 1 16-ounce can peeled tomatoes, drained and chopped

1 cup long-grain rice

2½ cups chicken or beef broth

¼ cup finely chopped parsley

Salt and freshly ground black pepper to taste

- In a large heavy skillet, combine the beef, onions, and garlic. Heat over low heat, stirring to break up the meat. Cook until the meat is no longer pink and the onions are softened. Drain any accumulated fat.
- Add the peppers and mushrooms to the skillet and sauté for 5 minutes. Add the Worcestershire sauce and tomatoes and cook until most of the liquid has evaporated and the mixture is fairly thick.
- Stir in the rice and broth. Simmer, partially covered, until the liquid has been absorbed and the rice is soft, stirring occasionally, about 20 to 25 minutes. Stir in the parsley, season with pepper and salt if needed, and serve hot.

Beef Stew

A good beef stew begins with well-trimmed beef chuck cut in healthy size chunks, marinated in wine and herbs, and braised to tenderness. Add separately cooked vegetables and a unique spice or herb for an imaginative touch. For the best taste, make stews a few days before serving to let the flavors mingle.

Serves 6 to 8

4 pounds boneless beef shoulder (chuck) steak, well trimmed of fat and cut in 2-inch cubes

For the marinade

1½ cups dry red wine
1 clove garlic, peeled and coarsely chopped

¼ cup chopped shallots
1 bay leaf

For the stew

¼ cup cubed salt pork (⅛ pound), or 3 slices bacon, cut up
¼ cup vegetable oil
½ cup plus 1½ tablespoons flour
1 teaspoon salt
½ teaspoon paprika
Freshly ground black pepper
2 medium onions, chopped

2 cups beef or veal stock, or use 1½ cups beef broth and ½ cup water
2 medium carrots, peeled and cut in ½-inch slices
2 tablespoons salted butter
¾ pound mushrooms, wiped clean, trimmed, and cut in half
¼ cup chopped parsley for garnish

- To make the marinade, combine all the marinade ingredients in a stainless steel, glass, or plastic container. Add the meat and marinate, covered, overnight.
- Remove the meat and pat it dry, reserving the marinade.

- To make the stew, in a heavy pan, sauté the salt pork cubes over low heat, stirring frequently, until crisp and most of the fat has been rendered. Remove the salt pork and add a tablespoon of the oil to the pan.
- Combine ½ cup of the flour, the salt, paprika, and pepper, and dredge the dry cubes of beef in the mixture, shaking off any excess.
- Brown a batch of the meat cubes on all sides over medium heat, shaking the pan to prevent the meat from sticking. Don't crowd the pan. Lower the heat if the meat browns too quickly. Add more oil as necessary. As each batch of meat is done, transfer it to a large heavy casserole with a lid.
- Add the reserved marinade to the sauté pan to deglaze it, scraping the browned bits off the bottom of the pan and incorporating them into the marinade. Reduce the sauce by half and pour it over the meat.
- Add the remaining oil to the pan and sauté the onions over low heat for 10 minutes, stirring often to prevent browning. When the onions are soft, add them to the meat along with the beef stock. Bring to a boil and place a covering of foil on the surface of the stew. Cover the pan and simmer for 1½ hours, or until the meat is fork tender.
- Skim any excess fat from the top surface. Remove ¼ cup of the braising juices and whisk in the remaining 1½ tablespoons flour until smooth. Add the mixture to the stew and bring to a simmer to thicken the braising juices slightly.
- Cook the carrots in boiling salted water until tender but not mushy. Drain and add to the stew.
- In a clean sauté pan, melt the butter and sauté the mushrooms over medium heat, tossing and stirring constantly, until they begin to brown and squeak, about 3 minutes. Add the mushrooms to the stew.
- Stir the stew and heat thoroughly before serving. Sprinkle with parsley and serve with boiled new potatoes or crusty French bread.

Beef Stroganoff

Beef Stroganoff is usually a fancy dish that combines mushrooms and a sour cream–enriched sauce served over beef tenderloin. But my mother made it as a special family dinner using beef chuck braised to tenderness. Noodles do a good job of soaking up the rich sauce.

Serves 6

3 pounds boneless lean stewing beef, cut in large pieces, *or* 6 blade chuck steaks, about ½ pound each

¼ cup flour

½ teaspoon salt

Freshly ground black pepper

¼ cup vegetable oil

½ cup finely chopped onions

1 teaspoon paprika

1½ cups beef stock, *or* ¾ cup each canned beef broth and water

2 tablespoons tomato paste

2 teaspoons Worcestershire sauce

1 teaspoon Dijon mustard

½ cup sour cream

½ cup heavy cream

Salt and freshly ground pepper to taste

2 tablespoons butter

¾ pound medium mushrooms, thinly sliced (3½ cups)

1 tablespoon lemon juice

2 tablespoons minced parsley

12 ounces broad egg noodles cooked, drained, and tossed with 2 tablespoons butter

- Trim the beef of all excess fat and sinew. Combine the flour, salt, and pepper and dredge the meat on all sides, shaking off any excess.
- In a large sauté pan with a lid, heat 2 tablespoons of the oil. In a few batches, sear the beef on all sides until well browned, stirring with a wooden spatula to prevent sticking. Add another tablespoon of oil as needed and don't crowd the meat as it browns. As each batch is finished, remove the meat with a slotted spoon to a bowl.
- Add the remaining oil to the pan and sauté the onions over low heat, stirring often, until softened but not colored, about 5 minutes. Stir in the paprika.
- Add the beef stock, whisking to incorporate the brown glaze on the bottom of the pan. Return the meat and any accumulated juices to the pan and bring the liquid to a boil. Place a piece of foil directly on the meat and

liquid so the meat is braised rather than steamed. Cover the pan and simmer for 1 hour or until fork tender.

▪ With a slotted spoon, transfer the beef to a serving platter and keep warm. Skim the fat from the braising juices in the pan. Add the tomato paste, Worcestershire sauce, mustard, sour cream, and cream to the pan. Whisk together and increase the heat. Bring to a boil and reduce the sauce over medium heat until slightly thickened. Season to taste with salt and pepper.

▪ While the sauce is cooking, melt the butter in another pan and sauté the mushrooms over medium-high heat, stirring constantly, until they begin to brown, about 3 minutes. Stir in the lemon juice.

▪ To serve, spoon the mushrooms onto the beef and top with the rich sauce. Sprinkle with minced parsley and serve over the noodles.

B

$\mathcal{B}$ISCUITS

You don't have to be a Southerner to love biscuits! These are a fast addition to any meal: with butter and jam for *breakfast,* an accompaniment to soup or salad for *lunch,* and a treat for *dinner* instead of potatoes or rice. In the South, their soft wheat flour with its low gluten (protein) makes light, feathery biscuits. If White Lily flour isn't available in your area, use a combination of flour and cornstarch to give the same fine, light texture. Here are two quick biscuit recipes, one with buttermilk and baking soda for added leavening, the other with milk and baking powder. Use a light hand so you don't develop the gluten—that can result in tough biscuits.

Buttermilk Biscuits

Makes 9 to 10 biscuits

2 cups White Lily all-purpose flour (not self-rising), *or* 1¾ cups all-purpose flour and ¼ cup cornstarch

2 teaspoons double-acting baking powder

¼ teaspoon baking soda

1 teaspoon sugar

1 teaspoon salt

4 tablespoons solid vegetable shortening

¾ to 1 cup buttermilk

Egg wash made of 1 egg yolk beaten with 2 tablespoons milk, (optional)

• Lightly grease a 9-inch cake pan or heavy baking sheet. Preheat the oven to 450 degrees.

• Sift the dry ingredients into a mixing bowl. Cut in the shortening until it resembles meal. Add the buttermilk gradually, tossing gently with a fork until the mixture is quite moist and forms a mass. Turn out onto a well-floured board and knead lightly a few times.

• Pat the dough to a ½-inch thickness. Use a 2½-inch cutter or glass, or an empty frozen juice can dipped in flour to cut out the biscuits. Re-form the scraps without overworking them and cut out more biscuits, 9 or 10 in all.

• Arrange the biscuits close together in the prepared pan for soft biscuits, or one inch apart on the baking sheet for crustier biscuits. Brush the tops lightly with the egg wash.

• Place the baking sheet on the middle oven rack and immediately reduce the temperature to 425 degrees. Bake until very lightly colored, about 15 minutes. The Biscuits should be pale. Serve hot with butter.

Baking Powder Biscuits

When you haven't any buttermilk on hand, these biscuits are just as delicious. Additions like minced chives or fresh herbs make these wonderful dinner companions.

Makes 9 to 10 biscuits

1¾ cups flour
¼ cup cornstarch
4 teaspoons double-acting baking powder
1 teaspoon salt
4 tablespoons solid vegetable shortening

1 to 2 tablespoons minced chives or fresh herbs (optional)
¾ cup milk, approximately
Milk or melted butter for brushing on the tops

- Preheat the oven to 425 degrees. Lightly grease a heavy baking sheet or 9-inch cake pan.
- In a bowl, sift together the flour, cornstarch, baking powder, and salt.
- Cut in the shortening until it resembles meal. Add the chives or herbs.
- Gradually add the milk, tossing gently with a fork until the dough is quite moist. Turn the dough out onto a floured surface and knead lightly a few times, just until the dough forms a mass.
- Press or roll the dough to a ½-inch thickness. Cut the biscuits with a 2½-inch cutter or glass, or an empty frozen-juice can dipped in flour to prevent sticking. Reform the scraps without overworking and cut out more biscuits, to make 9 or 10 in all.
- Arrange the biscuits on the prepared sheet or in the pan, and brush the tops lightly with milk.
- Place the baking sheet on the middle rack of the oven and reduce the temperature immediately to 400 degrees. Bake until very lightly colored, about 15 to 18 minutes. Serve hot with butter.

Blue Cheese Dressing

This recipe can be used to make a creamy dressing for green salads, a dip for chips and raw vegetable sticks and flowers, or a sauce for fried chicken wings.

Makes 3 cups

1 cup Mayonnaise (see page 174)
¾ to 1 cup buttermilk
1 cup crumbled blue cheese (Roquefort, Saga Blue, Blue Castello, or Gorgonzola (4 ounces)
Pinch of sugar
Pinch of cayenne pepper
Freshly ground black pepper
Salt, if needed
1 clove garlic, peeled, cut in half, and skewered with a toothpick

▪ In a bowl, combine the mayonnaise and ¾ cup buttermilk and whisk until smooth.

▪ Stir in the crumbled blue cheese, sugar, cayenne, and pepper. Mash the cheese with a fork to make the dressing a bit creamier. Add remaining buttermilk for a thinner dressing. Add salt to taste.

▪ Pour the dressing into a jar and add the garlic. Refrigerate at least 1 hour to let the garlic subtly flavor the dressing. Remove the garlic just before serving.

Blueberry-Cinnamon Cake

Even when blueberries are out of season, you can enjoy the combination of blueberries and cinnamon in this breakfast cake that's similar to muffins but with a streusel topping. Freeze blueberries in August to have on hand when the craving for Blueberry-Cinnamon Cake overcomes you in midwinter.

Serves 8

1½ cups flour

½ cup sugar

2 teaspoons double-acting baking powder

½ teaspoon salt

4 tablespoons unsalted butter, softened

1 egg, at room temperature

½ teaspoon vanilla extract

½ cup milk, at room temperature

1 cup (small ones are best) blueberries, fresh or frozen

For the topping

2 tablespoons unsalted butter

¼ cup flour

¼ cup brown sugar

¾ teaspoon cinnamon

- Preheat the oven to 375 degrees. Lightly grease a 9-inch round or square cake pan with butter or shortening.
- Sift together the flour, sugar, baking powder, and salt into a bowl. Cut in the butter until it resembles meal.
- Whisk together the egg, vanilla, and milk. Add the liquids and blueberries to the dry ingredients, stirring just until combined. Spread the batter in the prepared pan.
- To make the topping, combine the butter, flour, sugar, and cinnamon. Work with a pastry blender or your fingers until crumbly. Sprinkle over the batter.
- Bake the cake in the upper half of the oven until it begins to pull away from the sides of the pan and the center is springy, about 30 minutes. Serve slightly warm.

Blueberry Pie (Fresh)

It seems foolish to me to cook blueberries when they're perfect fresh. This summer pie combines my favorite berry with red currant jelly in a simple graham cracker crust. I like to top the pie with piped swirls of whipped cream. It's best to serve the pie the day it's made so the crust stays crisp.

Makes one 9-inch pie

For the graham cracker crust

1½ cups graham cracker crumbs
   (1 packet of 11 double crackers)

¼ cup sugar
6 tablespoons butter, melted

For the filling

1 cup red currant jelly
2 tablespoons orange liqueur
1½ teaspoons cornstarch

1 pint (about 3 cups) fresh blueberries,
   washed, dried, and stems removed

B

41

For the topping

1 cup heavy cream

2 tablespoons confectioners' sugar

- Preheat the oven to 375 degrees. Lightly grease a 9-inch pie plate with shortening.
- To make the crust, thoroughly combine the crumbs, sugar, and butter. Press the mixture evenly onto the bottom and sides of the prepared pie plate. Bake the crust on the middle rack of the oven until lightly browned, about 12 minutes. Cool completely on a wire rack.
- To make the filling, in a small saucepan melt the jelly over low heat. Combine the liqueur and cornstarch and stir to dissolve. Add to the melted jelly and heat to thicken. Cool slightly and combine with the blueberries, tossing gently to coat. Spoon into the cooled pie shell and refrigerate.
- To make the topping, in a mixing bowl beat the cream and sugar until stiff peaks form. Spoon or pipe the whipped cream in a decorative pattern over the cooled blueberry filling and refrigerate until serving. Garnish with a few fresh berries.

Blueberry Pie (Baked)

If you prefer your blueberries cooked, this is the summer pie for you.

Makes one 9-inch pie

Dough for 9-inch double-crust pie (see page 8)

For the filling

4 cups fresh blueberries (about 1⅓ pints), washed and stems removed

1 tablespoon freshly squeezed lemon juice

1 cup sugar

5 tablespoons flour

½ teaspoon cinnamon

2 tablespoons unsalted butter

Vanilla ice cream

- Preheat the oven to 450 degrees. Lightly grease a 9-inch pie plate with shortening.
- On a lightly floured surface, roll out the larger disc of dough to make a 13-inch circle. Carefully transfer the dough to the prepared pie plate and press onto the bottom and sides without stretching it. Trim the edges, leaving a ¾-inch overhang. Add any extra dough to the smaller disc of dough.
- To make the filling, combine the blueberries, lemon juice, sugar, flour, and cinnamon. Toss carefully but thoroughly. Transfer the filling to the lined pie plate. Dot the top with bits of butter. Brush the edges of the dough with water.
- Roll out the remaining dough to fit over the top. Lay it over the blueberries and press the top and bottom dough together to seal. Trim the edges and crimp to form a decorative edge. Cut vent holes in the top crust.
- Place the pie plate on a heavy baking sheet (to catch any overflow) and bake on the bottom rack of the oven for 10 minutes. Reduce the heat to 350 degrees and continue baking until the pie in nicely browned, about 30 minutes.
- Serve the pie slightly warm with vanilla ice cream.

Boston Cream Pie

This beloved classic is really a *cake*, and is only as good as its three simple components: vanilla cake, vanilla custard, and the Parker House addition of a chocolate glaze. It's like a chocolate eclair, but in cake form!

Make the filling ahead and refrigerate it until serving time when the cake can be quickly assembled. This cake conveniently uses the egg whites from the filling and has a light crumb to match the soft vanilla custard. The cake alone, without the filling or topping, makes a wonderful 8-inch, double-layer white cake (bake about 30 minutes).

Serves 10

For the vanilla filling

3 egg yolks

¼ cup sugar

3 tablespoons flour

Pinch of salt

1¼ cups half-and-half

1 teaspoon vanilla extract

1 tablespoon unsalted butter

For the cake layer

1½ cups flour

¼ cup cornstarch

2½ teaspoons double-acting baking powder

½ teaspoon salt

½ cup solid vegetable shortening

1 cup sugar

2 teaspoons vanilla

⅔ cup milk, at room temperature

3 egg whites, at room temperature

For the chocolate glaze

⅓ cup heavy cream

2 tablespoons unsalted butter

3 ounces semisweet chocolate, finely chopped

- To make the filling, in a heavy saucepan whisk together the yolks, sugar, flour, and salt. Add the half-and-half slowly, whisking until smooth. Cook the mixture over low heat, whisking constantly toward the end of the

continued on next page

cooking time until thick and smooth and the center tries to bubble, about 10 to 12 minutes.

- Strain the mixture into a bowl. Stir in the vanilla and butter. Cool, stirring occasionally to let the steam escape. Cover and refrigerate until you assemble the cake.
- Grease a 9-by-2-inch round cake pan with shortening, line the bottom with parchment paper, and grease and lightly flour the paper.
- Preheat the oven to 350 degrees.
- To make the cake, sift together the flour, cornstarch, baking powder, and salt three times.
- In a mixing bowl, beat the shortening and add the sugar gradually. Beat the mixture until light, and add the vanilla.
- On low speed, alternately add the sifted dry ingredients and milk, mixing just until thoroughly combined.
- In a separate bowl, beat the egg whites just until stiff but not dry. Fold the whites into the cake batter gently but thoroughly. Spread the batter evenly in the prepared pan.
- Bake the cake on the middle rack of the oven until golden, about 45 minutes. (The center should be springy and the cake should begin to pull away from the sides of the pan.) Cool 10 minutes before turning out onto a wire rack to cool completely. Cover lightly with a towel to prevent the cake from drying out.
- To make the glaze, heat the cream and butter in a heavy saucepan until bubbles appear around the edges. Remove the pan from the heat, add the chocolate, and cover. After 5 minutes, uncover and stir very gently until the mixture is smooth. Cool until thickened yet fluid enough to glaze the cake and drip over the sides.
- The cake is best assembled just before serving time since it will dry out in the refrigerator. Brush the crumbs from the edges of the cake. Cut the cake into two equal horizontal layers with a serrated knife. The finished top should remain the top. Carefully place the bottom layer on a cake plate.
- Spread the filling to within an inch of the edge of the bottom layer. Add the top layer with the finished, baked side up. The weight of the top layer will squeeze the pudding to the edges of the cake.
- Pour the glaze over the top and spread quickly with a flat metal spatula until it covers the top and drips over the edges. Serve right away or briefly refrigerate, uncovered, until serving time.

Bread Pudding

The old way is still the best for this simple, homey classic. If your children can butter toast, they can make this dessert and bake it while you prepare dinner. Bread pudding is best served warm, with maybe a bit of cream for added goodness, so make just enough for one sitting. For breakfast, this reminds everyone of French toast, another bread-and-custard favorite.

Apart from the toasted and buttered bread and the custard sauce basics, you can embellish the flavors to suit yourself. Spread fruit jam on the toast, or add drained crushed pineapple, or a chopped apple.

Serves 4

2½ tablespoons unsalted butter, softened

4 slices firm white bread

About 2 tablespoons fruit jam, *or* ½ cup drained crushed pineapple, *or* 1 apple, cored, peeled, and finely chopped (optional)

2 eggs

3 tablespoons sugar

Pinch of salt

¾ cup light cream

½ teaspoon cinnamon

Extra light cream for the top (optional)

- Butter a 1-quart shallow baking dish with ½ tablespoon of the butter. Preheat the oven to 350 degrees.
- Trim the crusts from the bread, toast lightly, and butter each slice. (Spread with the optional fruit jam.) Cut the bread in approximately 1-inch cubes and scatter in the prepared pan. (Add the optional pineapple or apple.)
- Whisk together the eggs, 2 tablespoons of the sugar, the salt, and cream. Pour the mixture over the bread and gently push the bread down. It's all right to have a few points of bread poking up.
- Combine the cinnamon and remaining sugar and sprinkle over the top of the pudding.
- Put the baking dish in a roasting pan and pour in enough hot water to come half way up the sides of the baking dish. Carefully place it on the middle rack of the oven and bake until nearly set and fairly firm, about 25 to 35 minutes. Cool 5 minutes before serving warm, with or without additional cream.

Broccoli Stir-fry

Broccoli takes on new dimensions when quickly stir-fried with a bit of ginger, garlic, and salt. This is, hands down, our favorite family vegetable, and one that adds a beautiful green to the dinner plate. If the broccoli is cleaned and cut ahead, it takes only a few minutes to stir-fry and steam in one pan at serving time.

Serves 4 to 6

1 bunch (about 1½ pounds) broccoli
3 tablespoons peanut or vegetable oil
¾ teaspoon salt
1 clove garlic, peeled and smashed with the flat of a knife

1 large slice fresh ginger, peeled and smashed with the flat of a knife
½ cup water

- Wash, clean, and prepare the broccoli by cutting off the stems and peeling the tough skin. Peel and cut the stems in ½-inch diagonal slices. Cut the tops in bite-size flowers.
- In a large sauté pan with a lid, heat the oil, salt, smashed garlic, and ginger until very hot. Remove the garlic before it burns. Add the prepared broccoli stems and flowers and stir quickly for 1 minute until coated with the oil.
- Add the water and cover immediately. Reduce the heat to medium and let the broccoli steam for about 5 minutes.
- Remove the lid, increase the heat, and cook until the water has nearly evaporated and the broccoli is cooked to the desired tenderness, about 1 minute. Remove the ginger and serve.

Brownies

Don't you tire of such superlatives as *"best* brownie," "world's *greatest* brownie," "the *perfect* brownie"? My family *loves* these brownies, which are very chocolatey, very fudgey, without nuts, and lightly iced.

The cocoa powder makes them easy to prepare, and the corn syrup keeps them fudgey. If you like a cakier brownier, eliminate the corn syrup.

Makes 24 brownies

½ pound unsalted butter, at room temperature

1 cup granulated sugar

1 cup brown sugar

2 tablespoons light corn syrup

1 teaspoon vanilla extract

4 eggs, at room temperature

1 cup flour

¾ cup unsweetened cocoa powder

½ teaspoon salt

Confectioners' sugar (optional)

For the chocolate icing

4 tablespoons unsalted butter, softened

1 cup confectioners' sugar

3 tablespoons unsweetened cocoa powder

Pinch of salt

1 teaspoon vanilla extract

1 to 2 tablespoons water or coffee

- Preheat the oven to 350 degrees. Butter the bottom of a 9-by-13-inch baking pan.
- To make the cake, cream the butter and sugars until light and fluffy. Beat in the corn syrup and vanilla. Add the eggs one at a time, beating until very light.
- Sift the flour, cocoa powder, and salt together and add in three parts to the creamed mixture. Mix on low speed just until thoroughly incorporated.
- Spread the batter evenly in the prepared pan and bake in the upper half of the oven until the sides are set and the middle remains a bit soft, about

continued on next page

35 minutes. Cool. Dust with confectioners' sugar and cut into squares, or cool completely and frost with chocolate icing.

- To make the chocolate icing, cream the butter, sugar, cocoa, salt, and vanilla, adding enough water or coffee to create a spreading consistency.
- Wait until the brownies are completely cool before icing. Cutting the iced brownies will be easier if you refrigerate them for 15 minutes to set the icing.

*B*utter Brickle

Butter Brickle is a combination of nut brittle and buttercrunch candy, both based on a butter-sugar syrup cooked to the crack stage. Spread the candy to a delicate thinness while hot, brush it with melted chocolate, and sprinkle the top with chopped nuts (pecans, almonds, or walnuts). It makes a nice gift in a bow-bedecked tin as well as great nibbling anytime.

Makes about 1½ pounds

¼ cup heavy cream
¼ cup water
8 tablespoons unsalted butter, cut into pieces
1 cup sugar
½ cup light corn syrup

½ teaspoon vanilla extract
6 ounces bittersweet chocolate, finely chopped
½ cup finely chopped, lightly toasted nuts (almonds, walnuts, or pecans)

- Lightly butter a baking sheet and a wooden spoon or spatula.
- In a large heavy pot, combine the cream, water, butter, sugar, and corn syrup. Heat and stir with a wooden spoon until the sugar dissolves. Increase the heat and boil to 295 degrees on a candy thermometer. Watch carefully and stir constantly toward the end when the temperature rises quickly and the candy begins to turn a golden color.

- Remove the pot from the heat and immediately stir in the vanilla. Pour the candy onto the greased baking sheet and quickly spread with the buttered spoon to a 12-inch square or to the desired thickness.
- Melt the chocolate in a heavy pot over warm water, stirring often, just until melted and smooth. When the candy is almost cool, brush the chocolate over the surface and sprinkle with nuts.
- Set the candy aside to let it cool completely before breaking it up into pieces.

Note: Some candy tips

Lightly toasting the nuts brings out the flavor and makes them taste better.

A candy thermometer is a big help in making sure you've cooked the syrup to the crack stage.

Sugar syrup can cause terrible burns, so be careful!

Tempering chocolate so it keeps its nice glossy finish has always seemed a bother to me. An alternative method is to melt the chocolate slowly in a heavy pan over water, stirring often. When it's beautiful, smooth, and glossy, use it immediately—no reheating or cooling. That's the chocolate I use for dipping glacéed fruits and nuts to get a professional look at home. Place the dipped fruits or nuts on waxed paper and simply peel off when the chocolate has set.

B

Butterscotch Sauce

Thick and rich with the taste of brown sugar, butter, and cream, this sauce can only be better when combining with chocolate! For a double treat, my children get ice cream sundaes with warmed chocolate fudge sauce *and* warmed butterscotch sauce. They both keep well in a jar in the refrigerator. The microwave makes heating these sauces a 20-second job.

Makes about 1½ cups

½ cup granulated sugar

½ cup brown sugar

¼ cup light corn syrup

4 tablespoons unsalted butter

2 tablespoons water

2 teaspoons white vinegar

Pinch of salt

¾ cup heavy cream (approximately)

- In a heavy saucepan, combine the sugars, corn syrup, butter, water, vinegar, and salt. Bring to a boil and cook over medium heat 1 minute or until it's like a heavy syrup. Off the heat, whisk in the cream, more for a thinner sauce, less for a thicker sauce. Cool before pouring into a jar and refrigerating. As it cools it will become thicker.

- For warm butterscotch sauce, heat uncovered in the microwave or put the jar in a saucepan of water and heat slowly over low heat.

Caesar Salad

This salad is only as good as its ingredients so take the time to wash and *dry* the lettuce, to grate *quality* cheese, and to sauté *fresh* bread cubes, and use freshly squeezed lemon juice and extra-virgin olive oil. If your family has mixed feelings about anchovies, cut them up and serve them on the side.

Serves 6

For the croutons

2 cups ¾-inch cubes French bread   ⅓ cup extra-virgin olive oil

continued on next page

For the salad

1 clove garlic, cut in half

2 medium heads romaine lettuce, washed and dried well

¾ teaspoon salt

Freshly ground black pepper

⅓ cup extra-virgin olive oil

1 egg, plunged in boiling water for 1 minute and then in cold water

3 tablespoons freshly squeezed lemon juice

6 anchovies, drained and cut up (optional)

½ cup freshly grated Parmesan cheese

- Sauté the bread cubes in the oil until browned and crisp. Set aside.
- Rub a salad bowl with the garlic halves and discard. Tear the lettuce in bite-size pieces and add. Sprinkle the lettuce with salt and pepper and drizzle with oil. Toss well.
- Break the coddled egg over the lettuce; add the lemon juice, anchovies, and the cheese. Toss well to coat the lettuce.
- Top with the croutons and *serve immediately* so they don't become soggy.

52

Caramel Corn

This snack is fun to make with children, and it tastes much better and fresher than the boxed version. A hot caramel syrup binds the popcorn and peanuts to make our traditional Halloween Caramel Corn, complete with a few hidden surprises added at the last minute—small plastic or metal figures or toy vehicles, "fortunes," or wrapped individual candies.

The sugar syrup needs a candy thermometer or a very practiced candy maker who can detect subtle changes in color and in the size of the bubbles to make a successful crack-stage caramel.

Serves 8 to 10

16 cups freshly popped popcorn (two batches, each made with ¼ cup kernels), unsalted
½ cup water
1 cup granulated sugar
½ cup brown sugar

⅓ cup light corn syrup
8 tablespoons unsalted butter
1 teaspoon vinegar or lemon juice
1½ cups cocktail peanuts
Prizes (optional)

53

- Put the popped corn in a large bowl.
- Using a large saucepan (the caramel will boil up a lot!), combine the water, sugars, corn syrup, butter, and vinegar. Stir well and heat to boiling. Stirring constantly over medium heat, bring the caramel mixture up to 285 degrees (soft-crack stage) on a candy thermometer.
- Working quickly and carefully, pour the hot caramel over the popcorn, stirring in the peanuts as you mix and toss. Spread on a baking sheet to cool. The caramel will harden as it cools. Break the caramel corn into pieces and toss with prizes.

Carrot Cake

As a child, I only had to hear the name to wonder why anyone would ruin a good cake with vegetables. One taste made me a believer. The carrots, nuts, and pineapple add texture to a moist cake fragrant with cinnamon and spices. Plain, or iced with a cream cheese frosting, carrot cake is no ascetic health food, but a cake of great versatility that can be made with grated butternut squash as well as carrots, or turned into an Indian carrot cake with the substitution of pistachio nuts for walnuts, fresh grated coconut for the pineapple, and a bit of ground cardamom with the cinnamon.

Serves 12 to 15

54

2 cups flour

2 teaspoons double-acting baking powder

1 teaspoon baking soda

½ teaspoon salt

2 teaspoons cinnamon

¼ teaspoon grated nutmeg

4 eggs, at room temperature

1¾ cups sugar

2 teaspoons vanilla extract

8 tablespoons unsalted butter, melted and cooled

½ cup vegetable or corn oil

3 medium (about ¾ pound) carrots, grated to make 2½ cups

1 8-ounce can crushed pineapple in natural juice, well drained

Grated zest of 1 orange

¾ cup coarsely chopped walnuts

½ cup raisins (optional)

Confectioners' sugar, *or* cream cheese frosting for the top

For the cream cheese frosting (optional)

4 ounces cream cheese, softened

2 tablespoons unsalted butter, softened

1½ cups confectioners' sugar

1 teaspoon orange juice to thin, if necessary

Walnuts for garnish (optional)

- Grease a 9-by-13-inch pan with shortening and dust it lightly with flour. Preheat the oven to 350 degrees.
- Sift together the flour, baking powder, baking soda, salt, cinnamon, and nutmeg.

- In another bowl, beat the eggs until light. Add the sugar gradually, beating until pale and light.
- On low speed, add the vanilla extract, butter, and oil slowly, beating until combined.
- Fold in the sifted dry ingredients until smooth and well mixed.
- Gently stir in the carrots, pineapple, orange zest, nuts, and raisins.
- Spread the batter in the prepared pan and bake on the middle rack of the oven until the cake pulls way from the sides of the pan and a toothpick inserted in the center comes out clean, about 50 to 60 minutes. Cool completely and dust with confectioners' sugar or frost with cream cheese frosting.
- To make the frosting, beat the cream cheese and butter together until smooth. Add the sugar and thin with orange juice if needed. Spread over the cooled cake. Decorate with walnuts if you like.

*C*arrot Slaw

For my non-cabbage eaters, this is a favorite salad at the height of picnic season. It's a favorite in the doldrums of winter as well, when vegetables aren't at their peak. The variations on this shredded carrot-and-mayonnaise slaw depend upon your whim and available ingredients. For an Indian touch, I add chopped pistachio nuts and a dash of cardamom with the currants and ginger. For children, I add cinnamon and skip the ginger.

Serves 6

1 pound carrots, skinned and grated or shredded to make 3 cups
½ cup Mayonnaise (see page 174)
1 tablespoon lemon juice
⅓ cup dried coconut flakes

⅓ cup currants
1 teaspoon sugar, or to taste
2 tablespoons minced crystallized ginger, *or* ½ teaspoon cinnamon

- Combine the carrots, mayonnaise, lemon juice, coconut, currants, and sugar. Add the ginger and toss with a fork. Refrigerate a few hours, toss, and serve.

Challah

As wonderful as fresh egg breads taste, they are even better the next day as toast. The eggs give them beautiful color and lightness. Whatever the ethnic origin—French brioche, Portuguese sweet bread, Jewish challah, Italian or Greek, braided or in loaves—egg breads are universally acclaimed.

Challah gives children a chance to show off their kneading and braiding skills and to decorate the top of the bread with "paint" (an egg wash) and "sprinkles" (poppy seeds, sesame seeds, coarse salt). Your time and patience will be richly rewarded.

Makes 2 loaves

1¼-ounce envelope (1 scant tablespoon) active dry yeast

Pinch of sugar

1¼ cups warm water (see page 19)

4½ cups flour (approximately)

2 tablespoons sugar

2 teaspoons salt

2 eggs, at room temperature

¼ cup vegetable oil

1 egg yolk and 1 tablespoon milk for a glaze

Poppy seeds, sesame seeds, or coarse salt for the top

- Grease 2 4½-by-8½ or 5-by-9 loaf pans or a heavy baking sheet with shortening.
- Add the yeast and pinch of sugar to ¼ cup of the warm water; allow it to proof until puffy and bubbly, about 10 minutes. If it doesn't proof, discard it and use a fresher batch of yeast. The envelope of yeast should be dated, and refrigerated to keep it fresh.
- Put 3½ cups of the flour, the sugar, and salt in a large bowl. Make a well in the dry ingredients and add the proofed yeast, eggs, oil, and remaining water. Stir well until the mixture forms a dough. Turn the dough out onto a floured surface and knead it, adding ½ cup more flour. Knead until smooth, springy, and no longer too sticky, adding remaining flour as needed.
- Oil a large bowl and add the dough, turning to coat all sides. Cover loosely with a towel and let rise in a warm place until the dough has doubled, about 45 minutes to 1 hour.

- Punch the dough down and divide it in half. Divide each half into 3 equal parts; roll each part into a 14-inch rope. To braid, pinch together one end of the 3 ropes. The left rope is placed over the center rope becoming the center rope. Then the right rope is placed over the center rope. Again, the left rope is placed over the center, then the right, continuing until the end. Tuck the ends under and place in the pans or on the baking sheet. Cover the breads loosely with a towel and allow to rise until doubled in size, about 45 minutes.
- Preheat the oven to 375 degrees.
- Combine the egg yolk and milk and brush over the tops of the breads. Sprinkle with seeds or salt. Bake on the middle rack of the oven until the bottom of the bread sounds hollow when turned over and rapped with your knuckles, about 40 to 50 minutes. The bread should be a beautiful golden color. Cool on a rack before slicing.

Cheese Ball or Log

As a cheese maker, I have great respect for the skill, integrity, and time it takes to make fine cheese. There is nothing better than a quality farmstead cheese of any nationality. Yet there are also times for festive cheese balls that are so popular for entertaining.

The traditional Cheddar spread rolled in nuts has been elaborated on in many versions: curried, with chutney and coconut; with blue cheese and candied pineapple, coated with pecans; with goat cheese and herbs, wrapped in prosciutto. The base is basically a butter, cheese, and cream cheese combination, imaginatively spiced and flavored, and assembled with an eye for color and presentation. Instead of rolling the cheese into a large ball or log, you might make small cheese "truffles" and serve them in fancy candy papers as hors d'oeuvres. Or you might roll the cheese in toasted sesame seeds instead of nuts.

Here's a favorite cheese ball that's always a hit with corn or tortilla chips.

Makes one 5-inch ball

8 tablespoons unsalted butter, softened

1 8-ounce container soft extra-sharp Cheddar cheese (Wispride or Cracker Barrel)

1 3-ounce package cream cheese

2 teaspoons chili powder, or to taste

½ teaspoon paprika

⅛ teaspoon cayenne pepper

Pinch of sugar

1 canned or brined hot pepper, finely minced (optional)

¾ cup chopped walnuts or pecans

¼ cup finely chopped parsley or cilantro (optional)

- In a mixer, blend the butter, cheddar cheese, cream cheese, spices, sugar, and hot pepper until smooth.
- Transfer to a piece of waxed paper and form into a rough 5-inch ball. Chill a few hours to make handling easier. The cheese will still be fairly soft.
- At serving time, roll the cheese ball in the nuts or a combination of nuts and parsley or cilantro. Arrange on a serving dish and serve with chips or crackers.

Cheesecake

Creamy rich and filling cheesecakes come in every flavor and with a multitude of crusts and toppings. Once you master a basic, all-purpose cheesecake, you can move on to variations in the crust, filling, and topping. Consider a crumb crust of graham crackers, chocolate wafers, gingersnaps, vanilla or lemon cookies; or half crumbs and half ground nuts. The basic filling of cream cheese, sugar, eggs, and cream may be flavored with citrus juice and zest, a few drops of almond extract, lots of minced crystallized ginger, or melted white or dark chocolate. Fresh fruit toppings add an impressive, colorful crown to a simple cheesecake.

Cracks form on the top surface when cheesecakes are baked at a temperature that's too high. Baking at an initially high temperature sets the crust, then a low temperature slowly cooks the filling to a rich creaminess. Cool completely before refrigerating.

Wrap cheesecakes well and store away from strong-smelling foods like garlic and onions. Cheesecakes can be made ahead and frozen if you wrap them well. If you have just one springform pan and need to make more than one cheesecake, put a foil-lined cardboard round in the bottom of the springform pan and press the crumb crust onto the buttered foil and sides. Fill and bake the cheesecake. When cooled, remove the sides of the springform and lift the cheesecake out on the cardboard round so you can reuse the pan.

If you change the size of the pan, adjust the baking time. A thicker cheesecake in an 8-inch or 9-inch pan will take longer. Check to see if it's set and no longer wet in the center before you turn off the oven to cool slowly.

Serves 12 to 14

For the crust

5 tablespoons unsalted butter, melted   2 tablespoons sugar
1½ cups graham cracker, chocolate
    wafer, or gingersnap crumbs

continued on next page

For the filling

1½ pounds cream cheese, at room temperature

1 cup sugar

3 eggs, at room temperature

1 tablespoon flour

½ cup heavy cream

For the flavorings (optional)

2 teaspoons vanilla extract

¼ teaspoon almond extract

Grated zest of 1 lemon or orange with a tablespoon of the juice

¼ cup minced crystallized ginger tossed with the flour

60

- Lightly brush the bottom and sides of a 10-inch springform pan with some of the melted butter. Preheat the oven to 400 degrees.
- To make the crust, thoroughly combine the melted butter, crumbs, and sugar. Press onto the bottom and 1 inch up the sides of the prepared pan. Set aside.
- To make the filling, in a mixing bowl beat the cream cheese until softened. Add the sugar gradually, beating until well creamed. Add the eggs, one at a time, beating until light. Add the flour and cream and mix until smooth. Add the flavoring.
- Spread the filling in the crust and smooth the top. Place the springform pan on a heavy baking sheet and bake on the middle rack of the oven for 10 minutes.
- Reduce the temperature to 225 degrees and continue to bake until the filling seems nearly set when you wiggle the pan, about 45 to 50 minutes.
- Turn off the oven and let the cake cool in the oven for 30 minutes. Open the oven door and let the cake cool 30 minutes more before transferring the pan to a wire rack to cool completely.
- Refrigerate until cold. Run a knife around the outside edge and remove the sides of the springform pan. Cover with plastic wrap to store in the refrigerator.

Variations: Optional toppings to put on at serving time
> Whole strawberries, points up, and brushed with melted apricot jam
>
> 1 pint fresh blueberries tossed in ¾ cup melted currant jelly to glaze
>
> Maple syrup brushed on top and garnished with whole pecans in a decorative pattern
>
> Chocolate curls; a vegetable peeler run over a milk chocolate bar will do this well.

Cherry-Almond Pie

George Washington's birthday wouldn't be complete without this cherry pie and its almond-streusel topping. It's a combination my son finds irresistible, especially à la mode. I call this "cheater's cherry pie" because of the prepared filling. Fresh sour cherries just aren't in season for George's February birthday. But *don't* cheat on the crust. Make your own for a far superior pie.

61

Makes one 9-inch pie

For the pie crust

1¼ cups flour
1 tablespoon sugar
¼ teaspoon salt
3 tablespoons unsalted butter

3 tablespoons solid vegetable shortening
3 to 4 tablespoons cold water

For the filling

1 21-ounce can cherry pie filling

3 or 4 drops almond extract

For the almond-streusel topping

½ cup flour
⅔ cup sugar

4 tablespoons unsalted butter
½ cup sliced or chopped almonds

continued on next page

- To make the crust, in a bowl or food processor, combine the flour, sugar, and salt.
- Add the butter and shortening and work with a pastry blender, or turn the food processor on and off, until the mixture resembles meal.
- Add the water slowly, tossing with a fork until the dough nearly comes together, or add all at once through the feed tube of the food processor with the motor running and process until the dough just begins to come together.
- Turn the dough out on a lightly floured surface and knead gently 2 or 3 times until it is more homogenized and forms a ball. Flatten into a disc and wrap well in plastic wrap. Chill until firm, at least 30 minutes.
- Roll the dough out on a lightly floured surface to form a circle approximately 13 inches in diameter. Transfer the dough to a lightly greased 9-inch pie plate and carefully press into the bottom and sides without stretching it. Trim the edge, leaving a 1-inch overhang. Turn the edge under, press together, and crimp to make a decorative edge. Chill the crust again before adding the filling.

- Preheat the oven to 425 degrees.
- To make the filling, combine the pie filling and the almond extract. Spread the filling in the chilled shell. Place the pie plate on a heavy baking sheet in case of overflow.
- To make the streusel topping, combine the flour and sugar in a deep bowl. Add the butter and work with a pastry blender until it resembles meal. Mix in the almonds. Sprinkle evenly over the filling.
- Bake the pie on the bottom shelf of the oven for 10 minutes. Reduce the temperature to 400 degrees and continue to bake until the crust is nicely browned and the filling is bubbly, about 30 minutes more. Reduce the oven temperature the last 10 minutes if the pie is browning too quickly.

CHICKEN

Plain or fancy, nothing beats chicken for its popularity, versatility, and price. Whether it is roasted, baked, fried, poached, or used in salads, stews, soups, pies, or even hot dogs, Americans have a love affair with this tasty bird. The terms roaster, fryer, game hen, capon, and fowl refer to the size, gender, and age of the chicken.

The rage in upscale restaurants has been free-range chickens, bred more humanely but not necessarily for enhanced flavor. My friends George Germon and Johanne Killeen, who grill chickens to perfection over wood and charcoal or in a wood burning oven at their Providence restaurants, think the free-range chickens are scrawny and overrated. They suggest finding a good supplier or a poultry farm where raising fowl is the primary business.

*T*rixie's Baked Chicken

I've made my grandmother Beatrice's chicken dish since I can remember helping in my mother's kitchen. It's perfect for a child's culinary repertoire since it's easy, foolproof, and a delicious contribution to a family dinner. It makes any young cook proud. As I've grown older, I've learned to trim the chicken more carefully (of all excess fat and excess skin), to add sesame seeds, herbs, or grated Parmesan cheese to the bread crumbs, and to go easy on the butter, but Trixie's Baked Chicken is still in my repertoire of family favorites.

Serves 4

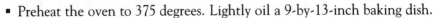

⅓ cup dry, unseasoned bread crumbs

1 teaspoon salt

½ teaspoon paprika

¼ teaspoon black pepper

2 tablespoons sesame seeds

1 3-pound chicken, well trimmed and cut into 8 pieces

2 tablespoons butter

• Preheat the oven to 375 degrees. Lightly oil a 9-by-13-inch baking dish.
• Combine the bread crumbs, salt, paprika, pepper, and sesame seeds on a piece of waxed paper. Coat the chicken pieces with the bread crumb mixture and place skin down in the prepared baking dish. Dot with bits of butter and bake 30 minutes.
• Turn the chicken skin side up and baste well with any accumulated juices and butter in the pan. Bake an additional 30 minutes, basting a few times, or until the chicken pieces are browned and crisp. Transfer the chicken to a platter and serve.

Chicken Almondine
(a.k.a. "Alligator Tails")

Children find the notion of eating "Alligator Tails" much more adventurous and exciting than eating Chicken Almondine, my 15-minute family favorite dinner. Even adults like the exotic notion of eating these buttery almond-scaled alligators at dinner parties. Calling them chicken almondine seems too *ordinaire*.

For speed and ease, buy boned and skinned chicken breasts. Dipped in an egg, milk, and flour batter, then in almonds and bread crumbs, they're ready to be quickly sautéed in lots of butter. These are wonderful with just a squeeze of lemon or, for added interest, with any condiments you have on hand: chutneys, Hot and Sweet Mustard (page 183), salsa sauces, Pepper-Mint Jelly (page 203), or Cranberry Relish (page 94).

Even faster and spicier is the deviled version. Brush the chicken with ⅓ cup Dijon mustard instead of dipping it in batter, then coat with the almonds and bread crumbs. This works with veal cutlets and fish fillets as well. When I dip batter- or mustard-coated pork cutlets in finely ground pecans and sauté them, it's Pork Pecandine.

Serves 6

6 to 8 boned, skinned chicken breast halves	1¼ cups sliced almonds
	½ cup dry bread crumbs
1 egg	Freshly ground pepper
½ cup milk	Pinch of cayenne pepper
½ cup flour	6 to 8 tablespoons salted butter
1 teaspoon salt	Lemon wedges for garnish

- Trim the chicken breasts of any fat. Cover the chicken with a piece of wax paper and, with a rolling pin, pound to flatten the chicken slightly to an even thickness.

continued on next page

- In a shallow dish or pie plate, combine the egg, milk, flour, and ½ teaspoon of the salt. Whisk until smooth. The consistency should be like heavy cream. Thin if necessary with a little more milk.
- On a piece of wax paper, combine the almonds, bread crumbs, the remaining salt, pepper, and cayenne pepper. Mix thoroughly.
- Dip each chicken breast in the batter, coating all sides and letting any excess dip off. Dip in the almond-crumb mixture and lay on a wire rack while making more. The breading will adhere best if you let the chicken (or meat or fish or vegetables) remain on the racks on a baking sheet in the refrigerator for at least 30 minutes.
- Melt 3 tablespoons of the butter in a large sauté pan. Sauté the chicken in two batches so you don't crowd the pan. When the butter is hot, add half the prepared chicken and sauté over medium heat about 4 minutes. Turn and sauté on the other side until nicely browned, about 4 minutes. Don't overcook. If the chicken browns too quickly, reduce the heat. When done, remove the chicken from the pan and keep it warm. Add more butter to the pan if needed, and cook the remaining chicken.
- Serve hot with a wedge of lemon or any condiments you like.

Chicken and Dumplings

This simple, satisfying Sunday dinner dish of my childhood has become a treasured weekday dinner served with salad. When time is short, you can cook the chicken ahead and quickly drop the dumplings into the braising juices to cook at the last minute. Additions of fresh or dried wild mushrooms to the chicken and fresh herbs in the dumplings give new life to an old dish that is still worth making.

All dark meat of chicken or just chicken breasts will ensure more even cooking. Wild mushrooms (boletes, also known as porcini or cèpes) give the sauce a rich, woodsy flavor, but you could use cultivated mushrooms.

Serves 4 to 6

3 tablespoons vegetable oil

8 pieces chicken, well trimmed of fat and excess skin

¼ cup flour seasoned with salt and pepper, for dredging

2 tablespoons butter

¼ cup minced shallots

½ pound fresh cultivated mushrooms, sliced (2½ cups)

2 tablespoons flour

2 cups chicken broth

1 cup water

¼ cup dried mushrooms soaked in 1 cup water for 30 minutes (optional)

Parsley stems, tied with string

¼ cup minced parsley for garnish

67

For the dumplings

1 cup cake flour (or use ⅞ cup all-purpose flour and 2 tablespoons corn starch as a substitute)

2 teaspoons double-acting baking powder

½ teaspoon salt

1 egg, at room temperature

¼ cup milk

1 teaspoon thyme or chives or fresh herbs, very finely minced (optional)

continued on next page

- In a large sauté pan with a lid, heat the oil. Dredge the chicken pieces lightly in the flour and brown well on all sides in the hot oil. Set the chicken aside and pour off any remaining oil. In the same pan, melt the butter over low heat and sauté the shallots and fresh mushrooms, stirring often to prevent them from browning. When they are soft, sprinkle with the flour, stir, and continue to cook for 1 minute. Off the heat, whisk in the chicken broth and water until smooth.
- If using dried mushrooms, remove them from the soaking water and chop well. Strain the liquid through a damp paper coffee filter or damp paper towel to remove any sand or grit. Add the mushrooms and liquid to the pan.
- Arrange the chicken pieces in the pan and add the tied parsley stems. Place a piece of foil directly on the surface of the chicken and liquid; then put the lid on the pan. Simmer until the chicken is tender (45 minutes for dark meat, 25 minutes for chicken breasts). Remove the foil and parsley stems and skim any fat from the top.

68

- When the chicken is nearly cooked, prepare the dumplings, which will cook in the same liquid. To make the dumplings, sift together the flour, baking powder, and salt three times. Mix the egg and milk with the herbs. Stir the egg-milk mixture slowly into the dry ingredients just until mixed. Don't overwork.
- Remove the chicken from the pan and arrange on a platter. Cover the chicken loosely with foil to keep warm while the dumplings cook.
- Drop the dumpling batter by rounded teaspoon into the simmering chicken-mushroom broth in the pan. Cover and simmer 10 minutes.
- Spoon the sauce with the mushrooms and the dumplings over the chicken. Sprinkle with parsley and serve hot.

CHICKEN SALADS

Every cook must have a number of family chicken salad recipes, from the basic celery and mayonnaise, to more exotic salads with additions of grapes and pecans, pea pods and ginger, or sun-dried tomatoes and capers. Moist, flavorful chicken cut in large chunks is the only trick to making any of them delicious, whether you use commercial or homemade mayonnaise.

Makes about 4 cups

To make chicken for salad

1 4- to 5-pound chicken	Parsley stems, tied with string
1 onion, cut in half	¼ cup oil
2 celery stalks, cut up	A few peppercorns
1 carrot, cut in chunks	Pinch of salt

- Place the chicken in a pot just large enough to hold it and the other ingredients. Cover with water; add the remaining ingredients.
- Bring the water to a boil and simmer, partially covered, for 1 hour. Cool the chicken in the liquid before removing it. Strain the poaching liquid, skim off any fat, and save the broth for another use. Take the skin off the chicken in large pieces. Pull the meat off the bones and cut in large chunks. Discard the bones. Place the meat in a bowl and cover with the chicken skin and a few tablespoons of the cooking broth to keep the chicken moist while you make the salad.

Chicken Salad with Mustard Mayonnaise

I serve this with boiled new potatoes, garden green beans, and cherry tomatoes. Or serve the salad in crusty French rolls for a picnic.

Serves 6 to 8

Approximately 4 cups boned cooked chicken chunks from 1 4-pound chicken (see page 63)

½ cup slivered cornichons (small French pickles)

3 to 4 stalks celery, chopped

2 tablespoons small capers in brine, drained

¼ cup minced parsley

For the mustard mayonnaise

70

3 tablespoons vinegar brine from cornichon jar, at room temperature

1 cup vegetable oil, *or* a combination of vegetable oil and olive oil

1 egg, at room temperature

1 tablespoon Dijon mustard, at room temperature

½ teaspoon salt

2 tablespoons hot water

Salt and freshly ground pepper to taste

6 slices bacon, cooked crisp and crumbled (optional garnish)

- Combine the chicken, cornichons, celery, capers, and parsley in a bowl; set aside.
- To make the mustard mayonnaise, pour the vinegar brine and oil into a measuring cup.
- In a bowl or food processor, combine the egg, mustard, and salt. Whisking constantly or with the motor running, add the oil mixture in a very slow, steady stream until a thick emulsion has formed. Add the hot water to set the mayonnaise. Store in the refrigerator unless using immediately.
- Add enough mustard mayonnaise to the chicken salad to bind it well. Season with salt and pepper to taste. Serve topped with optional bacon and any extra mayonnaise on the side.

Chicken Salad with Ginger Mayonnaise

Serves 6 to 8

Approximately 4 cups boned cooked chicken chunks from 1 4-pound chicken (see page 63)

2 cups peeled, julienned jicama, *or* 1 8-ounce can sliced water chestnuts, drained

2 cups diagonally sliced celery

3 to 4 scallions, white and green part, sliced thinly on a diagonal

For the ginger mayonnaise

3 tablespoons lemon juice, at room temperature

1 egg, at room temperature

1 teaspoon powdered ginger

½ teaspoon dry mustard

1 tablespoon sugar

¾ teaspoon salt

1 cup vegetable oil

3 to 4 tablespoons minced crystallized ginger

½ pound pea pods, strings removed, blanched, plunged in ice water, and dried

¾ cup whole toasted almonds

71

- Combine the chicken, jicama, celery, and scallions in a bowl; set aside.
- To make the ginger mayonnaise, in a bowl or food processor combine the lemon juice, egg, ginger, mustard, sugar, and salt. Whisking constantly or with the motor running, add the oil very slowly in a steady stream until a thick emulsified mayonnaise forms.
- Stir in the crystallized ginger and refrigerate unless using immediately.
- Add enough ginger mayonnaise to the salad to bind it well. At serving time, top with almonds and arrange the pea pods around the salad. Serve any extra mayonnaise on the side.

Chicken Soup

I enjoy chicken soup as a late afternoon energizer in a mug, a quick lunch with leftovers from the refrigerator (see Leftover Soup, page 161), a snack for children who enjoy it with dipping crackers, or a special first course for dinner. My mother-in-law freezes chicken soup in ice cube trays "for emergencies." Family factions still debate the relative merits of fresh dill and fresh gingerroot. I add thyme.

Serves 6 to 8

1 3- to 4-pound chicken or chicken parts, trimmed of excess fat
Water to cover
1 large onion, peeled (onion skin will darken the broth) and quartered
2 stalks celery, cut in a few pieces
1 or 2 carrots, cut in a few pieces

Parsley sprigs, tied for easy removal
A knob of fresh gingerroot, *or* sprigs of dill (tied with the parsley), *or* a few sprigs of fresh thyme
1 teaspoon salt
A few black peppercorns
Salt to taste

• Place the whole chicken, breast down, or the chicken parts in a large heavy pot. Add water to cover and slowly bring to a boil. Skim the surface and lower the heat to a simmer.

• Add the onion, celery, carrots, parsley, ginger, salt, and pepper. Simmer, partially covered, for 1½ hours.

• Let the soup cool slightly before removing the chicken and vegetables. Pour the broth through a fine mesh strainer. Skim the fat from the soup (this is easier if you chill it to allow the fat to congeal) and add the cooked carrots and any chicken from the bones.

Note: If you want to use the soup for stock, you can reduce it by half to intensify the flavor by cooking, uncovered, over medium-high heat. Do not add salt to the soup.

Chili

I was once a judge in a chili cook-off, so I know how diverse chili recipes can be: some with beans (not technically correct); some with meat (*con carne*) such as venison, beef, or pork; some with clams; some with beer or tequilla; some with tomatoes, and even cocoa. But any version *always* contains hot chili peppers. Our family favorite is topped with chopped onions and shredded cheese, and served on rice or macaroni, or with tortilla chips as an hors d'oeuvre. It even tops hot dogs (chili dogs) or open-face toasted cheese sandwiches. Made in triple quantities, chili has become the warming dish at end-of-the-season soccer parties.

Serves 10 to 12

2 tablespoons oil
2 large onions, chopped
3 cloves garlic, peeled and minced
2½ pounds ground beef
¼ cup fine yellow cornmeal
1 28-ounce can tomatoes in tomato purée
2 cups water
¼ cup red wine vinegar
¼ cup tomato paste
3 to 4 tablespoons chili powder
1 tablespoon ground cumin
1 tablespoon dried oregano
1 tablespoon salt

1 tablespoon paprika
2 teaspoons sugar
2 teaspoons ground coriander
1 bay leaf
Black pepper and cayenne pepper to taste
1 1-pound can dark kidney beans, drained
1½ pounds elbow macaroni, cooked and drained
1 pound Longhorn cheddar cheese, grated
1 cup chopped red onion

• In a large pan, heat the oil and sauté the onions for 5 minutes over low heat, stirring to prevent them from coloring. Add the garlic and sauté, stirring, for 1 minute.

• Add the ground beef and sauté, breaking it up and stirring until the beef is no longer pink. Drain off all the accumulated fat.

continued on next page

- Mix in the cornmeal. Add the tomatoes with purée, the water, vinegar, chili powder, cumin, oregano, salt, paprika, sugar, coriander, and bay leaf. Slowly bring the mixture to a boil and simmer, uncovered, for 30 minutes, stirring occasionally.
- Stir in the beans and heat thoroughly. Remove the bay leaf and add the black pepper and cayenne pepper to taste. Serve hot over the macaroni. Sprinkle the top with cheese and onions.

CHOCOLATE CHIP COOKIES

74

The basic chocolate chip cookie recipe (on the back of the chocolate chip packages) is a simple gem when made with quality ingredients like real butter and good chocolate. My mother-in-law taught me that the way to my husband's heart was to double the amount of chocolate chips in the basic recipe. Use mini-chips, maxi-chips, or hand-cut chunks of chocolate; add oats, walnuts, pecans, unsalted peanuts, or macadamia nuts. The dough can be pressed into a pan to make cookie bars when time is short.

Inspired by a trip to Hershey, Pennsylvania, I made a new chocolate chip cookie that became a family favorite even for those who objected to nuts interfering with the decadence of pure chocolate. See what you think!

Chocolate Chip Cookies à la Hershey

Makes 5 dozen cookies

½ pound unsalted butter, softened
¾ cup granulated sugar
¾ cup brown sugar
2 eggs, at room temperature
1 teaspoon vanilla extract
2½ cups flour
¼ cup Hershey's unsweetened cocoa
1 teaspoon baking soda

½ teaspoon salt
1 teaspoon instant coffee granules (optional)
2 8-ounce Hershey Bars with Almonds (*or* Special Dark if you prefer a darker chocolate and don't like nuts, *or* 1 of each)

- Preheat the oven to 375 degrees.
- In a mixing bowl, beat the butter until soft. Add the sugars gradually and beat until light. Add the eggs, one at a time, and the vanilla.
- Combine the flour, cocoa, baking soda, salt, and coffee granules. Gradually add to the butter-sugar mixture and mix well.
- Chop the chocolate bars in chunks or pieces and add to the dough. Shape the dough into 1½-inch balls and arrange on a heavy ungreased baking sheet.
- Place the baking sheet on a rack in the upper half of the oven and immediately reduce the temperature to 350 degrees. Bake until the edges are firm and the centers are still slightly soft, about 8 to 10 minutes. Cool 1 minute before removing with a spatula to a wire rack. Don't overbake them!

Variation: To make *Chocolate Chip Cookie Bars:* Grease a 10-by-15-inch jelly-roll pan and spread the dough evenly in the pan to the edges. Bake until set but still slightly creamy if you insert a toothpick in the center, about 25 minutes. They will firm as they cool. Cut into about 3 dozen cookie bars.

Chocolate Fudge

Every Good Boy Deserves Fudge (and every good girl!) was the musical mnemonic of my childhood. Fudge is still the favored reward for my son's diligence at the piano. Or, fudge *balls*, rolled in cocoa powder and served in candy papers, make an elegant end to a special dinner, or a decadent addition to a dessert table.

Makes 1½ pounds

⅔ cup heavy cream

2 cups sugar

2 tablespoons light corn syrup

4 tablespoons unsalted butter

3 1-ounce squares unsweetened chocolate, chopped

1 teaspoon vanilla extract

2 teaspoons instant coffee granules

3 tablespoons unsweetened cocoa powder

Pinch of salt

60 decorative individual candy papers (available at paper and candy supply stores)

• Combine the cream, sugar, corn syrup, butter, and chocolate in a heavy 2-quart saucepan. Bring to a boil over medium heat and stir constantly until the chocolate and sugar melt.

• Lower the heat and boil until the mixture reaches 235 degrees on a candy thermometer (soft-ball stage).

• Remove from the heat and cool, without stirring, for 30 to 35 minutes or until the chocolate is cool enough to touch. Add the vanilla, coffee granules, and salt. Beat until the chocolate loses its gloss and begins to thicken.

• Spread the fudge on a sheet of wax paper. Set aside until cool and firm, about 1 hour.

• Form the fudge into about 60 1-inch balls, roll them in cocoa, shaking off any excess, and carefully place them in the candy papers. Layer the candy in a covered tin with wax paper between layers, and store in the refrigerator. Serve at room temperature.

$\mathscr{C}$hocolate Layer Cake

After years of making many different kinds of chocolate cakes, some with cocoa or melted chocolate, some with buttermilk or coffee, some with brown sugar or white, we decided this is the one we like best. It uses unsweetened cocoa and a combination of buttermilk and coffee.

All cocoa is not the same. If the cocoa has been alkalized or "Dutched," the cake will use baking powder as leavening (see Note 1). If it hasn't been alkalized, baking soda is used to react with the acidic cocoa and leaven the cake. Buttermilk, another acid ingredient, gives cakes an unmistakable soft, fine crumb.

Serves 12

For the cakes

2 cups flour

¾ cup unsweetened cocoa powder (non-Dutch processed)

1½ teaspoons baking soda

½ teaspoon salt

¾ cup solid vegetable shortening

1¾ cups sugar

2 eggs, at room temperature

1 teaspoon vanilla extract

½ cup strong coffee, at room temperature

1 cup buttermilk, at room temperature

For the frosting

6 tablespoons unsalted butter, softened

¼ cup plus 2 tablespoons solid vegetable shortening

3 cups confectioners' sugar

Pinch of salt

½ cup unsweetened cocoa

⅓ cup warm coffee or water

1 teaspoon vanilla extract

Coffee as needed to thin to a spreading consistency

- Grease two 9-by-2-inch cake pans (or 3 8-inch pans) well with shortening and flour the bottoms lightly. Preheat the oven to 350 degrees.
- To make the cakes, sift together the flour, cocoa, baking soda, and salt.

continued on next page

- In a mixing bowl, beat the shortening. Add the sugar gradually and beat until well creamed. Add the eggs, one at a time, beating until very light, about 5 minutes. Add the vanilla.
- On low speed, add the dry ingredients alternately with the coffee and buttermilk, mixing just until thoroughly combined.
- Divide the batter between the pans and push it up against the sides with a knife to help it rise evenly.
- Bake the cakes on a rack in the upper half of the oven until the centers are springy and the cakes begin to pull away from the sides of the pan, about 35 to 40 minutes (about 30 to 35 minutes for 8-inch pans).
- Cool the cakes in the pans for 15 minutes before turning them out onto a wire rack to cool completely. Cover loosely with a towel to prevent the cakes from drying out. Frost when completely cool.
- To make the frosting, beat the butter and shortening together in a mixing bowl until well creamed. Beat in the sugar and salt.
- Whisk the cocoa and warm liquid together and add, with the vanilla, to the mixing bowl. Beat until light and fluffy, adding more coffee, a tablespoon at a time, until the frosting is the consistency of mayonnaise. Use immediately to frost the cooled cake layers.

Note 1: If using Dutch-processed cocoa, use only ¾ teaspoon baking soda and add 1½ teaspoons baking powder to the recipe.

Note 2: *Tips for frosting cakes:* Layer cakes are easily frosted and more portable if you put them on a foil-covered cardboard round the diameter of the cake layer. Cardboard rounds (of various diameters) are available at bakery or candy supply stores.

Chocolate Pudding

My childhood chocolate pudding was a vanilla pudding with lots of dark chocolate dropped in and stirred through. It has since evolved into something a little more sophisticated that's still easy and that my family finds even more irresistible: *baked* chocolate pudding.

Serves 8

¾ cup strong coffee

1 cup sugar

3 1-ounce squares bittersweet chocolate, chopped

4 tablespoons unsalted butter, cut in pieces

1 teaspoon vanilla extract

2 eggs, separated

1 cup flour

1 teaspoon double-acting baking powder

¼ teaspoon salt

Whipped cream for garnish

• Butter 8 ½-cup ramekins or custard cups. Preheat the oven to 350 degrees.

• In a heavy saucepan, combine the coffee and sugar and heat until the sugar is dissolved. Add the chocolate, cover, and set aside for 10 minutes.

• When the chocolate has melted, uncover and stir to combine. Whisk in the butter and vanilla. Lightly beat the egg yolks and add to the chocolate, stirring until smooth.

• Sift the flour, baking powder, and salt together. Sift the dry ingredients, a little at a time, over the chocolate and combine before adding more. Beat the egg whites until stiff but not dry (better under- than overbeaten) and fold into the chocolate mixture.

• Fill the prepared cups ¾ full and place in a large baking pan. Pour hot water into the baking dish to come halfway up the sides of the ramekins. Place the pan on the middle rack of the oven and cover loosely with foil.

• Bake until the puddings are no longer wiggly when you shake them and the tops look done, about 30 minutes. Remove the ramekins from the water bath and let the puddings cool on a rack where they will deflate slightly.

• These puddings are best served warm, topped with a large spoonful of whipped cream. If made ahead and refrigerated, they can be warmed in the microwave, or put them in a wide saucepan of hot water.

Chocolate Pudding Cake

This compensates for a dinner of leftovers or simple omelets or soup. It combines a brownielike cake with a fudge sauce that sinks to the bottom of the pan as the cake bakes. Easily made by hand in a single bowl, chocolate pudding cake can be whipped up in a few minutes and baked during dinner. It's best served warm and topped with whipped cream.

Serves 6 to 8

1 cup flour

⅔ cup granulated sugar

3 tablespoons unsweetened cocoa powder

2 teaspoons double-acting baking powder

¼ teaspoon salt

¼ cup milk

4 tablespoons unsalted butter, melted

1 egg

1 teaspoon vanilla extract

80

For the topping

⅓ cup granulated sugar

⅓ cup brown sugar

¼ cup unsweetened cocoa powder

½ teaspoon instant coffee granules

1½ cups very hot water

1 cup heavy cream

2 tablespoons confectioners' sugar

½ teaspoon vanilla extract

- Preheat the oven to 350 degrees. Lightly butter an 8-inch round or square baking dish or casserole.
- Sift together the flour, sugar, cocoa, baking powder, and salt. Combine the milk, butter, egg, and vanilla. Whisk together and stir into the dry ingredients, mixing just until combined. Spread the thick batter in the prepared pan.
- To make the topping, in the same bowl combine the sugars, cocoa, and coffee powder. Sprinkle over the cake batter.
- Pour the hot water over the topping and place the pan on the middle rack of the oven. Bake until the cake is firm, about 40 minutes. The puddinglike sauce will have sunk to the bottom and will be soft. Cool 15 minutes.

• Whip the cream, adding the sugar and vanilla, until soft peaks form. Serve the warm cake in dessert dishes with the chocolate sauce spooned over the top. Garnish with the sweetened whipped cream.

Cinnamon Toast

Cinnamon-sugar is a kitchen staple, to use for this favorite breakfast or teatime toast as well as for sprinkling on applesauce or sliced bananas and yogurt.

Makes one slice

For the cinnamon-sugar

1 cup sugar   1 tablespoon ground cinnamon

For the cinnamon toast

1 slice quality bread of your choice (I   1 to 2 teaspoons unsalted butter
    use white or oatmeal) (see p. 187)   1 to 2 teaspoons cinnamon-sugar

• To make the cinnamon-sugar, combine the sugar and cinnamon. (Cinnamon-sugar can be stored indefinitely in a covered jar.)
• To make the cinnamon toast, toast the bread very lightly.
• Butter the toast generously to the edges and sprinkle with some of the cinnamon-sugar.
• Place the toast on a baking sheet or the tray of a toaster oven and broil briefly just until the cinnamon-sugar is bubbly and the toast is golden.

CLAM CHOWDERS

For red Manhattan or white New England clam chowder, use one of the following:

Shucked minced clams with their juice, available fresh or frozen in seafood markets.

4 quarts fresh clams in their shells (steamed in ½ cup water just to open) to yield 2 cups minced clams; strain the cooking broth.

Canned minced clams in juice.

Remember that clams are naturally salty, so add salt to the chowder only at the end.

Manhattan Clam Chowder

In Boston, this is practically heresy!

Serves 6 to 8

3 tablespoons butter
1 cup finely chopped onion
½ cup finely chopped carrot
½ cup finely chopped celery
½ teaspoon crushed fennel seeds
1 teaspoon anchovy paste
½ teaspoon dried oregano
1 bay leaf

1 28-ounce can plum tomatoes, whole
    or crushed
2 tablespoons tomato paste
4 cups water
2 cups (1 pound) minced clams with
    their juice
Salt and freshly ground pepper to taste
¼ cup freshly minced parsley

- In a large heavy pot, melt the butter and sauté the onions, carrots, and celery over low heat, stirring often to prevent them from coloring, about 10 to 15 minutes. When the onions are very soft, add the fennel seeds and anchovy paste and continue to sauté 2 or 3 minutes more.
- Add the oregano, bay leaf, tomatoes, tomato paste, and water. Bring to a boil and simmer, partially covered, for 40 minutes. Break up the whole tomatoes in small bits.
- Add the clams and their juices and simmer about 5 minutes. Season with salt and pepper to taste. Stir in the parsley and serve hot with French bread.

Note: Fresh scallops can be substituted for clams, though it would then be scallop chowder. Be sure to remove the tough, opaque muscle or "foot" remaining on the side of some scallops.

New England Clam Chowder

Serves 6 to 8

2 cups (1 pound) minced clams in their juice

2½ cups water (approximately)

3 tablespoons butter

2 tablespoons finely diced salt pork

1 medium onion, finely chopped

1 stalk celery, trimmed and finely chopped

3 tablespoons flour

1 bay leaf

Sprig of fresh thyme

1 or 2 all-purpose potatoes, peeled, and cut into ½-inch cubes

2 cups light cream or half-and-half

1 teaspoon paprika

Salt, if needed

Freshly ground black pepper

84

- Strain the clams and reserve the juices. Add water to the juice to yield 3 cups. Set the clams and liquid aside.
- In a large heavy pot, melt the butter and sauté the salt pork until crisp. Remove the salt pork from the pot and reserve. Add the onions and celery and simmer over low heat until very soft, stirring often to prevent them from coloring, about 10 to 15 minutes. Stir in the flour and sauté for 1 minute more.
- Slowly whisk in the reserved 3 cups of water and clam juice. Add the bay leaf and thyme. Bring to a boil slowly, whisking occasionally as it thickens.
- Add the potatoes and simmer 10 minutes or until partially cooked. Add the clams and simmer until the clams are cooked and the potatoes are soft, about 5 to 10 minutes.
- Add the cream and heat, but don't boil. Remove the bay leaf and thyme and season with paprika, salt, and pepper.

Club Sandwich

I'm still indebted to my childhood friend Eleanor Kahlo for inviting me to Woodstock Country Club where we dined on the best handmade potato chips, sodas, and club sandwiches I can remember, and just by signing her parents' names on the check! Our mouths could hardly fit around the double stack of white pullman bread, hand-sliced roast turkey or chicken breast, crisp bacon, juicy Indiana farm tomatoes and lettuce, all held together with rich, homemade mayonnaise. Few restaurants do justice to the club sandwich, but at home, you can make the best.

Makes 1 sandwich

3 slices quality bread, plain or toasted
2 tablespoons Mayonnaise (see page 174)
6 thin slices roast chicken or turkey breast

Salt to taste
4 thin slices red, ripe tomatoes
2 lettuce leaves, washed and dried
4 strips bacon, cooked until crisp

85

- Spread 1 tablespoon of the mayonnaise on 1 slice of bread. Top with 3 slices chicken. Salt lightly; add 2 slices of tomatoes, 2 strips of bacon, and a lettuce leaf.
- Spread the remaining mayonnaise on the second slice of bread and lay on the lettuce. Layer the remaining chicken, salt, tomatoes, bacon, and lettuce leaf on the second slice of bread. Cover with the third slice of bread.
- Cut in half diagonally and hold each half together with a long frilled toothpick. Enjoy with the traditional accompaniment—potato chips and a soda.

COLESLAWS

Whatever type of coleslaw you like, consider shredding the cabbage(s) with a sharp knife instead of a processor. Machines make life easier but can turn coleslaw into an indistinguishable mush of vegetables. Here are a few coleslaw recipes I always come back to.

Creamy Coleslaw

Serves 4 to 6

For the dressing

½ cup Mayonnaise (see page 174)
½ cup sour cream
3 tablespoons cider vinegar
1½ tablespoons sugar (or to taste)
1 teaspoon dry mustard
¾ teaspoon salt or celery salt
Freshly ground black pepper
Pinch of cayenne pepper

1 small (1½- to 2-pound) head green
    cabbage, shredded (5 to 6 cups)
1 small carrot, grated
1 or 2 stalks celery, thinly sliced
2 or 3 scallions, white and some green
    parts, thinly sliced
¼ cup currants (optional)

- To make the dressing, combine all the dressing ingredients.
- Toss the dressing with the shredded, grated, and sliced vegetables and currants. This is best served the day it's made. Mix well before serving.

Coleslaw Vinaigrette

Here's a colorful salad that tastes as good the next day as the day it's made, and it travels well for picnics on hot summer days.

Serves 4 to 6

1 small (1½- to 2-pound) head green cabbage, shredded (5 to 6 cups)

1 small red onion, thinly sliced

2 teaspoons salt

2 stalks celery, sliced

2 small peppers (green, red, or yellow), cored, seeded, and chopped

1 teaspoon caraway seeds

¼ cup finely chopped parsley

For the dressing

2 tablespoons red wine vinegar

2 teaspoons Dijon mustard

⅓ cup vegetable oil

Freshly ground black pepper

- Combine the cabbage and onions with the salt and let them drain in a colander for 30 minutes with a plate and weight on top.
- To make the dressing, combine the vinegar and mustard in a small bowl. Whisking constantly, add the oil in a thin steady stream until the vinaigrette thickens. Add pepper to taste.
- Rinse the cabbage and onions under water, drain well, and dry in a clean towel.
- Combine the drained cabbage and onions, the celery, peppers, and caraway seeds. Toss with the vinaigrette. Add salt to taste. This coleslaw keeps well in the refrigerator for a few days. Add the parsley just before serving so it stays green.

Sweet-and-Sour Seeded Coleslaw

Serves 8 to 10

1 small (1½-pound) head *each* green and purple cabbage, shredded (12 cups)

1 red pepper, cored, seeded, and chopped

1 green pepper, cored, seeded, and chopped

1 carrot, peeled and grated

2 celery stalks, thinly sliced

½ cup finely chopped onion

For the dressing

¾ cup sugar

⅓ cup cider vinegar

¼ cup vegetable oil

1 teaspoon salt

1 tablespoon dry mustard

1 tablespoon poppy seeds

½ teaspoon celery seeds

½ teaspoon caraway seeds

⅛ teaspoon cayenne pepper

- To make the dressing, combine in a saucepan the sugar, vinegar, oil, salt, dry mustard, seeds, and cayenne pepper. Bring to a boil and stir to dissolve the sugar. Cool.
- In a large bowl, combine the vegetables and add the dressing. Toss well to mix thoroughly. Cover and refrigerate overnight. Mix well before serving.

Corn Bread

Here's our basic favorite.

Makes one 9-inch square pan

1 cup flour
1 cup fine yellow cornmeal
¼ cup sugar
1 tablespoon double-acting baking powder

1 teaspoon salt
1 cup milk, at room temperature
1 egg, at room temperature
2 tablespoons butter, melted
Butter to serve on top

- Thoroughly grease a 9-inch square metal baking pan with butter. Preheat the oven to 400 degrees.
- In a bowl, combine the flour, cornmeal, sugar, baking powder, and salt.
- In another bowl, combine the milk, egg, and melted butter. Mix the wet and dry ingredients together lightly with a fork just until combined. Don't overwork it.
- Spread the batter evenly in the prepared pan and bake on the middle rack of the oven until the corn bread is lightly colored and begins to pull away from the sides of the pan, about 18 to 20 minutes. Cool slightly and cut into 9 squares. Serve hot with lots of butter.

C

Corn Fritters

These fritters, also known as corn oysters or pancakes, are a standby at corn season. They make breakfast, and even dinner, something special when they're cooked in lots of butter and served with sausage or bacon. This recipe, which serves four, has been known to satisfy just one hungry teenage son.

Makes 16 fritters

4 to 5 ears of fresh corn, cut and then scraped (2 cups)

2 eggs, separated

½ cup flour

1 tablespoon sugar

½ teaspoon salt

½ teaspoon double-acting baking powder

Grating of nutmeg

3 to 4 tablespoons salted butter

- Cut the kernels of the corn with the sharp side of a knife and scrape the pulp with the dull side to make 2 cups.
- In a bowl, combine the corn kernels, egg yolks, flour, sugar, salt, baking powder, and nutmeg.
- Beat the egg whites until peaks form and fold carefully but thoroughly into the corn batter to lighten it.
- Heat a griddle or heavy sauté pan and add a tablespoon of butter. Make 4 fritters in each batch, dropping the corn batter from a large serving spoon (about 3 tablespoons for each fritter). Heat until browned underneath; turn to cook the other side. Add more butter before cooking another batch. These are best served hot from the griddle with maple syrup.

Corn on the Cob

As simple as it seems, there *is* more than one way to cook and eat corn. As a midwestern girl, I ate a lot of corn: raw from the fields the way the farmers ate it; soaked in water and roasted in a pit; cooked and rolled in butter and maple syrup; but mostly, boiled in water very briefly and then rolled in butter and sprinkled with salt.

The new corn hybrid with "starch blockers" tastes like it was just picked from the fields even when it's been shipped from another state. The sugar doesn't convert to starch so the corn is deliciously sweet.

Serves 6

Water

1 tablespoon salt

2 teaspoons sugar

6 ears of corn, husked

Butter

Salt and freshly ground pepper to taste

- Bring a large pot of water to a boil; add the salt and sugar.
- Drop the ears of corn into the water. Bring the water back to a boil, cover, and remove from the heat. Let the corn sit for 5 minutes before removing it from the water.
- Serve with butter, salt, and pepper.

Corned Beef Hash

Hash is that wonderful combination of likeable, available ingredients—potatoes, meat, and onions. Homemade hash puts leftover potatoes or meat to good use. I love roast beef hash with a little Worcestershire sauce or A-1 Sauce; and hash with ham is a brunch favorite; but corned beef hash with eggs is my first love. Whichever meat you like (or have on hand), the proportions are the same.

Serves 4

3 medium boiling potatoes (white or red), peeled and cut in ¼-inch cubes

4 tablespoons salted butter

1 small onion, finely chopped

½ pound lean corned beef or other cooked meat, ground or chopped in very small cubes

Freshly ground black pepper to taste

Salt, if needed

6 eggs (optional)

• Cook the potatoes in boiling salted water until softened but still firm, about 4 minutes. Drain well and set aside.

• In a heavy sauté pan, melt the butter and add the onion. Sauté for 1 minute. Add the corned beef and potatoes and cook, turning occasionally with a spatula, until the bottom begins to brown, about 7 minutes. Season with pepper and salt to taste.

• If adding eggs, make 6 "nests" in the hash and crack 1 egg into each. Turn the heat to low and cover. Let the eggs cook about 3 minutes; turn off the heat. Let the eggs sit, covered, until the heat of the hash cooks the eggs until opaque, or to your liking.

Cranberry Bread

Cranberry bread was our introduction to New England—a gift from our new neighbors, the Grahams, when we moved east from California. I've made their recipe ever since. Cranberry bread needn't be only a Thanksgiving harvest treat, since it's possible to make it year-round with frozen cranberries.

Makes 1 loaf

2 cups flour
1½ teaspoons double-acting baking powder
½ teaspoon baking soda
½ teaspoon salt
1 egg, at room temperature
1 cup sugar

⅔ cup fresh orange juice
Grated zest of 1 orange
3 tablespoons unsalted butter, melted
½ cup coarsely chopped walnuts
1 cup cranberries, cut in half or very coarsely chopped

- Grease well and lightly flour a 4½-by-8½-inch loaf pan. Preheat the oven to 350 degrees.
- Sift together the flour, baking powder, baking soda, and salt. Set aside.
- Beat the egg and add the sugar gradually, beating until light. Slowly add the orange juice, zest, and butter.
- Add the dry ingredients to the egg mixture in a few parts, blending just until thoroughly combined. Stir in the nuts and cranberries.
- Turn the batter into the prepared loaf pan and bake on the middle rack of the oven until the bread begins to pull away from the sides of the pan, a toothpick inserted in the center comes out clean, and it sounds quiet, about 60 to 70 minutes. Cool the bread in the pan for 15 minutes before turning it out onto a rack to cool completely.

Cranberry Relish

Makes 2½ to 3 cups

12 ounces fresh cranberries
Juice and grated zest of 2 juice oranges
1 cup sugar

Pinch of salt
¾ cup finely chopped walnuts (optional)

- Coarsely chop the cranberries by hand or in a food processor.
- In a stainless steel or enamel saucepan, combine the cranberries, orange juice, grated zest, sugar, and salt. Bring to a boil and simmer, stirring, until thickened, about 8 to 10 minutes.
- Cool the relish 15 minutes before adding the nuts. Cool completely before refrigerating in a covered jar.

Cranberry Salad Mold

Gelatin molds have not generally been part of my culinary world, but here is an exception. It is an appealing alternative to cranberry sauce and a great accompaniment to the rich, heavy, and hot dishes of Thanksgiving.

Serves 8

2¼ cups water
2 cups whole cranberries
¾ cup sugar
1 6-ounce (or 2 3-ounce) package(s) lemon gelatin
2 tablespoons freshly squeezed lemon juice
2 tablespoons port (optional)

1 8-ounce can unsweetened crushed pineapple with its juice
½ cup sour cream
½ cup finely chopped celery
½ cup chopped pecans or walnuts
1 cup seedless red grapes, cut in half
Orange slices for garnish

- Lightly oil a 6-cup decorative ring mold and turn it upside down on a paper towel.
- In a saucepan, combine the water, cranberries, and sugar, and cook until the cranberries begin to pop, stirring occasionally, about 5 minutes.
- Stir in the lemon gelatin until dissolved. Add the lemon juice, port, pineapple with its juice, and sour cream. Whisk to blend well.
- Pour the mixture into a bowl and chill over ice or in the refrigerator until it drops in clumps from a spoon (warming will unset it if you chill it too long). Fold in the celery, nuts, and grapes and pour into the prepared ring mold.
- Chill until firm, at least 4 hours. Dip the mold in warm (not hot) water or rub with a sponge dipped in hot water to loosen the gelatin. Put a serving plate over, invert the mold and plate, and shake the mold to remove the salad. Be patient—it may take a few minutes to unmold. Use more warm water and try again if necessary. Decorate the plate with orange slices.

Creamed Spinach

Use fresh or frozen spinach for equally good results, or try this with 4 cups shredded and drained zucchini.

Topped with an egg (poached, or hard-boiled and chopped) and served on toast, creamed spinach is great brunch food or a satisfying dinner.

Serves 4 to 6
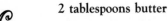

2 pounds fresh spinach, cooked until wilted and chopped, *or* 2 10-ounce packages frozen chopped spinach, defrosted and squeezed to extract the liquid

2 tablespoons butter

1 tablespoon flour

Salt and freshly ground black pepper to taste

Grating of nutmeg

1 cup light cream

- In a heavy saucepan, melt the butter and add the cooked and drained spinach. Sauté a few minutes over low heat.
- Stir in the flour, salt, pepper, and nutmeg; sauté for 1 minute more.
- Add the cream and stir to mix well. Bring to a simmer and cook a few minutes to a desired consistency. Adjust the seasoning to taste.

Crumb Pie

In the winter, when fruit pies aren't in season, crumb pie, similar to shoofly or gravel pie, is a great choice.

Be sure to bake the pie on the bottom rack of the oven so the crust gets browned.

Dough for 1 9-inch single-crust pie
(see page 10)
1 cup hot water
½ cup brown sugar

½ cup dark corn syrup
½ teaspoon baking soda
2 eggs

For the crumbs

1 cup flour
¾ cup dark brown sugar
¼ cup rolled oats
1½ teaspoons cinnamon
¼ teaspoon nutmeg
¼ teaspoon powdered ginger

¼ teaspoon salt
½ cup chopped pecans or walnuts (optional)

Ice cream or whipped cream

- Preheat the oven to 425 degrees. Lightly grease a 9-inch pie plate with shortening.
- On a lightly floured surface, roll out the dough to a 13-inch circle. Carefully transfer it to the pie plate, pressing it into the bottom and sides without stretching the dough. Trim the edge, leaving a 1-inch overhang. Turn the dough under and crimp to make a decorative border. Refrigerate the bottom crust while you make the filling.
- To make the filling, whisk together the water, brown sugar, corn syrup, baking soda, and eggs in a small bowl.
- To make the crumbs, combine the flour, brown sugar, oats, spices, and salt in another bowl. Work in the butter with a pastry blender until crumbly. Add the nuts.
- Alternately layer the wet and dry ingredients in the unbaked pie shell, ending with a thick layer of crumbs.
- Bake on the lowest rack of the oven for 15 minutes. Reduce the oven temperature to 375 degrees and continue to bake until set and golden, about 35 to 40 minutes. Serve warm with ice cream or whipped cream.

CUCUMBER SALADS

For cucumber salads, I much prefer the long English seedless cucumbers. Since they aren't waxed, you can leave the pretty dark skin intact.

Sweet-and-Tart Cucumber Salad

Serves 4 to 6

1 English cucumber, scored with the tines of a fork and very thinly sliced
1¼ teaspoons salt
3 tablespoons sugar, or to taste
½ cup white vinegar

2 tablespoons water
2 tablespoons minced parsley
1 to 2 tablespoons finely chopped mint or dill
Freshly ground black pepper to taste

• Combine the sliced cucumbers and 1 teaspoon of the salt in a colander. Set aside to drain for 30 minutes, tossing occasionally. Rinse, and dry on a clean dish towel.

• Combine the cucumbers in a bowl with the sugar, vinegar, water, parsley, mint, the remaining salt, and pepper. Adjust the seasoning to taste. Transfer the salad to a glass jar and refrigerate until serving time.

Cucumber Salad with Sour Cream and Lime Dressing

Serves 4 to 6

1 English cucumber, scored and thinly   1½ teaspoons salt
   sliced or shredded

For the dressing

¾ cup sour cream
2 tablespoons lime juice
½ teaspoon black pepper
½ teaspoon ground cumin

½ teaspoon ground coriander
¼ teaspoon sugar
⅛ teaspoon cayenne pepper

- Combine the cucumber and 1 teaspoon of the salt in a colander. Set aside to drain for 30 minutes, tossing occasionally. Rinse and dry well on a clean dish towel.
- To make the dressing, combine in a bowl the sour cream, lime juice, black pepper, cumin, coriander, the remaining salt, sugar, and cayenne pepper. Add the cucumbers and toss well. Adjust the seasoning to taste. Refrigerate and serve chilled.

Curried Turkey, Lamb, or Chicken

This curry dish is a wonderful answer to leftover turkey, chicken, or roast lamb. A quick curry sauce binds the meat, which can be served on rice with bowls of toppings on the side. Children will learn to love the exotic spices when they can sprinkle or spoon on coconut, raisins, nuts, yogurt, or chutney themselves.

This curry borrows unique flavors from Thai and Indonesian cooking. Peanut butter and tomato paste thicken and enrich the sauce that's made with chicken stock and yogurt. Curry powders are blends of sweet and hot spices: tumeric, cardamom, allspice, coriander, mustard, ginger, saffron, cumin, and pepper. Find a good spice market and taste or smell already prepared curry blends to find a sweet or hot one you like. Two or three tablespoons minced crystallized ginger added at the end is a fine substitute for the grated fresh gingerroot and sugar.

Serves 4

2 tablespoons butter

1 large onion, chopped

1 clove garlic, minced

1 stalk celery, finely chopped

1 tablespoon grated fresh gingerroot

1 tablespoon curry powder, to taste

1½ tablespoons flour

3 tablespoons peanut butter

2 teaspoons tomato paste

1 teaspoon sugar

1 cup chicken stock or broth

1 cup plain yogurt

4 cups cut-up cooked turkey, lamb, or chicken

⅓ cup currants or raisins

Condiments (shredded coconut, peanuts, yogurt, chutney)

- Heat the butter in a large sauté pan. Add the onion, garlic, celery, and ginger, and sauté over low heat for 10 minutes, stirring often to prevent the vegetables from coloring or sticking.
- Stir in the curry powder and flour, mixing well. Add the peanut butter, tomato paste, sugar, stock, and yogurt; whisk until smooth. Heat until thickened. Add the meat and raisins. Heat thoroughly, stirring.
- Serve hot on rice or in pita pockets (page 204) and with coconut, peanuts, yogurt, and chutney as condiments.

CUSTARD

Custard at its most basic is milk thickened with egg. Baked custards make a nutritious breakfast topped with a spoon of Granola (see page 136) as well as a dessert topped with a spoon of maple syrup.

Baked Cup Custard

For a richer custard, use half-and-half instead of milk and add an extra egg yolk. I sometimes substitute maple syrup or honey for the sugar. Use a water bath for slower, more even baking and to keep the custard soft and smooth throughout. Scalding the milk will reduce the baking time by 10 minutes.

Serves 6

2 eggs, at room temperature
1 egg yolk
¼ to ⅓ cup sugar
¼ teaspoon salt

2 cups milk, scalded and cooled slightly
½ teaspoon vanilla extract
Freshly grated nutmeg (optional)

continued on next page

- Preheat the oven to 325 degrees. Place 6 custard cups in a roasting pan or baking dish.
- In a bowl, whisk the eggs and yolk together. Add the sugar and salt; whisk to combine. Add the milk slowly, whisking until smooth; then add the vanilla.
- Divide the custard among the cups and dust with grated nutmeg.
- Place the pan on the middle rack of the oven and pour enough hot water in the pan to come ¾ of the way up the sides of the custard cups.
- Bake until a knife inserted around the edges comes out clean, about 35 minutes (10 minutes more if you haven't scalded the milk). The custard will continue to cook as it cools and the center will become firm.
- Remove the cups from the hot water and cool on a wire rack before refrigerating.

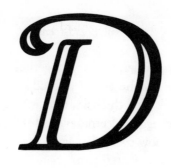

Date-Nut Bread

Greasing a pan and dusting it with flour is usually sufficient to prevent cakes or breads from sticking, but lining the pan with parchment paper for any fruited or rich bread or loaf cake is a guarantee there won't be problems in turning it out.

Makes 1 loaf

1 cup coarsely chopped pitted dates (about 5½ ounces)

1 cup boiling water

2 cups flour

1 teaspoon baking soda

1 teaspoon baking powder

½ teaspoon salt

4 tablespoons unsalted butter, softened

½ cup firmly packed brown sugar

2 eggs, at room temperature

1 teaspoon vanilla

½ cup coarsely chopped pecans or walnuts

▪ Grease a 4½-by-8½-inch loaf pan, line it with parchment paper, and grease the paper. Preheat the oven to 350 degrees.

▪ Put the dates in a bowl and pour the boiling water over them. Stir in the baking soda. Let the mixture cool completely.

continued on next page

- Sift the flour, baking powder, and salt together.
- In a mixing bowl, cream the butter and add the granulated sugar and brown sugar, beating well. Add the eggs, one at a time, beating until light. Add the vanilla with the eggs. Alternately add the dry ingredients and the date mixture, mixing on low speed just until combined. Fold in the nuts. Transfer the batter to the prepared pan.
- Bake on the middle rack of the oven until the bread begins to pull away from the sides of the pan, a toothpick inserted in the center comes out clean, and it sounds quiet, about 1 hour.
- Remove the bread from the oven and cool in the pan on a rack for 15 minutes. Run a knife around the edge of the pan, turn out the bread, carefully remove the parchment paper, and place on a rack to cool completely. Cut in thin slices with a serrated knife.

104

*D*eviled Eggs

These favorites start with what my youngest child calls "butter eggs": perfect hard-cooked eggs with a bright yellow yolk that is the consistency of butter. The "devil" comes from dry or prepared mustard.

Peeling the egg shell for deviled eggs (or egg salad) is made much easier if you hard-boil *older* eggs. When you're poaching eggs and want them to stay together, use very *fresh* eggs.

Makes 24 deviled eggs

12 to 14 eggs (extras in case a few don't peel well)

1 teaspoon salt

4 teaspoons prepared yellow or Dijon mustard, *or* 2 teaspoons dry mustard

½ teaspoon salt, or to taste

Pinch of cayenne pepper

Snipped chives or other fresh herbs (optional)

4 to 6 tablespoons Mayonnaise (see page 174)

Toppings (capers, smoked salmon, dill, parsley, sun-dried tomatoes, black olives, chutney, anchovies, smoked oysters, or caviar)

- Put the eggs in a pan with enough cold water to cover. Add 1 teaspoon salt and bring the water to a boil. Take the pan off the heat, cover, and set aside for 12 to 13 minutes. Immediately transfer the eggs to a bowl of cold water and let more cold water run over them for 1 minute. (This will cool them down and keep the yolks bright yellow.) Crack and carefully peel the shells; cut the eggs in half horizontally. (Cutting a tiny horizontal piece off the bottom will prevent the eggs from sliding off the serving plate.)
- Carefully remove the yolks. Combine the yolks in a bowl with the mustard, salt, cayenne pepper, optional herbs, and enough mayonnaise to bind the ingredients and form a paste. Season to taste with more salt, a squeeze of lemon juice, some caper juice if capers are the garnish, a pinch of curry if chutney is the topping, or a spoonful of sour cream if caviar is the topping.
- To stuff the whites, place a spoonful of filling in each egg half and smooth the top, or transfer the filling to a pastry bag fitted with a large star tip and pipe the filling into the cavity. Decorate the tops with something as simple as parsley or as exotic as smoked oysters to make these eggs ideal for either family eating or cocktail parties.

$\mathcal{D}$ill Beans

Excess garden green beans can be a winter treasure if you take a little time to pickle them in season. Pick them very small, pack them in canning jars, pour a brine over them, and process them in a large kettle of water for 15 minutes. Use pint or quart canning jars with new, reliable lids. Coarse Kosher salt is pure and should be used rather than regular table salt which will cloud the brine.

This recipe comes from friend and *Boston Globe* food reporter Sheryl Julian, who introduced me to the joys of spicy dill beans years ago.

Makes 1 quart

1¼ pounds straight and garden-fresh green beans

2 cloves garlic, peeled and bruised

¼ teaspoon cayenne pepper

½ bunch fresh dill (approximately)

1¼ cups water

1¼ cups white vinegar

2 tablespoons coarse Kosher salt

1 quart or 2 pint jars and lids

• Thoroughly wash and dry 1 quart or 2 pint canning jar(s) and lid(s), running under boiling water and draining to dry.

• Fill a kettle large enough to hold the canning jar(s) upright or lying down with enough water to cover the jar(s) by 1 inch, but do not yet place the jars in the kettle. Bring the water to a boil.

• Tightly pack the green beans into the jar(s). Allow enough space at the top for the garlic and dill. Add the garlic and cayenne pepper, and pack the fresh dill to the top.

• In a saucepan, bring the water, vinegar, and salt to a boil. Pour the brine over the vegetables to within ¼ inch of the top.

• Wipe the rim of the jar clean to insure a good seal. Screw on the top(s) tightly.

• Carefully place the jar(s) in the boiling water, completely submerged. Check the seals to be sure there is no leakage. Remove and adjust the lids if necessary. Boil for 15 minutes. Remove the jar(s) from the water with tongs and let them cool, undisturbed, on a towel or trivet. When you hear the magical "ping," you'll know that the seal is tight and there is a vacuum of air in the jar. When you push down on the lid top, it should be tight and unyielding. Give the top another turn to tighten it and store at least 2 months to allow the beans to mellow before chilling and eating.

DOUGHNUTS

To cut calories, I've baked doughnuts in the oven, but there's nothing as good as fried doughnuts.

If you don't have a doughnut cutter, you can make doughnut "holes" by dropping rounded teaspoons of dough in the hot oil. We like the "holes" even better since proportionately they have even more sugar coating. Dougnuts are at their irresistible best just after they're made, so unless you're feeding a slumber party, the football team, or trick-or-treaters, restrain yourself and make a reasonable number or you might eat every delicious and fattening bite yourself!

Remember to keep the oil hot (375 degrees) and don't crowd the pan, so the doughnuts brown quickly without absorbing too much oil.

*B*uttermilk Doughnut "Holes"

Makes 2 dozen "holes"

1¼ cups flour

¾ teaspoon double-acting baking
   powder

¼ teaspoon baking soda

¼ teaspoon salt

Grating of nutmeg

Pinch of cinnamon

1 egg, at room temperature

⅔ cup sugar

⅓ cup buttermilk

1 tablespoon unsalted butter, melted

Vegetable oil for frying

• Sift the flour, baking powder, baking soda, and salt together. Add the nutmeg and cinnamon.

• In a bowl, whisk together the egg, ⅓ cup of the sugar, the buttermilk, and melted butter. Combine with the dry ingredients and mix until smooth.

• In a deep, heavy skillet, add oil to a depth of 2 inches. Heat the oil to 375 degrees (a candy/frying thermometer is very useful).

• Using two teaspoons, scoop up batter with one and slide it off into the hot oil with the other. Let the doughnuts fry until nicely browned, about 2 minutes, turning halfway through cooking. They will flip themselves over if they're rounded enough. With a slotted spoon, transfer them to a brown bag or paper towels to drain.

• Put the remaining ⅓ cup sugar in a bowl or small brown bag. While the doughnuts are still hot, shake them in the sugar to coat. Cool on a wire rack and enjoy immediately.

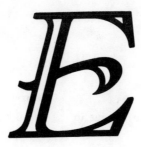

*E*clairs

Eclairs, cream puffs, and profiteroles are all based on the French *choux* pastry. A dough of flour, water, butter, and eggs is baked in a hot oven until puffed, which leaves a hollow shell for rich fillings. Chocolate eclairs are fingers of dough with a vanilla custard filling and a chocolate glaze. Cream puffs are round, usually filled with vanilla custard, and dusted with confectioners' sugar. The smaller profiteroles are also round but are filled with ice cream and topped with chocolate sauce. *Choux* pastry can also make delicious bite-size hors d'oeuvres to be stuffed with savory fillings.

Makes 12 eclairs or cream puffs or 60 cocktail puffs

For the filling

Vanilla Pudding (see page 283) substituting 2 cups light cream for the 3 cups milk, to make a stiffer and richer filling

continued on next page

For the pastry

1 cup water	½ teaspoon salt
8 tablespoons unsalted butter, cut in chunks	1 cup flour
	5 eggs
1 tablespoon sugar	1 teaspoon vanilla for sweet pastries

For the chocolate glaze

4 ounces semisweet chocolate chips   2 tablespoons unsalted butter

E

~~~

- Make the vanilla pudding, cover, and chill in the refrigerator until ready to fill the Eclairs.
- Preheat the oven to 425 degrees. Butter a heavy baking sheet and run it under cold water.
- To make the pastry, combine in a heavy saucepan the water, butter, sugar, and salt. Bring to a boil and remove from the heat. Add the flour all at once, stirring until a ball of dough forms.
- Place the saucepan over medium heat and stir constantly with a flat wooden spatula or spoon for 5 minutes, scraping the bottom and turning the dough to allow some water to evaporate. Don't let the bottom brown.
- Remove the saucepan from the heat and transfer the dough to a deep bowl or the bowl of a food processor. Add one egg, stirring well until it's incorporated and the dough is smooth. Then repeat the process, adding the remaining eggs one at a time. After all the eggs are added, the dough should be thick enough to hold its shape when piped from a pastry bag into finger shapes or when formed into puffs with two spoons.
- Using a pastry bag with a plain tip, pipe the dough into 12 to 15 finger shapes or 60 ¾-inch cocktail puffs on the prepared baking sheet, spacing them 2 inches apart. Or make larger cream puffs using two soup spoons, scooping up the dough with one and pushing it off with the other. Dip your finger in water and smooth out any peaks or rough tops.
- Place the baking sheet on the middle rack of the oven and reduce the oven temperature to 400 degrees. Bake until well browned, about 20 to 30 minutes, depending on the size of the pastry. Reduce the oven temperature to 375 degrees after 15 minutes to prevent the bottoms from browning too

much. (If the puffs aren't browned and dried enough, they will collapse.) Poke a small hole in the side or end of each with a sharp knife to let the steam escape. Turn the oven off and open the door to let the pastries dry out a few minutes more. Cool on a wire rack.

▪ At serving time, fill a pastry bag fitted with a ½-inch plain tip with the cold Vanilla Pudding. Insert the tip in the steam hole in the side or end of each pastry and fill. Refrigerate the pastries while you prepare the glaze.

▪ To make the glaze, combine the chocolate and butter over, not in, hot water. Heat just until melted, stirring frequently until smooth. Cool slightly and drizzle over the tops of the pastries. These can be refrigerated for a few hours but are best eaten right away since the wet filling will make the pastry soggy.

Note: The unfilled and unglazed eclair or puff pastry can be made ahead and frozen. At serving time, remove from the freezer and place on a cookie sheet. Place in a *cold* oven, and then set the temperature to 300 degrees. Bake until warmed, about 10 to 15 minutes. Cool on a rack before filling and drizzling with chocolate.

111

Egg Salad

Makes enough for 4 sandwiches

6 hard-cooked eggs, peeled and coarsely chopped

1 cup finely chopped celery

½ cup Mayonnaise (see page 174), or more to taste

Salt to taste

Optional additions

1 tablespoon mustard, chutney, minced onions, pickle relish, *or* finely chopped pepper

▪ Combine the eggs, celery, and mayonnaise with any optional additions. Season with salt to taste and refrigerate.

Eggnog

Eggnog is best made just before you plan to serve it, since the whipped eggs and cream will deflate when sitting in the refrigerator. If you must, make the base ahead and refrigerate it, then fold in the whipped cream before serving. For an after-dinner drink, add espresso.

Makes 10 to 12 one-cup servings

6 eggs
1 cup sugar
3 cups whole milk
¼ to ½ cup bourbon
¼ to ½ cup rum
¼ to ½ cup brandy

2 teaspoons vanilla extract
2 cups strong espresso, chilled (optional)
2 cups heavy cream
Grating of nutmeg

• Beat the eggs until frothy. Gradually add ½ cup of the sugar, beating until light and frothy.
• Slowly stir in the milk, liquors, vanilla, and espresso.
• In a separate bowl, beat the cream, gradually adding the remaining ½ cup sugar, and beating until thick and glossy. Fold thoroughly into the eggnog and transfer to a punch bowl or pitcher to serve topped with a grating of nutmeg.

Eggplant Parmesan

Italian Parmesan dishes have filtered into nearly every American home kitchen because of their universal appeal. This is a summer version, when garden eggplants and tomatoes are at their peak.

Serves 6 to 8

1 medium eggplant (1½ pounds), cut in ½-inch slices (about 16)
Salt
¼ cup flour
½ cup olive oil
1 cup ricotta cheese
1 egg
¼ cup grated Parmesan cheese
Salt and pepper to taste
3 or 4 ripe garden tomatoes, about the same diameter as the eggplant, cut in the same number of slices as the eggplant

½ cup fresh bread crumbs
1 clove garlic, minced
½ teaspoon oregano
2 tablespoons minced fresh parsley
2 cups grated Monterey Jack cheese (about 6 ounces)
1 pound spaghetti, cooked and tossed with butter, *or* 1 loaf crusty bread, sliced

E

113

- Lightly salt the eggplant slices on both sides and lay on paper towels to drain for at least 30 minutes.
- Rinse the eggplant and dry with paper towels. Dust lightly with the flour.
- In a large sauté pan, heat ¼ cup of the oil until very hot. Add half the eggplant slices and sauté, turning once, until both sides are lightly browned and the eggplant is softened, about 5 minutes on each side. Transfer the slices to a jelly-roll pan and arrange close together. Add the remaining oil to the pan and sauté the remaining eggplant slices.
- Preheat the oven to 400 degrees.
- In a bowl, combine the ricotta cheese, egg, Parmesan cheese, and salt and pepper to taste. Evenly divide the mixture, putting a dollop on each eggplant slice.
- Top the cheese mixture on each with a tomato slice.
- Combine the bread crumbs, garlic, oregano, and parsley. Sprinkle over the tomato slices.
- Evenly divide the grated Monterey Jack cheese, mounding some cheese over the crumbs on each eggplant slice.
- Bake the eggplant on the middle rack of the oven until the cheese is melted and bubbling, about 15 minutes. Serve over spaghetti or with crusty bread.

*E*ggplant Relish

This remains one of my favorite do-ahead party hors d'oeuvres. When I have leftover relish, I use it like a tomato sauce, served over spaghetti that's tossed with butter and a bit of cream.

Makes about 1 quart

1 medium eggplant (1½ pounds), cut in ½-inch cubes

2 teaspoons salt

6 tablespoons vegetable oil or a combination of olive oil and vegetable oil

1 onion, thinly sliced

1 clove garlic, minced

3 tablespoons tomato paste

1 cup water

¾ cup chopped celery

12 pimiento-stuffed green olives, cut in half

1 to 2 tablespoons capers (rinsed and drained if very salty)

¼ cup red wine vinegar

2 tablespoons sugar

Lots of freshly ground black pepper

Salt to taste

2 tablespoons finely chopped parsley

Lemon wedges

• Toss the eggplant cubes with the salt, place in a colander, weight with a plate, and drain for at least 30 minutes. Dry with paper towels.

• In a large sauté pan or heavy pot, add 4 tablespoons of the oil and heat until quite hot. Add the eggplant and lower the heat, cooking slowly and scraping the bottom often with a spatula or wooden spoon to prevent sticking, about 15 minutes. The eggplant should be fairly soft.

• Remove the eggplant to a bowl and add the remaining 2 tablespoons of oil to the pan. Sauté the onions for a few minutes; then add the garlic and sauté, stirring often, until the garlic is soft but not colored. Add the tomato paste and water and stir to combine. Add the celery and cook about 5 minutes more. Return the eggplant to the pan and add the olives, capers, vinegar, and sugar. Stir to combine.

• Simmer the relish, partially covered, until the eggplant is tender and the sauce is thick, about 20 minutes. Add more water if needed. Add freshly ground pepper and salt to taste. Cool, cover, and refrigerate. At serving time, stir in the parsley and serve with crackers. Garnish with a few lemon wedges.

*E*GGS FOR BREAKFAST

As a mother who foolishly asks her family every Saturday morning, "What kind of eggs do you want?" I get four different answers: "Eggs in a cup" (soft boiled with buttered toast broken into the oozing yolk), "Scrambled" (with lots of butter and just a touch of bacon fat to give the eggs a bacon flavor), "Poppy Eggs" (my father's famous sunny-side up fried eggs, cooked slowly and covered briefly so "the white isn't runny but the yellow is), and the fourth answer, "None!" I prefer omelets with just about any filling and fresh herbs, so here is the cook's preference. Whichever eggs you make, don't overcook them.

E
~~~

115

Omelets

I've been known to send rapturous notes on paper napkins to restaurant chefs who make omelets well. I think it's the surprise that a dish this simple and delicious, but usually so badly done, has been well executed! When I'm out for breakfast, I always request that the chef not overcook the omelet since I have an aversion to eggs that taste like cardboard. And even with this request, I've been known to send back omelets and ask again. When I see that browned, dry look, I wonder why I didn't stay home and make my own omelet or order pancakes. Omelets can be a joy to eat and a convenient way to use leftover vegetables or cheese for a simple dinner.

Serves 1

E

116

¼ teaspoon salt, or to taste
Freshly ground black pepper

2 eggs, beaten with 2 teaspoons water
1 tablespoon butter

Filling of choice

3 tablespoons cheese (chevre or grated cheddar), creamed spinach or sautéed mushrooms, minced fresh

herbs, sour cream and caviar, smoked salmon and capers, sautéed peppers and onions, diced ham

- Add the salt and pepper to the eggs and mix well with a fork.
- Heat a 10-inch nonstick omelet or sauté pan and add the butter. The pan should be so hot before adding the eggs that they're noisy as they hit the hot (but not burned) butter.
- Immediately turn the heat to low, or if using an electric range, remove the pan from the heat. Stir the eggs quickly, tilting the pan to keep the bottom surface covered. The eggs should look lumpy and will set in less than 1 minute.
- While the eggs are still creamy, add the filling of choice, and heat until warm. Roll the omelet onto a plate with the filling in the center. The heat of the eggs will warm the filling more. Serve immediately or cover loosely with foil and keep warm in a 200-degree oven while you make more.

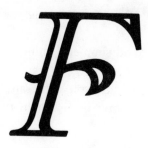

*F*ish Chowder

Serves 6

3 tablespoons butter
1 cup finely chopped onion
1 clove garlic
1 cup chopped red, yellow, orange, or green pepper
1½ tablespoons flour
2 sprigs of fresh thyme, *or* a pinch of dried thyme
1 cup milk
1 8-ounce bottle of clam juice

1½ pounds fresh lean fish fillets (scrod, haddock, salmon), cut in large chunks
1 cup freshly cut corn kernels (cut the kernels from the cob with the sharp side of the knife and scrape the pulp with the dull side)
1 cup light cream
1 teaspoon sugar
Salt, pepper, and cayenne pepper
¼ cup minced parsley

▪ In a heavy saucepan or casserole, melt the butter and add the onion. Sauté over low heat until the onion is very soft but not colored, about 10 minutes. Stir often. Add the garlic and peppers and sauté for 5 minutes more, stirring to prevent coloring. Stir in the flour and add the thyme. Whisk in the milk and clam juice and cook until slightly thickened.

continued on next page

- Add the fish and corn and simmer 4 minutes, or until the fish is just opaque and cooked.
- Add the cream and sugar. Season with salt, pepper, and a pinch of cayenne to taste. Heat but don't boil. Stir in the parsley and serve hot.

Fish Sticks

Serves 2 or 3

¼ cup flour
⅓ cup dry bread crumbs (approximately)
Salt and freshly ground black pepper
1 egg

1 teaspoon water
1 pound fresh white fish fillets (haddock, scrod, sole, flounder), cut on a diagonal to make "sticks"
2 to 3 tablespoons salted butter, melted

- Preheat the oven to 475 degrees.
- On a large piece of wax paper, make a pile of the flour and another pile of the bread crumbs. Season the bread crumbs with salt and pepper. Whisk the egg and water together in a pie plate.
- Coat all sides of the fish sticks with flour, shaking off the excess. Dip the floured fish in the egg and then coat on all sides with the bread crumbs. Lay the sticks on a wire rack as you continue to make more.
- Brush a heavy baking sheet with some of the melted butter. Arrange the fish on the baking sheet and drizzle the tops with the remaining butter.
- Baking time will depend on the thickness of the fish. Thin fillets should take just 2 or 3 minutes; scrod, 5 or 6 minutes; and a fish that's 1-inch thick may take 10 minutes. Bake in the upper half of the oven just until the fish is opaque. Don't overcook it. A few *seconds* of broiler heat at the end will give the crumbs a nice color.
- Serve with lemon wedges, Mayonnaise (see page 174), or Tartar Sauce (see page 270).

"French" Dressing

I'm not sure what makes this salad dressing French except that it's very good. This recipe comes from a favorite aunt (and great home cook) I visited every summer of my childhood. Lunches were always eaten over-looking Lake Michigan and the sand dunes and nearly always included green salad with cottage cheese, topped with this dressing.

I'm reminded to make this dressing when I get down to the end of the ketchup (Aunt Margie spells it catsup) jar and can't get the remains out. I add the vinegar to the jar and shake it up to start the dressing.

Makes 1½ cups

⅓ cup cider vinegar
2 tablespoons sugar
⅓ cup Ketchup (see page 155)
½ teaspoon salt
½ teaspoon Worcestershire sauce
¼ teaspoon pepper

Pinch of cayenne pepper
⅔ cup vegetable oil
2 tablespoons fresh lemon juice
1 clove garlic, peeled and skewered on
  a toothpick

F

119

- In a deep bowl, combine the vinegar, sugar, ketchup, salt, Worcestershire sauce, pepper, and cayenne pepper.
- Add the oil very slowly, as in making mayonnaise, whisking constantly, until the dressing is thickened and emulsified.
- Stir in the lemon juice and pour the dressing into a glass jar. Add the toothpicked garlic and refrigerate. Remove the garlic from the dressing before serving.

ℱrench Fries

French fries are made with potatoes, oil, and salt. Russet or Idaho potatoes are best. Boiling potatoes are pretty good too, but sweet potatoes do *not* work unless they're dipped in a batter. Scrub the potato skins but you needn't peel them. Slice or julienne the potatoes and keep them in water until ready to fry. But be sure to dry them *thoroughly* before adding them to the hot oil to prevent dangerous spattering.

Whether you use vegetable, peanut, or even olive oil, it must be heated in a large, deep frying pot to 375 degrees. Fry the potatoes in small batches to avoid crowding the pot and lowering the temperature too drastically. Electric fryers with lids make good sense since they keep the oil at a consistent temperature and contain the spattering. When the potatoes are golden, remove them with a slotted spoon to a paper towel-lined jelly-roll pan to drain. Salt to taste and keep warm in a single layer, uncovered, in a 300-degree oven. To reuse the oil, strain it through a fine mesh strainer and store it in a jar in the refrigerator.

Variation: For homemade potato chips use a hand slicer and carefully slice the potato directly into the hot fat, only a few at a time so you don't crowd the pot. Fry to a golden brown. Drain well and salt to taste. These are an addiction that may be hard to break.

*F*rench Toast

If you like to sit down for a relaxed breakfast rather than be the kitchen slave for your ravenous morning eaters, you can get a head start and keep the French toast warm in a 250-degree oven. Don't cover the cooked toast or it will get soggy.

Serves 4

3 eggs
1 cup light cream
3 tablespoons confectioners' sugar
1 teaspoon vanilla extract
½ teaspoon salt

8 slices firm white bread or French bread cut on a diagonal
4 tablespoons salted butter
Confectioners' sugar, fruit preserves, or maple syrup

- In a pie plate or shallow baking dish, whisk together the eggs, cream, sugar, vanilla, and salt. Thoroughly soak 2 slices of bread at a time on each side.
- In a large sauté pan, melt 1 tablespoon of butter at a time. Add the soaked bread and sauté on *low* heat until golden, about 4 to 5 minutes. Turn and sauté on the other side until puffed and golden. Soak more bread, melt more butter, and continue to sauté the remaining bread.
- Serve with a topping of sifted sugar, fruit preserves, or maple syrup.

F

FRIED CHICKEN

The fried chicken dilemma goes on: Southern fried chicken with its dusting of flour? Batter-dipped fried chicken à la Kentucky? Or a buttermilk-marinated fried chicken? For any of them, the important thing is to have the oil hot so the chicken will be crisp, and to have the chicken pieces in small, roughly equal sizes to assure even cooking. That's why I usually fry just chicken wings or just drumsticks. Dark meat generally takes about 5 minutes longer to cook than white. Be sure to thoroughly trim the chicken of all excess skin and fat and to pat the chicken dry.

Serves 6

To prepare the chicken

4 pounds chicken wings, tips removed, small drumsticks, or small pieces
1½ teaspoons salt

½ teaspoon black pepper
1 teaspoon paprika

To fry the chicken

2 to 3 cups vegetable oil, or to a depth of at least 1 inch

- Thoroughly trim the chicken of excess fat and excess skin. Pat the chicken dry with paper towels and sprinkle with the salt, pepper, and paprika.
- Add oil to a cast iron pan with a cover, large enough to hold 5 or 6 chicken pieces at a time without crowding. Make sure there is at least 1 inch of oil in the bottom of the pan. Heat the oil to a temperature of 370 degrees on a frying thermometer before adding the chicken.
- Preheat the oven to 225 degrees.

- Carefully add 5 or 6 chicken pieces (Southern, buttermilk marinated, or batter-coated) to the hot oil, skin side down, without crowding. Cover and reduce the heat to medium-high. Turn a few times until golden brown and cooked through. White meat will take 12 to 15 minutes, dark meat 18 to 20 minutes. Be sure to bring the oil temperature back to 370 degrees each time you add another batch of chicken.
- Drain the chicken on paper towels and place in a single layer on a jellyroll pan. Keep warm in the preheated oven as you make more chicken. Serve hot.

$\mathcal{S}$outhern Fried Chicken

1 cup flour

- Put the flour in a brown bag and add the seasoned chicken pieces, a few pieces at a time, shaking to coat lightly with flour. Remove with tongs and place on a baking sheet while the oil is heating.
- Follow directions for frying.

$\mathcal{B}$uttermilk Marinated Fried Chicken

2½ cups buttermilk
1 tablespoon sugar
3 strips of lemon or orange zest (use a vegetable peeler)

1 clove garlic, peeled and skewered with a toothpick
1 cup flour

continued on next page

- In a large bowl, combine the buttermilk, sugar, zest, and garlic. Add the seasoned chicken, turning to coat all sides. Marinate a few hours, turning the chicken occasionally. At frying time, remove the garlic and zest from the bowl. Place the flour on a piece of waxed paper. Shake the excess buttermilk from the chicken pieces and add, a few at a time, to the flour, turning to lightly coat the chicken. Remove with tongs and place on a baking sheet while the oil is heating.
- Follow directions for frying.

*B*atter-dipped Fried Chicken

F

124

1 egg
¾ cup milk (approximately)
1 cup flour
1 teaspoon double-acting baking powder

½ teaspoon salt
Pinch of cayenne pepper

- Combine the egg, milk, flour, baking powder, salt, and cayenne pepper, and whisk until smooth. Add more milk if necessary until the batter is the consistency of heavy cream. Don't dip the pieces of chicken in the batter until you're ready to fry them.
- Follow directions for frying.

Fried Rice

A little more rice or vegetables or eggs will stretch this dish to serve more people. Fresh pineapple on toothpicks is the dessert of choice, with a few fortune cookies, of course!

Serves 4 to 6

¼ cup vegetable oil
1 small onion, chopped
2 stalks celery, chopped
2 eggs, slightly beaten
4 cups cold cooked rice
2 tablespoons soy sauce
½ teaspoon sugar
2 cups diced cooked pork, chicken, or shrimp

1 8-ounce can sliced water chestnuts, drained
½ cup frozen petite peas
3 scallions, white and green parts, sliced thinly on a diagonal
Salt and freshly ground black pepper to taste

- In a large skillet, heat the oil and sauté the onion over low heat for 5 minutes. Add the celery and sauté a few more minutes, stirring to prevent the vegetables from coloring.
- Add the eggs, stirring quickly until they're cooked and in small pieces.
- Add the rice, soy sauce, and sugar, and break up any clumps. Add the pork and cook, stirring, until heated through and the rice begins to brown on the bottom.
- Stir in the drained water chestnuts, peas, and scallions; heat thoroughly. Add salt and pepper to taste.

Fruit Compote

¾ pound mixed dried fruit (apricots, prunes, pears, peaches, figs)
½ cup white wine or orange juice
2 cups water (approximately)
3 strips of orange zest (use a vegetable peeler)

1 cinnamon stick
3 to 4 whole cloves
¼ cup sugar, or to taste
Fresh pineapple chunks, red seedless grapes, or orange sections (optional)
2 tablespoons fruit liqueur (optional)

For the topping

½ cup whipped cream
¼ cup sour cream

2 tablespoons confectioners' sugar

F

126

- In a saucepan, combine the dried fruits, wine, water, orange zest, cinnamon stick, and cloves. Bring to a boil over medium heat. Reduce the heat, partially cover, and simmer 15 minutes or until the fruits are softened. Add more water if needed. Stir in sugar to taste. Cover and cool.
- Remove the cinnamon stick, cloves, and orange zest. Add the fresh fruit and fruit liqueur.
- To make the topping, combine the heavy cream, sour cream, and sugar. Beat on high speed until thickened.
- Serve the compote slightly warm or at room temperature. Spoon into individual serving dishes and top with a dollop of the cream.

$\mathcal{F}$RUIT SALAD

Citrus fruit salads can be made well ahead of serving, but most fruit salads are best made just before serving. Pineapple and melons hold well, but bananas and strawberries will discolor and become mushy, so add them at the last minute. A squeeze of lemon or lime juice will prevent apples from discoloring; a dash of fruit liqueur and a touch of sugar will give added flavor to even the best fruit.

$\mathcal{S}$ummer Fruit Salad

Serves 6

3 cups melon balls or cubes

3 to 4 peaches or nectarines, pitted, peeled, and cut in chunks

2 cups pitted sweet cherries (there's a gadget for this) or seedless grapes

2 cups pineapple cubes

½ pint fresh blueberries or raspberries, *or* 1 pint fresh strawberries, hulled and cut in half if large

2 tablespoons freshly squeezed lemon or orange juice

1 tablespoon sugar, or more to taste

1 banana

Lettuce (optional)

Poppy Seed Dressing (see page 211), *or* Sweet Yogurt Dressing (see page 300) (optional)

▪ Combine all the salad ingredients except the banana, lettuce, and dressing. Toss well. Cover and refrigerate no more than one hour.

continued on next page

- Before serving, peel the banana, score lengthwise with a fork and cut in diagonal slices. Add to the salad and toss gently.
- Serve in a bowl or on a bed of lettuce with a pitcher of dressing as a topping.

*F*ruit Soup

Cherries, peaches, nectarines, and Italian plums each make a refreshing soup, but their water contents vary, so the consistency differs from soup to soup. If the soup is too thick, thin it with orange juice or fruit liqueurs. If it's thin, thicken it slightly with a cornstarch mixture.

F

Serves 6 to 8

2 pounds fresh fruit (cherries, peaches, nectarines, plums), pitted and cut in chunks

3 cups water

1 cup orange juice

½ cup sugar, or to taste

Pinch of salt

1 teaspoon cornstarch mixed with 1 tablespoon water, to thicken if needed

¼ cup fruit liqueur (optional)

½ cup heavy cream

Fresh blueberries or raspberries for garnish (optional)

- In a large saucepan, combine the fruit, water, and orange juice. Bring to a boil and simmer until the fruit is very soft.
- Purée the soup in a blender in small batches, beginning on low and increasing the speed until smooth. Return the soup to the saucepan. Add the sugar to taste and the salt. If necessary add the cornstarch and water mixture, heating until thickened.
- Off the heat, stir in the fruit liqueur. Let the soup cool and refrigerate until chilled.
- At serving time, beat the cream until just thickened. Serve the soup in bowls with a swirl of cream and a few fresh berries on top.

$\mathcal{F}$ruit Turnovers

My mother-in-law gave me this dough recipe for *hamantaschen*, the tricornered pastries served on the Jewish holiday of Purim, but the dough is exceptional for any fruit turnovers or filled cookies. This is a rich dough that's difficult to handle unless you chill it thoroughly. Baking powder and yeast are both used as leavening, with yeast also acting as a moisture barrier.

Makes 24 to 30 turnovers

For the dough

1½ teaspoons active dry yeast

¼ cup warm water

Pinch of sugar

2¾ cups flour

½ teaspoon double-acting baking powder

¼ teaspoon salt

8 tablespoons unsalted butter, softened

½ cup solid vegetable shortening

¾ cup sugar

1 egg

½ cup flour (approximately), for rolling out the dough

For the filling

1½ cups thick fruit preserves

1 cup dried fruit compote, drained and processed to chunks with ½ cup walnuts

1 cup pitted, chopped dates (about 5½ ounces), simmered with 1 cup water

in a small covered pan until soft and thick, about 5 minutes. Stir in ½ cup finely chopped walnuts and ¼ teaspoon cinnamon

Confectioners' sugar for the top (optional)

- To make the dough, sprinkle the yeast over the warm water. Add a pinch of sugar and stir. Let the yeast proof and bubble while you continue with the dough.
- Sift together the flour, baking powder, and salt; set aside.
- Beat the butter and shortening until light. Add the sugar gradually, beating until fluffy and light. Beat in the egg.

continued on next page

- Alternately add the dry ingredients and the yeast mixture and mix until a stiff but sticky dough forms. Wrap the dough well in wax paper and then place it in a plastic bag. Refrigerate for a few hours or overnight to chill thoroughly.
- Lightly grease a heavy baking sheet with shortening. Preheat the oven to 400 degrees.
- Divide the dough into 24 pieces.
- Form the pieces into balls and roll each out to a ¼-inch thickness, using the extra flour to prevent sticking. Cut out a 3½-inch circle from the larger circle with a large glass or pastry cutter.
- Place a rounded teaspoon of filling in the center of the dough. Brush the edges of the dough with a little water. Fold the dough over the filling without stretching it to make a semicircle and press the edges together with the tines of a fork. Arrange on the prepared baking sheet.
- Use the remaining scraps of dough to make more turnovers.
- Place the baking sheet on the middle rack of the oven and immediately reduce the temperature to 375 degrees. Bake until lightly browned, about 15 to 17 minutes. Remove the turnovers to a wire rack to cool. Before serving, dust the tops with confectioners' sugar.

Note: These are best eaten the day they're made. To crisp, place on a baking sheet and heat about 5 minutes in a preheated 375-degree oven. Remove the turnovers to a wire rack to cool.

*F*udge Sauce

Makes two 8-ounce jars

4 tablespoons unsalted butter
¾ cup brown sugar
½ cup granulated sugar
1 cup heavy cream

2 tablespoons light corn syrup
¾ to 1 cup cocoa (depending on desired
   thickness)
1 teaspoon instant coffee granules

- In a heavy saucepan, melt the butter. Add the sugars, cream, and corn syrup and heat to boiling, stirring until smooth and the sugar is dissolved.
- Off the heat, whisk in the cocoa and coffee granules until smooth. As it cools, the sauce will thicken.
- When cooled, spoon into 2 lidded jars and refrigerate. To reheat for ice cream, remove the lid(s) from the jar(s) and heat slowly in a pan of water, or microwave to warm.

F

Gingerbread

Serves 8 to 10

8 tablespoons unsalted butter, softened
½ cup plus 1 tablespoon sugar
1 egg, at room temperature
½ cup dark molasses
2 cups flour
1½ teaspoons powdered ginger
1½ teaspoons cinnamon
⅛ teaspoon ground cloves

½ teaspoon salt
½ cup hot water
1 teaspoon baking soda
2 tablespoons minced crystallized ginger (optional)
¾ cup small fresh blueberries (optional)
Whipped cream for the top

- Grease a 9-by-2-inch square cake pan with a teaspoon of the butter. Preheat the oven to 375 degrees.
- Beat the remaining butter until soft and light, adding ½ cup of the sugar gradually and beating until well creamed. Add the egg, beating until fluffy; then beat in the molasses.
- Sift together the flour, spices, and salt.
- Combine the water and baking soda and stir to dissolve.

continued on next page

- On low speed, alternately add the dry ingredients and the water to the creamed molasses mixture, beating until thoroughly combined and scraping the bowl a few times. Fold in the ginger (or the blueberries, for a brunch cake).
- Spread the batter in the prepared pan and bake on a rack in the upper half of the oven until the cake begins to pull away from the sides of the pan and its center is springy, about 30 to 35 minutes. While warm, sprinkle the top with the remaining tablespoon of sugar.
- Serve the cake warm from the pan with a dollop of whipped cream.

*G*raham Crackers

Ask any child where graham crackers come from and he or she will say, "a box," but almost never from a home oven. Yet these nutritious crackers, developed by Dr. Sylvester Graham in the early nineteenth century as a health food for his patients, are fun and easy to make. Spread with peanut butter and honey, they are a favorite family snack or quick lunch when served with yogurt. Graham crackers are the favorite treat of my daughter's soccer team.

Makes 30 double crackers

1½ cups all-purpose flour
1½ cups whole wheat flour
1 teaspoon double-acting baking
  powder
½ teaspoon baking soda
¼ teaspoon salt

½ cup unsalted butter, softened
1 cup brown sugar
½ cup granulated sugar
1 teaspoon vanilla extract
½ cup milk, at room temperature
Flour for rolling out the dough

- Stir together the flours, baking powder, baking soda, and salt. Cream the butter and sugars until light. Add the vanilla and beat until fluffy.
- Alternately add the flour mixture and the milk to the butter mixture until a stiff dough forms. Wrap the dough well in plastic wrap and chill thoroughly for a few hours or overnight.
- Lightly grease 2 heavy baking sheets with solid shortening. Preheat the oven to 350 degrees.
- Divide the dough into 5 pieces, rolling out one at a time and keeping the others refrigerated. Using the extra flour, roll each piece as evenly as possible into a 5-by-15-inch rectangle (about ⅛-inch thick). Using a ruler and knife or pastry wheel, trim the dough to make straight edges; cut the dough into 6 crackers by cutting once lengthwise down the middle and in 3 even cuts horizontally. With a dull knife, make lines in each cracker to mark its halves and quarters. With a fork, make the characteristic holes in the crackers. Transfer the crackers with a spatula to the prepared baking sheet.
- Bake on the middle rack of the oven until golden, about 12 to 14 minutes. While one batch is baking, roll out another piece of dough and use the other baking sheet to speed up the process. Transfer the crackers with a spatula to a wire rack to cool and crisp.
- Store the cooled graham crackers in an air-tight tin.

G

Granola

We always have a large jar of granola available as a topping for "plain" cereal or yogurt. Each batch is delicious and unique because the ingredients usually vary slightly. Add your own favorites to the roasting pan, keeping the ratio of dry to wet ingredients about 7 to 1.

Makes 16 cups

8 cups old-fashioned or quick rolled oats

1 cup brown sugar

½ cup flour, preferably whole wheat

1 cup grated dry, unsweetened coconut

1 cup dry milk powder

1 cup wheat germ *or* bran *or* bran cereal *or* GrapeNuts cereal

1 cup slivered almonds

¼ cup sesame seeds

⅔ cup corn oil or vegetable oil

⅓ cup water

½ cup light corn syrup or honey

¼ cup maple syrup

2 teaspoons vanilla extract

1 teaspoon salt

1 cup raisins *or* chopped pitted dates (optional)

- Preheat the oven to 300 degrees.
- Combine the dry ingredients in a large roasting pan and stir well.
- Heat the remaining ingredients, except the raisins, in a saucepan and pour into the roasting pan. Toss to mix the ingredients thoroughly.
- Bake until golden, stirring 3 or 4 times, about 1 to 1½ hours. Turn out the granola onto a brown paper bag to cool completely. Mix in the raisins or dates. Store in a large jar or airtight container.

Grape Jelly

Jellies use the liquid extracted from cooking fruit and straining it through cheesecloth. *Jams* use the crushed or ground fruit pulp as well as the juice for a thicker consistency. *Preserves* use large chunks or whole pieces of fruit cooked in a sugared, slightly thickened syrup.

The fruit used in any of these toast-toppers must be ripe and flavorful. Summer and fall surplus fruit can provide wonderful winter and spring treats. Commercial pectins, liquid or powdered, are thickening agents that eliminate the guesswork in jelly making. However, the techniques for using them are different: liquid pectin is added to the boiling juice and sugar mixture; powdered pectin is mixed with the fruit juice before it's heated. Both require 1 minute of hard boiling (a boil that can't be stirred down) to maximize their gelling power.

Although frozen grape juice concentrate can be used in jelly, Concord grapes have the best flavor for authentic grape jelly. Their distinctive perfume in the produce department always takes me by surprise in reminding me it's autumn, school, and peanut-butter-and-jelly days once again.

Makes eight 8-ounce jars

4 pounds ripe Concord grapes	Cheesecloth
¾ cup water	8 8-ounce canning jars with bands and
6 cups sugar	lids, washed and rinsed in boiling
1 tablespoon lemon juice	water
3 ounces liquid pectin	

- Wash the grapes and pick off most of the stems. Place in a large, deep pot and partially crush the grapes with a wooden spoon to extract some of the juice. Since wood absorbs and gives off flavors, don't use the wooden spoon you've been using for the onion soup and lamb stew. The grape juice will permanently color the wooden spoon purple so you'll recognize it easily when you use it in the future.

continued on next page

- Add the water to the crushed grapes and bring to a boil over high heat. Reduce the heat and simmer for 10 minutes.
- Dampen a double thickness of cheesecloth with water and line a strainer with it. Set the strainer over a large bowl to catch the juice. Pour the hot fruit and juice into the cheesecloth and let the juice drip through without disturbing it. Pressing the fruit to extract more juice will result in a cloudy jelly but a higher yield. You should have approximately 3½ cups of juice. The grape juice will permanently color the cheesecloth as well as the spoon.
- Add the juice to a large, deep pot and stir in the sugar and lemon juice. Bring to a boil over high heat, stirring occasionally, until you can't stir down the boiling.
- Add the pectin and heat to a rolling boil. Boil hard for 1 minute.
- Remove the pan from the heat and immediately skim off the foam on top. Pour the jelly into the hot sterilized jars to within ⅛ inch of the top.
- Wipe the rims clean and top with the hot sterilized lids. Screw the bands on and cool, undisturbed, on a trivet until you hear the "ping" that lets you know the jars are safely sealed. If a vacuum has formed, the lids should be tight and not give way when pressed.
- Let the jelly sit, undisturbed, overnight. Check to be sure the bands are tight before labeling and storing.

Note: To make homemade grape juice from the remaining pulp, squeeze the solids in the cheesecloth ball. To each ½ cup of pulpy juice, add 3 cups of water, 1 tablespoon lemon juice, and ½ cup of sugar, or to taste. Stir well to dissolve the sugar. Serve chilled.

G

Green Bean Salad

When the summer green bean crop overwhelms me and it's too hot to "put up" dill beans, I make this simple salad. Onion, mustard, and vinegar give the salad pizzazz, although vinegar (or any acid) turns green vegetables a terrible, almost khaki color. To avoid this, cook the green beans and make the dressing, but don't toss them together until serving time. This goes well with grilled sausages and boiled new potatoes.

Serves 4

1 pound small, tender green beans, ends trimmed
3 tablespoons vegetable oil
½ cup finely chopped onions
½ teaspoon celery seeds
2 teaspoons Dijon mustard

3 tablespoons cider vinegar
¼ teaspoon salt
Black pepper
Pinch of sugar
Lettuce leaves and cherry tomatoes for garnish

G

139

- Cook the green beans in boiling salted water to cover by 1 inch until tender, about 3 minutes. Drain and plunge into a bowl of ice water to stop the cooking and keep them a beautiful green color. When cool, drain and dry on a clean dish towel.
- To make the dressing, sauté the onions in the oil until very soft, stirring to prevent them from coloring, about 4 minutes. Add the celery seeds and cook 1 minute more. Off the heat, whisk in the mustard, and then the vinegar. Season with salt, pepper, and sugar. Don't refrigerate.
- At serving time, arrange the green beans on lettuce leaves and pour the dressing over the top. Garnish with cherry tomatoes.

Grilled Cheese Sandwich

On the days my children come home from school for lunch, they look forward to a grilled cheese sandwich, a bowl of vanilla yogurt with sliced bananas and cinnamon-sugar, and a glass of chocolate milk. Grilled cheese, they say, "warms them up and cheers them up!"

Makes 1 sandwich

2 slices quality bread
4 to 6 slices cheese

1 tablespoon salted butter

- Heat a small pan over medium heat.
- Arrange the cheese between the slices of bread. Add half the butter to the hot pan. When it sizzles, lay the bread and cheese in the pan. Immediately reduce the heat to low. Top the sandwich with bits of the remaining butter. When the underside is browned, turn the sandwich over.
- Cover with a small plate to weight down the sandwich and soften the cheese. When the second side is golden and the cheese begins to ooze from the sides, remove the sandwich from the pan, cut it in half, and serve.

Variations

My children like 2 kinds of cheese, Monterey Jack and Cheddar.

I like ham, a slice of tomato, or a teaspoon of chutney sandwiched between the cheeses.

Sometimes I brush the inside of the bread with mustard first.

My mother used to grill the sandwich in a waffle iron, with the waffle pattern!

I sometimes make a French *croque monsieur* with my ham and cheese sandwich by dipping it in an egg-milk mixture, à la French toast, and then sautéing it in butter.

Open-face sandwiches with toasted bread, English muffins, or pita bread halves aren't exactly *grilled* in a toaster oven or under the broiler, but they taste nearly as good and have fewer buttery calories.

*H*am Loaf

Here's a great addition to a brunch buffet, or the answer to too much leftover ham.

Serves 6

4 slices bacon
1 pound boiled ham, ground or minced
1 cup fresh bread crumbs
¼ cup finely chopped parsley
¼ cup finely chopped scallions
1 egg, lightly beaten

2 tablespoons water
2 tablespoons minced crystallized ginger
1 tablespoon Dijon mustard
3 hard-boiled eggs, peeled (optional)

For the glaze

3 tablespoons orange marmalade or apricot jam

2 teaspoons Dijon mustard

continued on next page

- Preheat the oven to 375 degrees. Line the bottom of a 4½-by-8½-inch loaf pan with 2 slices of the bacon.
- Combine the ham, bread crumbs, parsley, scallion, egg, ginger, water, and mustard. Stir to mix well and pack into the loaf pan. If using hard-boiled eggs, pack ⅓ of the ham mixture in the pan, put the whole eggs down the center, end to end, and pack in the remaining ham mixture. Press the mixture down to fill the gaps. Top with the remaining bacon.
- Bake the loaf on a rack in the upper half of the oven for 30 minutes. Pour off any accumulated fat.
- To make the glaze, combine the marmalade and mustard and spread over the top. Return the loaf to the oven and bake for 20 to 30 minutes more.
- Cool 5 minutes and remove the loaf from the pan. Slice and serve warm, or cool and refrigerate to serve chilled with French bread.

142

*H*amburgers

Next to a charcoal grill, the best way to cook hamburgers is in a heavy cast-iron skillet that gets hot and gives hamburgers a good browning. For the best ground beef, ask your butcher to custom grind a nicely marbelized piece of beef chuck or sirloin, or grind it yourself by trimming the meat well, cutting it in chunks, and putting it through a meat grinder two times.

Makes 4 hamburgers

1½ pounds *freshly ground* lean ground chuck or sirloin

Freshly ground black pepper

1 teaspoon salt or a mix of seasoned salts (onion, garlic, or celery)

1 tablespoon salted butter

4 toasted hamburger buns

Lettuce, tomato, and onion slices (optional)

Condiments: Mayonnaise (see page 174), Ketchup (see page 155), Mustard (see page 183), or Hot Dog (or Hamburger) Relish (see page 146)

- Heat a cast-iron skillet or heavy pan until very hot.
- Season the ground beef with pepper and salt and mix without overworking. Form into 4 patties.
- Just before cooking the hamburgers, add the butter to the pan; as soon as it melts, add the beef patties. They should sizzle immediately.
- Reduce the heat to medium and cook the patties for 2 to 4 minutes on each side, depending on the desired doneness. Turn just one time. A well-seared and browned outside and a juicy pink inside is *our* ideal.
- Serve on lightly toasted buns with toppings and condiments of your choice.

H ermits

Makes 36 bars

8 tablespoons unsalted butter, at room temperature	⅛ teaspoon ground allspice
1 cup brown sugar	⅛ teaspoon ground nutmeg
1 egg, at room temperature	½ cup sour cream
1½ cups flour	½ cup currants or chopped raisins
½ teaspoon baking soda	½ cup quick or old-fashioned rolled oats
½ teaspoon salt	¼ cup sesame seeds
1 teaspoon ground cinnamon	3 tablespoons sugar

- Grease a 10-by-15-inch jelly-roll pan with butter or shortening. Preheat the oven to 350 degrees.
- Beat the butter with the sugar until creamed and light. Add the egg and beat until very light and fluffy.
- Sift together the flour, baking soda, salt, and spices. Alternately add the dry ingredients and the sour cream to the egg-sugar mixture, blending just until thoroughly combined. Stir in the currants, oats, and sesame seeds.
- Spread the batter evenly to the edges of the prepared pan. Bake on a rack in the middle of the oven until the center is springy, about 15 to 18 minutes. Sprinkle with sugar while still warm. Cool and cut into 36 bars.

Honey Cake

Honey cake is one delicious result of my beekeeping interest and the fall honey harvest. The excess honey from one hive assures honey cakes throughout the year, not only for a sweet New Year. Seek out a local beekeeper who'll sell you some ripe, flavorful honey and tell you about the fascinating society of bees and their golden treasure.

In substituting honey for sugar, use ⅔ cup honey for each cup of sugar and reduce the amount of liquid by ¼ cup for each cup of honey used.

Makes one 9- by-13-inch cake

H

144

1½ cups all-purpose flour	2 eggs
½ cup rye flour	½ cup sugar
½ teaspoon salt	4 tablespoons unsalted butter, melted
1 teaspoon cinnamon	¼ cup vegetable oil
½ teaspoon powdered ginger	½ cup honey
¼ teaspoon ground allspice	¼ cup warm water
⅛ teaspoon ground nutmeg	1 teaspoon baking soda
½ teaspoon instant coffee granules	½ cup sliced almonds

- Grease and flour a 9-by-13-inch baking pan. Preheat the oven to 325 degrees.
- In a bowl, sift the flours, salt, spices, and coffee granules.
- In a separate bowl, beat the eggs, adding the sugar gradually until very light and soft peaks form. Add the melted butter, oil, and honey on low speed, mixing until smooth and trying not to deflate the egg mixture too much.
- Combine the water and baking soda, mixing until dissolved. Alternately fold the water and the dry ingredients into the egg mixture until the batter is smooth and homogenous.
- Spread the batter evenly in the prepared pan. Bake on the middle rack of the oven for 35 minutes. Open the oven and sprinkle the top of the cake with the sliced almonds. Continue to bake for an additional 15 minutes or until the cake is nicely browned and a toothpick inserted in the center comes out clean.
- Cool completely on a wire rack before cutting into 24 1-by-2½-inch "fingers."

Honey-Glazed Carrots

Cooked and glazed in one pan, these carrots are simple to prepare and a complement to chicken, pork, beef, or fish.

Serves 4

1 cup orange juice
1 cup water
2 tablespoons butter
1½ tablespoons honey

½ teaspoon salt
1 pound carrots, peeled and cut in matchsticks or thin diagonal slices
Grating of nutmeg

- In a large sauté pan, combine the orange juice, water, butter, honey, and salt. Heat until the butter has melted. Add the carrots, tossing to coat well.
- Cook uncovered over medium-low heat, stirring occasionally, until the carrots are tender and the liquid is nearly evaporated and forms a glaze, about 25 to 30 minutes. Watch them carefully at the end of the cooking time to make sure they don't burn; reduce the heat or add more water if necessary. Season with nutmeg, additional salt, or honey to taste.

Hot Chocolate

Makes 1 large mug

1 scant tablespoon unsweetened cocoa powder
1 firmly packed, rounded tablespoon brown sugar

¼ teaspoon instant coffee granules (optional)
1½ cups hot milk, or to taste
2 marshmallows (optional)

- Combine the cocoa, brown sugar, and coffee in a large mug and mix well. Add ¼ cup of the hot milk and stir until smooth. Stir in the remaining milk, and enjoy. Top with marshmallows if you like.

Hot Dog (or Hamburger) Relish

Makes four 1-pint jars

4 cups ground or chopped green cabbage

4 pickling cucumbers (1 pound), chopped or shredded

2 sweet red peppers, cored and ground or chopped

2 green peppers, cored and ground or chopped

1 large onion, ground or chopped

¼ cup coarse Kosher salt

2 cups cider vinegar

1¼ cups sugar, or more to taste

½ cup light corn syrup

2 teaspoons mustard seeds

1½ teaspoons celery seeds

½ teaspoon turmeric

4 1-pint jars and lids

146

- In a large bowl, combine the ground or chopped vegetables. Add the salt and mix thoroughly. Let the vegetables stand for at least 2 hours, stirring occasionally.
- Put the vegetables in a strainer and rinse thoroughly under cold water. Drain well, pressing out all the liquid. Place in a large pot.
- Add the remaining ingredients and slowly bring to a boil. Reduce the heat and simmer for 3 to 5 minutes.
- Run the four 1-pint jars and their lids under boiling water and drain.
- Ladle the hot relish into the jars, wipe the rims clean, and cover tightly. Transfer the jars to a trivet and leave undisturbed until you hear the "ping" that lets you know that the jars are sealed. Cool, label, and refrigerate.

*I*ce Cream

Makes about 1 quart

3 egg yolks	1 cup milk, scalded
½ cup sugar	1 teaspoon vanilla extract
Pinch of salt	1½ cups heavy cream

- To make the base for the ice cream, combine the yolks, sugar, and salt in a heavy pan. Whisk until light and the sugar dissolves.
- Add the hot milk slowly, whisking until smooth. Heat over low heat, stirring constantly, until thickened and the custard coats the back of a spoon. Don't let it boil. Strain the mixture into a bowl and cool before adding the vanilla and cream.
- Chill the base completely in the refrigerator before making the ice cream according to your machine's directions.
- Remove the ice cream from the freezer 15 minutes before serving to soften it.

Variations

Chocolate: Stir the scalded milk into ⅓ cup unsweetened cocoa powder and whisk until smooth before adding to the eggs and sugar.

continued on next page

Coffee: Add 1 to 2 tablespoons instant espresso powder to the hot milk.

Chocolate Chip: Add 1 cup chocolate mini-chips to the chilled base.

Mint: Substitute ½ teaspoon mint extract for the vanilla extract.

Maple/Nut: Add ½ cup maple syrup to the eggs in place of the sugar. Add ½ cup chopped walnuts or pecans to the base.

Fruit (Strawberry, Blueberry, Peach): Use only ½ cup milk to make the custard and add 2 cups crushed or peeled and mashed sweetened fruit to the chilled base before making the ice cream.

Ginger: Heat the milk with ¼ cup chopped and peeled fresh gingerroot. Strain before adding to the egg-sugar mixture.

I
~~~
148

*I*ce Cream Cake Roll

This makes a great birthday cake, bedecked with candles. Use the Jelly Roll recipe (see page 153) to make a vanilla cake roll. Cut in 1-inch slices and wrapped individually, ice cream cake "sandwiches" are great after-school snacks.

Serves 10 to 12

For the cake

½ cup flour

¼ cup unsweetened Dutch-processed cocoa powder

¾ teaspoon double-acting baking powder

¼ teaspoon salt

3 eggs

¾ cup sugar

1 teaspoon vanilla extract

¼ cup vegetable or corn oil

2 tablespoons water

½ cup chocolate wafer crumbs or chocolate sprinkles

1 quart ice cream, softened enough to make it spreadable

- Grease a 10-by-15-inch jelly-roll pan with shortening, line it with parchment paper, and grease and lightly flour the paper, shaking out any excess flour. Preheat the oven to 400 degrees.
- Sift together the flour, cocoa, baking powder, and salt twice. Set aside.
- Beat the eggs, gradually adding the sugar and beating until light and frothy. Add the vanilla and continue beating until the mixture is pale and doubled in volume.
- On low speed, stir in the oil and water, mixing just until incorporated, deflating the mixture as little as possible.
- Fold in the dry ingredients gently but thoroughly until no bits of flour are visible. Turn the batter into the prepared pan and carefully spread it to the edges.
- Place the pan in the center of the oven and immediately reduce the oven temperature to 375 degrees. Bake until the cake is springy to the touch, about 15 minutes.
- While the cake is baking, sprinkle a 10-by-15-inch area of a clean dish towel with the chocolate wafer crumbs.
- Remove the cake from the oven and let it cool in the pan for 3 minutes. Run a knife around the edge of the pan and place it next to the prepared towel. *Quickly* turn the pan over onto the crumbs (to avoid a mess). Carefully remove the parchment paper and trim the short edges of the cake. Loosely cover the cake with the used parchment paper. Roll the cake up in the towel, starting from the long edge. Set it aside to cool completely.
- Unroll the cake and remove the parchment paper. Spread the softened ice cream to the edges of the cake. Reroll the cake and ice cream tightly without the towel. Wrap in foil and freeze until very firm.
- Remove the cake from the freezer 10 minutes before serving time to let the ice cream soften. Cut the cake in diagonal slices and serve plain or with Fudge Sauce (see page 131) or Butterscotch Sauce (see page 50). Sweetened fresh berries make a nice sauce for an ice cream-filled vanilla cake roll.

I

Note: If not using Dutch-processed cocoa powder, add ⅛ teaspoon baking soda to the dry ingredients and use only ½ teaspoon baking powder.

Iced Tea

The mint patch gets picked every summer morning for this thirst quencher. Strong infusions of tea and mint can sit on reserve, ready for more water to make gallons of tea for a large crowd. Use three mild herbal tea bags, but just two for stronger tea blends. Don't let the tea bags steep for more than 10 minutes or the tea will become bitter.

Makes ½ gallon

2 or 3 tea bags
4 to 5 sprigs of fresh mint, bruised
1 cup boiling water

3 tablespoons sugar, or to taste
7 cups cold water
Fresh mint or lemon for garnish

- Place the tea bags and mint in a measuring cup or large glass. Add the boiling water and cover with a plate to steep for 10 minutes.
- Remove the mint and squeeze the tea bags before discarding. Add sugar to the glass and stir to dissolve. Cool slightly.
- Pour the tea into a ½ gallon pitcher and add the cold water to fill. Serve over ice and garnish with fresh mint or lemon.

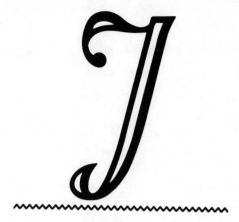

Jambalaya

Jambalaya is a one-dish meal that combines many Creole ingredients: tomatoes, peppers, shellfish, ham, and spicy pepper. Choose a combination of chicken, clams, ham, sausage, or shrimp. In tomato season, use 1 cup of peeled, seeded, and chopped garden tomatoes, but when fresh tomatoes are pink and tasteless, use a 1-pound can of peeled tomatoes, drained and chopped.

Serves 6 to 8

2 tablespoons oil

8 pieces chicken, trimmed of all excess fat and skin

4 tablespoons salted butter

½ cup finely chopped onion

2 cloves garlic, minced

½ cup finely chopped green pepper

½ cup finely chopped celery

1 cup peeled, seeded, and chopped fresh tomatoes, *or* 1 1-pound can peeled tomatoes, drained and chopped

¼ cup finely chopped parsley

1½ cups long-grain rice

3½ cups boiling water

1 teaspoon salt

¼ to ½ teaspoon cayenne pepper

¼ teaspoon dried thyme, *or* a few fresh sprigs of thyme

1 bay leaf

Pinch of ground cloves

Freshly ground black pepper

¼ pound boiled ham, julienned

½ pound uncooked shrimp, peeled and deveined

Chopped parsley for garnish

continued on next page

- In a large, heavy sauté pan, heat the oil and brown the chicken well on all sides. Remove and set aside.
- In the same pan, melt the butter. Add the onion and sauté over low heat for 5 minutes until softened, stirring often to prevent coloring. Add the garlic and sauté a few more minutes, stirring constantly. Add the pepper and celery and sauté a few minutes. Add the tomatoes and cook until the mixture has thickened and most of the liquid has evaporated. Stir in the parsley and rice and sauté until the rice is hot.
- Pour the boiling water over the rice mixture and stir in the spices and seasoning. Return the chicken to the pan. Bring the liquid to a boil, cover, and simmer until the chicken is cooked and most of the liquid has been absorbed by the rice, about 35 minutes.
- Add the ham and shrimp to the rice, cover, and continue cooking until the shrimp is pink and the ham is heated through, about 5 minutes.
- Fluff the jambalaya with a fork to distribute the ingredients and serve sprinkled with additional parsley.

Jelly Roll

The goodness of any food this simple depends upon the quality of its few ingredients. This roll cake is a moist genoise leavened with baking powder as well as eggs, and good for any roll or ice cream cake. Fill with a good fruit jam, or lemon curd, or mincemeat to give the cake a distinctive taste.

Serves 10 to 12

For the cake

½ cup light cream
4 tablespoons unsalted butter
1½ cups flour
2 teaspoons double-acting baking powder
¼ teaspoon salt
4 eggs, at room temperature
1 cup sugar

1½ teaspoons vanilla extract

3 tablespoons confectioners' sugar
¾ to 1 cup thick fruit preserves (apricot, cherry, plum), mixed with 1 tablespoon orange liqueur, if you like

153

- Grease a 12-by-17-inch jelly-roll pan, line it with parchment paper, and grease and lightly flour the paper. Preheat the oven to 375 degrees.
- To make the cake, in a small saucepan combine the cream and butter. Heat until the butter is melted. Set aside to cool to room temperature.
- Sift the flour, baking powder, and salt; set aside.
- Beat the eggs until frothy; then add the sugar slowly, beating on medium-high speed until very light and pale, about 5 minutes. Beat in the vanilla.
- Sift ⅓ of the dry ingredients at a time over the egg mixture and, with a spatula, thoroughly but gently fold the dry ingredients in alternately with the cooled cream until no lumps of flour are visible.
- Turn the batter into the prepared pan and gently spread it into the corners and sides of the pan.

continued on next page

- Place the pan on the middle rack of the oven and reduce the temperature to 350 degrees. Bake until the cake is golden and begins to pull away from the sides of the pan, about 18 minutes. Cool 5 minutes on a wire rack.
- Sift the confectioners' sugar over a clean dish towel. Put the cake pan on the edge of the towel and quickly turn it over to cover the sugar. Remove the cake pan and carefully peel the parchment paper from the cake. Trim the short edges of the cake and re-cover the cake with the loosened parchment paper. Roll the cake in the towel beginning from the long side. Set it aside to cool for 30 minutes before filling.
- Unroll the cake and remove the parchment paper. Spread the cake with the fruit preserves and tightly reroll the cake, using the towel as a guide. Arrange the cake, seam-side down, on a long platter. Cover well with plastic wrap so the cake doesn't dry out. Let the flavors develop a few hours before serving.
- Cut the cake in 1-inch diagonal slices and serve with fruit or ice cream on the side, if you like.

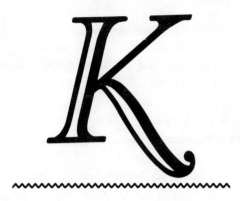

*K*etchup

Here's a straightforward ketchup that uses up excess garden tomatoes and is great on hamburgers. We don't like sweet ketchup, but if you do, add the optional brown sugar.

Makes 1½ to 2 pints

3 pounds ripe plum tomatoes, quartered

1 medium onion, coarsely chopped

⅓ cup white or cider vinegar

¼ cup light corn syrup

¼ cup brown sugar (optional)

1 cinnamon stick

1 teaspoon salt

½ teaspoon paprika

½ teaspoon mustard seeds

½ teaspoon celery seeds

¼ teaspoon crushed black peppercorns

Pinch of cayenne pepper

3 tablespoons tomato paste

2 1-pint canning jars and lids

▪ In a large enamel or stainless steel pot, combine all the ingredients. Bring to a boil over high heat, stirring and breaking up the tomatoes as they soften.

continued on next page

- Reduce the heat and simmer the tomatoes, partially covered, until thick, about 1 hour. Stir often to prevent burning.
- Remove the cinnamon stick and put the mixture through a food mill, pressing hard on the vegetables.
- Return the strained sauce to the pot and cook down for a thicker consistency.
- Rinse the jars and lids with boiling water. Drain to dry. Ladle the ketchup into the jars and seal. Cool and refrigerate. The ketchup will keep a few weeks in the refrigerator.

K

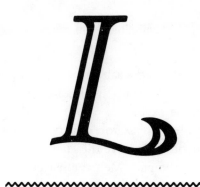

*L*amb Stew

Meaty lamb shanks, or "baby legs" of lamb as we call them, make a delicious stew.

Serves 4

¼ cup plus 1 tablespoon flour

1 teaspoon salt

½ teaspoon paprika

Freshly ground black pepper

4 meaty lamb shanks, about 1 pound each, cracked

3 tablespoons vegetable oil

2 tablespoons butter

2 medium onions, chopped

1 large carrot, peeled and chopped

1 clove garlic, minced

2½ cups chicken stock, *or* 2 cups chicken broth and ½ cup water

¼ cup freshly squeezed lemon juice

1 bay leaf

1½ tablespoons Dijon mustard

Grated zest of 1 lemon

1 clove garlic, minced

3 tablespoons chopped fresh mint leaves or parsley

Salt and freshly ground black pepper to taste

continued on next page

- Combine ¼ cup of the flour, the salt, paprika, and pepper on a piece of wax paper. Thoroughly trim the lamb shanks of excess fat and dredge them in the flour, shaking off the excess.
- Heat the oil in a large, heavy casserole or pan and brown the shanks well on all sides over medium heat. Remove the lamb to a platter, pour out any oil, and add the butter to the pan. Melt the butter over low heat.
- Add the onions and sauté for 5 minutes, stirring to prevent them from coloring. Add the carrots and garlic and sauté 5 minutes more over low heat, stirring often.
- Return the lamb to the casserole and add the stock, lemon juice, and bay leaf. Bring to a boil and cover with foil placed directly on the surface of the meat. Reduce the heat to low, cover, and simmer the lamb until fork tender, about 2 hours. Turn the meat a few times while cooking.
- Skim the fat from the braising juices and remove the bay leaf. Ladle ¼ cup of the juices into a small bowl. Add the mustard and the remaining 1 tablespoon of flour and whisk until smooth. Return the mixture to the pan and heat until the liquid simmers and thickens. Stir in the lemon zest, garlic, and mint. Serve hot, seasoned with salt and pepper to taste.

L

Lasagna

Lasagna is no spur-of-the-moment dish, particularly if you make your own delicate egg pasta, slowly cook a thick tomato-meat sauce, and even make your own cheese (*and* milk the goats, as I've done!). There are shortcuts that make a fine lasagna: commercial pasta, ricotta cheese, and prepared jars of thick "spaghetti" sauce. But making your own sauce allows you to add the ingredients you like. The sauce can be made ahead, the noodles even cooked ahead and put in a bowl of cold water until assembly time, and the cheese grated and waiting.

Some lasagnas include a bechamel (white sauce) as well as a tomato sauce. I add cream to the ricotta filling to provide that same richness.

Serves 10

For the tomato-meat sauce (Makes approximately 1½ pints)

1 pound lean ground beef

1 pound sweet Italian sausage, casing removed

1 large onion, finely chopped

2 cloves garlic, peeled and minced

½ pound fresh cultivated mushrooms, chopped

½ teaspoon fennel seeds

1 28-ounce can Italian tomatoes in purée

3 tablespoons tomato paste

1 cup dry red wine or water

Bay leaf

Salt and freshly ground pepper to taste

¼ cup minced parsley

For the cheese filling

1 pound ricotta cheese

½ cup freshly grated Parmesan cheese

1 or 2 eggs

1½ cups heavy cream

Salt and freshly ground pepper to taste

9 lasagna noodles (about ½ pound), cooked *al dente*, about 10 to 12 minutes, cooled in cold water, and drained on paper towels

1 pound mozzarella or Monterey Jack cheese, grated

continued on next page

- To make the sauce, heat a large, heavy pot or sauté pan, and add the ground beef, sausage, onion, and garlic. Sauté until the meat is no longer pink, breaking up the lumps and stirring occasionally, about 10 minutes. Drain any excess fat from the pan.
- Add the mushrooms and fennel seeds to the meat mixture and sauté until the mushrooms are softened, about 5 minutes. Add the tomatoes, tomato paste, wine, and bay leaf. Mix well, cover, and simmer the sauce for 30 minutes.
- Remove the cover and continue to cook until quite thick, about 30 minutes more. Remove the bay leaf and season with salt and pepper.
- To make the filling, combine the cheeses, egg(s), and 1 cup of the cream. Reserve the remaining cream for the top layer of cheese. Season with salt and pepper.
- To assemble the lasagna, spread a very thin layer of tomato sauce over the bottom of a 9-by-13-inch baking pan. Preheat the oven to 350 degrees.
- Lay 3 strips of the cooked, drained noodles in the bottom of the pan. Spread ⅓ of the ricotta mixture over the noodles, then ⅓ of the grated mozzarella and ½ of the tomato-meat sauce.
- Lay 3 more strips of lasagna noodles in the pan, another ⅓ of the ricotta mixture and another ⅓ of the mozzarella. Spread the remaining tomato-meat sauce over the cheese. Top with the remaining 3 lasagna noodles.
- To the remaining ricotta mixture, add the remaining ½ cup of cream. Pour the cheese mixture over the top of the lasagna noodles and spread to cover well. Sprinkle with the remaining mozzarella cheese.
- Bake on the middle rack of the oven until lightly colored and bubbly, about 45 minutes. Let the lasagna settle for about 10 minutes before cutting and serving.

Note: The lasagna can be partially baked for 30 minutes, cooled, wrapped well, and frozen. To heat, defrost and place in a preheated 350-degree oven, covered with foil, until heated through, about 30 minutes. Remove the foil and bake until lightly colored and bubbly, about 15 minutes more.

LEFTOVERS

Years ago, I bought a dozen small (10-ounce) earthenware casseroles to deal with leftovers that didn't go into soups or omelets. The leftover lasagna, stuffed cabbage, meatloaf and mashed potatoes, or fish sticks and macaroni and cheese can be welcome treats weeks later if frozen in individual casseroles and quickly heated for lunches, after-school snacks, babysitters, or simply delicious homemade TV dinners.

With the other leftovers, I make this quick soup.

Leftover Soup

Serves 3 to 4

2 13¾-ounce cans beef or chicken broth

2 cups water

½ cup quick rolled oats

2 cups leftovers, chopped (rice, pasta, vegetables, meat, chicken, tomatoes)

1 tablespoon fresh minced herbs or sliced scallions

2 tablespoons minced parsley

Salt and freshly ground black pepper

■ In a saucepan, combine the broth and water. Bring to a boil and stir in the oats. Cook 1 minute.

■ Add the leftovers and heat through. Stir in the herbs and parsley. Season with salt and pepper and serve hot.

*L*emon Chiffon Pie

Chiffon pies are usually in a crumb crust and are set with gelatin. Unflavored powdered gelatin needs to soak in liquid and expand before it's heated, but not boiled, in warm liquid. If gelatin is added to a cold base, it will seize into clumps of chewy gelatin.

Beating sugar into the egg whites makes a meringue that is much easier to incorporate into the flavored base than simple beaten egg whites.

Makes one 10-inch pie

For the crust

1½ cups cookie crumbs (graham cracker, vanilla wafer, or ginger crisp

3 tablespoons sugar

6 tablespoons unsalted butter, melted

For the lemon filling

1 envelope unflavored gelatin (¼ ounce)

¼ cup cold water

1 cup sugar

½ cup freshly squeezed lemon juice

4 eggs, separated

Pinch of salt

½ cup heavy cream

- Lightly butter a 10-inch pie plate. Preheat the oven to 375 degrees.
- To make the crust, combine the crumbs, sugar, and butter. Mix thoroughly and press onto the bottom and sides of the prepared pie plate.
- Bake on the middle rack of the oven until lightly colored, about 10 to 12 minutes. Cool completely on a wire rack before filling.
- To make the filling, pour the water into a saucepan and sprinkle the gelatin over it; let the gelatin soften for 5 minutes. Stir in ½ cup of the sugar, the lemon juice, egg yolks, and salt.
- Cook over low heat, stirring constantly, until the gelatin and sugar just dissolve, but don't boil.
- Chill the mixture over ice water or in the refrigerator, stirring occasionally, until it mounds when dropped from a spoon. If you forget and the mixture sets, heating slightly in warm water will de-gel it.

- Beat the egg whites in a separate bowl until foamy. Very gradually beat in the remaining ½ cup of sugar until a glossy, thick meringue forms.
- Fold the lemon mixture and whites together until smooth and homogenous. Mound in the cooled pie shell and refrigerate a few hours until set.
- At serving time, whip the heavy cream and spread over the top of the filling.

*L*emon-Meringue Pie

Makes one 10-inch pie

Dough for one 10-inch single-crust pie
  (see page 6)

For the lemon filling

1 cup sugar	1¼ cups water
6 tablespoons flour	1 tablespoon unsalted butter
¼ teaspoon salt	¼ cup freshly squeezed lemon juice
3 egg yolks, lightly beaten	Grated zest of 1 lemon (optional)

For the meringue topping

3 or 4 egg whites	6 tablespoons sugar
¼ teaspoon cream of tartar	

- Lightly grease a 10-inch pie plate with shortening. Roll out the chilled dough to form a 14-inch circle and transfer carefully to the prepared pie plate by folding in quarters or rolling up on the rolling pin. Without stretching the dough, press it onto the bottom and sides of the plate. Trim the dough, leaving a 1-inch edge. Fold the edge under and crimp to make a decorative high edge. Cover and refrigerate for 30 minutes to chill.
- Preheat the oven to 375 degrees.

continued on next page

- Put a piece of greased foil, butter-side down, in the chilled pie shell and fill with dried beans or raw rice to keep the crust down while prebaking. Bake the crust on the bottom rack of the oven for 15 minutes. Remove from the oven and carefully remove the foil and beans. Store the beans in a jar and use over and over again for other prebaked pastry shells. Prick the bottom of the shell with a fork. Return the shell to the bottom rack of the oven and bake until lightly browned, about 10 to 15 minutes more. Cool completely before filling.

- To make the filling, combine the sugar, flour, and salt in a heavy saucepan. Combine the egg yolks and water and whisk into the dry ingredients. Cook over low heat until thickened and smooth, whisking often to prevent lumps, about 8 to 10 minutes. The mixture should bubble in the center.

- Off the heat, add the butter and stir to melt. Add the lemon juice and lemon zest. Cool 10 minutes, stirring a few times, while you make the meringue topping.

- Preheat the oven to 400 degrees.

- To make the meringue, add the egg whites to a clean bowl and beat on high speed until foamy. Add the cream of tartar and continue to beat until soft peaks form. Add all but one tablespoon of sugar very gradually, beating until the meringue is stiff and glossy.

- Pour the hot filling into the cooled pie shell.

- Drop spoonfuls of meringue over the filling and spread with a metal spatula to completely cover the filling. Anchor the meringue by making sure it touches all the sides of the crust. Make swirls or decorations in the meringue with a knife or spoon. Or transfer the meringue to a pastry bag with a large star tip and make rosettes, crisscross patterns, or a coil pattern over the entire filling, making sure the meringue touches all sides of the crust.

- Sprinkle the remaining tablespoon of sugar over the top and bake until the tips or peaks of meringue are lightly colored, about 8 to 10 minutes. Cool on a wire rack before refrigerating. Serve chilled, preferably the same day that it is made.

Lemon Squares

Makes 24 squares

For the crust

2 cups flour

16 tablespoons (½ pound) unsalted butter, softened

½ cup confectioners' sugar

¼ teaspoon salt

Grated zest of 1 lemon

For the filling

4 eggs

1½ cups sugar

½ cup freshly squeezed lemon juice

¼ cup flour

½ teaspoon double-acting baking powder

¼ teaspoon salt

3 to 4 tablespoons confectioners' sugar for sifting over the top

- Preheat the oven to 350 degrees.
- To make the crust, mix all the ingredients in a bowl or food processor until a ball of dough forms. Wrap the ball in plastic wrap and refrigerate until chilled to make handling easier.
- Press the dough evenly onto the bottom and ¾ inch up the sides of an ungreased 9-by-13-inch pan.
- Bake on the middle rack of the oven until lightly colored, about 15 to 20 minutes. Cool on a wire rack while you make the filling. Leave the oven set at 350 degrees.
- To make the filling, beat the eggs until light. Add the sugar gradually and continue beating on medium-high speed until very light and airy, about 5 minutes. On low speed, mix in the lemon juice, flour, baking powder, and salt just until combined.
- Pour the mixture over the crust and bake until the filling is set and lightly colored, about 25 minutes. Immediately sift the confectioners' sugar over the top. Cool and cut into 24 squares.

Lemonade or Limeade

Lemonade used to come not from a frozen can or even a canister but from real lemons! Do you remember the "lemon shake-ups" at the state and 4-H fairs that were made with lemons, sugar, water, and ice? They were simple, thirst-quenching, and delicious. After you've tried the real thing, it's hard to accept artificially flavored and overly sweetened lemon drinks.

Serves 4

¾ cup sugar
1 cup boiling water
3 cups cold water

½ cup freshly squeezed lemon or lime juice

- Add the sugar to a 1½ quart pitcher. Add the boiling water and stir to dissolve the sugar. Cool slightly so the pitcher won't crack when cold water is added. Add the cold water gradually and stir.
- Add the lemon or lime juice to the pitcher. Stir, chill, and serve over ice in a tall glass.

*L*entil Soup

Here's one of many hearty, warming soups that gets us through the long, cold winter. With homemade bread and a salad, it's a favorite weekend lunch. I associate lentils with Indian cuisine, so I flavor the soup with a bit of curry powder and top it with yogurt.

Serves 6

3 tablespoons butter

1 medium onion, finely chopped

2 stalks celery, trimmed and finely chopped

1 small carrot, peeled and finely chopped

1 green pepper, seeded, cored, and finely chopped

2 tablespoons flour

2 teaspoons curry powder

1 cup green or red lentils

4 cups beef broth

4 cups water

2 tablespoons tomato paste

2 tablespoons lemon juice

Salt, black pepper, and cayenne pepper to taste

½ cup plain yogurt or sour cream for the topping

L

- In a large pot, melt the butter and sauté the onion, celery, carrot, and pepper over low heat, stirring to prevent them from coloring, about 12 minutes.
- Stir in the flour, curry powder, and lentils; sauté for 1 minute more.
- Slowly stir in the broth and water, and bring to a boil.
- Stir again, scraping the bottom to unstick any lentils, and cover. Simmer, partially covered, for 1 hour, stirring occasionally. Stir in the tomato paste and continue to simmer, partially covered, for 30 minutes more. Add the lemon juice, salt, black pepper, and cayenne pepper to taste.
- Serve the soup hot with a dollop of yogurt or sour cream.

*L*obsters

Here's a wonderful food the home cook can introduce to children in a safe environment (spread with newspapers). The technique for eating lobster can be mastered at home before attempting it in public.

For cooking lobster, follow the rules given below.

- Make sure the lobster is alive!
- Keep the lobster in the refrigerator until cooking time.
- Fill a pot large enough to hold the lobster(s) with enough water (with a tablespoon of salt and vinegar) to cover the lobster(s).
- When the water comes to a boil, add the lobster(s) and let the water return to a boil. Cook according to the table.

Pounds	Cooking Time
1	8 minutes
2	12 minutes
3	16 minutes

- Provide a hammer, nutcracker, and little cocktail picks for cracking the lobster and extracting the meat.
- Serve hot with melted butter or cold with homemade Mayonnaise (see page 174) and a squeeze of fresh lemon juice.

MACARONI AND CHEESE

How many pounds of macaroni and cheese do children consume before they move on to more adventurous culinary staples? I have two favorite recipes: one that's as fast as the packaged stove-top kind most kids like, and an adult version that's a baked casserole.

Macaroni and Cheese—Quick and Easy

Serves 2 or 3

1 cup (4 ounces) elbow macaroni

3 tablespoons unsalted butter

3 to 4 ounces Colby or Longhorn Cheddar, *or* American cheese, grated to make 1½ cups

1 tablespoon flour

¾ cup milk

Salt and freshly ground black pepper

Grating of nutmeg

continued on next page

- Cook the macaroni in boiling salted water until tender, about 8 to 10 minutes. Drain well, return the macaroni to its cooking pot, and add the butter, stirring until it melts.
- Toss the cheese and flour together in a bowl to mix thoroughly.
- Add the cheese to the macaroni and stir. Stir in the milk. Cook for a few minutes over low heat, stirring until a smooth, thickened sauce forms and coats the macaroni. Season with salt, pepper, and nutmeg, and serve hot.

*M*acaroni and Cheese Casserole

M

170

Serves 6

2 cups (½ pound) elbow macaroni
4 tablespoons unsalted butter
Salt and pepper
2 tablespoons flour

½ pound Cheddar cheese, grated to make 3 cups
2 cups (approximately) half-and-half
⅓ cup dry, unseasoned bread crumbs

- Preheat the oven to 375 degrees. Butter a 2-quart shallow casserole or baking dish.
- Cook the macaroni in boiling salted water until tender, about 8 to 10 minutes. Drain well and toss with 3 tablespoons of the butter.
- Spread ⅓ of the macaroni in the prepared dish and sprinkle with salt, pepper, 1 tablespoon of the flour, and 1 cup of the cheese. Add another ⅓ of the macaroni, salt, pepper, the remaining flour and another cup of cheese. Add the remaining macaroni, salt, pepper, and cheese, and press down gently.
- Pour the half-and-half over the macaroni and cheese until you can see it just reach the top. Sprinkle with bread crumbs and dot with the remaining tablespoon of butter.
- Bake on the top rack of the oven until bubbly and golden, about 35 minutes.

Marinated Mushrooms

Marinated mushrooms make either a wonderful, not-too-filling appetizer easily eaten with a toothpick or a nice addition to a green salad.

When storing mushrooms or any fruits and vegetables, paper bags are better than plastic. Paper "breathes" and absorbs moisture. Plastic holds in moisture and permits mold to develop. So, when you return from the market, transfer fruits and vegetables to a brown bag. Or wrap mushrooms, lettuce, parsley, celery, and herbs loosely in paper towels to absorb moisture and then place them in an open plastic bag.

Makes 1 pint

½ cup white vinegar
½ cup water
3 tablespoons olive or vegetable oil
1 teaspoon salt
1 teaspoon sugar
1 small onion, thinly sliced

1 clove garlic, peeled and cut in half
6 black peppercorns
1 pound firm white cultivated mushrooms, wiped cleaned and trimmed
½ bay leaf
A few sprigs of thyme

171

- In a saucepan, combine all the ingredients except the mushrooms, bay leaf, and thyme. Bring to a boil and add the mushrooms. Bring back to a boil and cook the mushrooms over medium heat about 5 minutes, or to the texture you like (taste one).
- Place the bay leaf and thyme in the bottom of a 1-pint glass jar. Pour the mushrooms and marinade into the jar and let them cool before covering and refrigerating. The mushrooms will develop more flavor if you wait a day before serving them.

Mashed Potatoes

Use old-fashioned tools for this old-fashioned favorite and mash the lumps out of the potatoes with a food mill or potato masher. Don't try mashed potatoes in a food processor or you're likely to end up with inedible glue.

Serves 6 to 8

4 large baking potatoes (2 pounds), peeled, cut in quarters, and put in a bowl of water to prevent discoloration until you cook them
4 tablespoons butter, cut in tablespoons

¾ cup heavy cream, heated
Salt and freshly ground black pepper to taste

172

- Cook the potatoes in a pot of boiling salted water until tender, about 15 to 20 minutes. Drain well.
- While hot, toss with the butter and put through a food mill or mash in a bowl with a potato masher or use a mixer with a flat attachment. When the potatoes are mashed, add the cream slowly, adding more or less to achieve the desired consistency. Add salt and pepper to taste. Serve immediately.

For baked mashed potato rosettes (Makes about 20 rosettes)

Mashed potatoes
½ cup milk or light cream
2 tablespoons dry bread crumbs

2 tablespoons butter, melted
Salt and freshly ground pepper

- Preheat the oven to 375 degrees. Butter a shallow baking dish.

- To the cooled mashed potatoes, add the milk or cream slowly to make a mixture that's smooth but stiff enough to hold a shape when piped from a pastry bag. Season with salt and pepper.
- Transfer the potato mixture to a large pastry bag fitted with a large star tip and pipe rosettes of potatoes into the prepared dish. Sprinkle the tops with the bread crumbs and drizzle with butter.
- Bake on the top rack of the oven about 15 minutes until lightly browned and heated through. Serve immediately.

Note: These can be made a few hours ahead of serving, covered lightly, and refrigerated. Bring to room temperature before baking.

Mayonnaise

A whisk, blender, or food processor will each do a fine job of thickening the mayonnaise as long as the egg is at room temperature. If you forget to bring the egg to room temperature, put it in hot water for a few minutes to warm it up. Cold eggs won't emulsify the oil and vinegar.

Makes 1¾ cups

1 whole egg, at room temperature
1 tablespoon lemon juice or vinegar
1 teaspoon salt
½ teaspoon dry mustard

Pinch of cayenne pepper
1½ cups vegetable oil or a combination
of vegetable oil and olive oil

174

- In a bowl, blender, or food processor, combine the egg, lemon juice, salt, dry mustard, and cayenne pepper.
- While whisking, blending, or processing, add the oil in a very thin, steady stream. A thick emulsified mayonnaise will form. Adjust the seasoning to taste, adding another tablespoon of lemon juice or additional salt as needed. Store in the refrigerator in a covered jar.

Variations

Before adding the oil, add ¼ cup finely chopped herbs, chives, scallions, or a clove of garlic.

Add 3 tablespoons Dijon mustard or a few anchovies, all at room temperature.

Substitute orange juice and zest for the lemon juice.

Thin the mayonnaise with 1 teaspoon of Worcestershire sauce or 2 teaspoons soy sauce.

Add 1 tablespoon sesame oil to the oil and 2 tablespoons toasted sesame seeds to the finished mayonnaise.

Give it some zip with 1 teaspoon powdered ginger and a pinch of sugar. Fold ¼ cup minced crystallized ginger into the finished mayonnaise.

For Pepper-Mint Mayonnaise (for chicken salad), add 1 seeded hot pepper, a handful of fresh mint leaves, and 1 teaspoon sugar to the bowl of the food processor.

Meatballs and Spaghetti

Serves 6 to 8

For the meatballs

1 pound ground beef
½ pound ground lean pork (ask your butcher to custom grind lean pork chops)
½ cup dry bread crumbs
2 eggs
2 tablespoons water
¼ cup finely chopped parsley

1 small onion, finely chopped
1 clove garlic, minced
¼ cup grated Parmesan cheese
1 teaspoon salt
½ teaspoon freshly ground pepper
½ teaspoon fennel seeds, crushed
Grating of nutmeg

For the sauce

1 15-ounce can chunky tomato sauce
½ cup water or dry red wine
1 bay leaf

1 teaspoon oregano
Salt and freshly ground pepper to taste

For the spaghetti

1 pound spaghetti
4 tablespoons unsalted butter

1 cup grated Parmesan cheese

- Preheat the oven to 425 degrees. Lightly oil an 8-by-12-inch shallow baking dish.
- To make the meatballs, thoroughly mix all the ingredients for the meatballs. Form the mixture into 24 meatballs and place in the prepared baking dish.
- Bake 15 minutes and turn the meatballs. Bake another 15 minutes and pour off any excess fat. Reduce the oven temperature to 350 degrees.
- Meanwhile, make the sauce. Combine the tomato sauce and water. Add the seasonings and pour the sauce over the drained meatballs. Cover the

continued on next page

baking dish loosely with foil; bake 15 minutes. Turn the meatballs and bake for 15 minutes more.

▪ While the meatballs are cooking, bring a large quantity of salted water to a boil. Add the spaghetti and cook for 8 to 10 minutes, or to the desired doneness. Drain well and toss with the butter and half the Parmesan cheese.

▪ Transfer the spaghetti to a large serving dish or platter and top with the meatballs and sauce. Sprinkle the top with the remaining Parmesan cheese.

MEAT LOAF

The choice of spices and ingredients makes meat loaf a versatile standard that can take on nearly any ethnic identity.

$\mathcal{M}$

176

Mexican Meat Loaf

Serves 4 to 6

1½ pounds lean ground beef
1 small onion, finely chopped
1 clove garlic, minced
¼ cup Ketchup (see page 174)
¾ cup fresh bread crumbs
3 tablespoons water
2 canned or fresh hot peppers, seeded and finely chopped (optional)

2 teaspoons chili powder
1 teaspoon ground cumin
1 teaspoon salt
½ teaspoon oregano
½ teaspoon black pepper
1 egg, lightly beaten
Commercial salsa and chopped fresh cilantro for garnish (optional)

▪ Preheat the oven to 350 degrees. Lightly oil the bottom of a 4½-by-8½-inch loaf pan.

▪ Combine the beef, onion, garlic, ketchup, bread crumbs, water, hot peppers, and spices. Beat the egg and combine with the meat loaf mixture.

Pack the mixture into the prepared loaf pan, mounding it slightly in the center.

- Bake for 1 hour, basting occasionally with the accumulated juices.
- Remove the meat loaf from the oven and let it sit 10 minutes. Pour off any excess liquid. Slice and serve with salsa and cilantro.

$\mathcal{M}$iddle Eastern Meat Loaf

This meat loaf is full of flavor from lamb, parsley, mint, and cinnamon. For added texture, substitute ½ cup bulgur for the bread crumbs and add ¼ cup toasted pine nuts. Macaroni and cheese or scalloped potatoes make a great accompaniment, and Pepper-Mint Jelly is a good condiment.

Serves 6 to 8

1 pound fresh ground beef
1 pound fresh lean ground lamb (ask your butcher to custom grind a few lean chops)
½ cup minced parsley
¼ cup minced scallions, some green as well as white parts
2 tablespoons minced fresh mint leaves
1 cup fresh bread crumbs, or ½ cup fine bulgur

1 teaspoon salt
½ teaspoon cinnamon
½ teaspoon paprika
Freshly ground pepper
2 eggs, lightly beaten
¼ cup water
¼ cup toasted pine nuts (optional)
Fresh mint for garnish

- Preheat the oven to 350 degrees. Lightly oil the bottom of a 4½-by-8½-inch loaf pan.
- In a large bowl, thoroughly combine all the ingredients except the mint for garnish. Pack the mixture into the prepared loaf pan, mounding it slightly in the center. Bake 1¼ hours, basting occasionally with the accumulated juices. Remove the pan from the oven and let the meat loaf sit for 10 minutes. Pour off any excess liquid. Slice and serve garnished with mint.

$\mathcal{M}$exican Wedding Cakes

My stomach hurts just remembering the excessive quantities of Mexican Wedding Cakes I ate at my childhood chum's house. These delicate buttery morsels were always around at holiday times, and fit for any wedding, Mexican or not. Ground pecans, or "pecan meal," can be ordered by mail and stored in the freezer for these cookies as well as for pancakes or pie crust enrichments. One reliable and friendly source: Sunnyland Farms, Albany, Georgia 31706.

Makes 4 to 5 dozen

½ pound unsalted butter, softened
5 tablespoons confectioners' sugar plus
   1 cup for rolling the cookies
1 teaspoon water

1 teaspoon vanilla extract
½ teaspoon salt
2 cups flour
1 cup (3 ounces) ground shelled pecans

- In a mixing bowl, cream the butter and 5 tablespoons of the confectioners' sugar. Add the water, vanilla, salt, flour, and pecans and mix until a stiff but sticky dough forms. Chill the dough 30 minutes to make rolling easier.
- Preheat the oven to 350 degrees. Lightly grease a heavy baking sheet with solid shortening.
- Roll the dough in your hands to form 1-inch balls. Place the balls 2 inches apart on the prepared baking sheet.
- Bake in the middle of the oven until the cookies are barely colored, about 20 minutes.
- While warm, roll the cookies in the remaining 1 cup of confectioners' sugar and cool completely on a wire rack. Roll the cookies a second time in any remaining sugar. Store in an airtight tin.

Molasses Cookies

The sugar-rolled balls of dough sweetened with molasses or honey make perfectly round crackle-topped cookies that keep well.

Makes 4 dozen cookies

8 tablespoons unsalted butter, at room
    temperature
1⅓ cups sugar
¼ cup dark molasses or honey
1 egg, at room temperature

2 cups flour
½ cup quick rolled oats
1½ teaspoons baking soda
1 teaspoon cinnamon
½ teaspoon salt

- Cream the butter and gradually add 1 cup of the sugar, beating until light. Add the molasses and beat until well mixed. Add the egg and beat until light.
- Combine the flour, oats, baking soda, cinnamon, and salt. Combine with the creamed mixture to form a dough. Wrap the dough in plastic wrap and chill at least 30 minutes to make handling easier.
- Preheat the oven to 375 degrees.
- Roll pieces of the dough in your hands to form 1-inch balls; roll the balls in the remaining ⅓ cup of sugar. Place the balls 2 inches apart on an ungreased heavy baking sheet.
- Place the baking sheet on a rack in the middle of the oven and immediately reduce the oven temperature to 350 degrees. Bake until the cookies are very lightly colored and the tops no longer look wet, about 8 to 10 minutes. Don't overbake.
- Transfer the cookies with a spatula to a wire rack to cool completely.

MUFFINS

Bran or Oatmeal Muffins

Oat bran is a wonderful alternative to the more familiar wheat bran. The oat flavor and goodness of bran are combined in one. I sometimes add a few chopped raisins or currants to the muffin batter and sprinkle the tops with sugar. Don't overmix or beat the batter or you'll end up with leaden muffins.

Makes 10 muffins

1 cup unprocessed bran or quick rolled oats
⅔ cup milk
1 egg
½ cup brown sugar
¼ cup vegetable oil
¼ cup chopped raisins or currants (optional)

1 cup flour
2 teaspoons double-acting baking powder
¼ teaspoon baking soda
½ teaspoon salt
1 teaspoon granulated sugar for the tops

• Preheat the oven to 425 degrees. Grease 10 2½-inch muffin tins well with shortening or line them with paper baking cups.
• In a bowl, combine the bran and milk. Let stand a few minutes. Stir in the egg, brown sugar, and oil. Mix thoroughly. Stir in the raisins.

- Sift together the flour, baking powder, baking soda, and salt.
- Combine the wet and dry ingredients, stirring with a fork just until mixed. A few lumps are fine.
- Divide the batter equally among the muffin tins, filling them about ¾ full.
- Put the muffin tins on the middle rack of the oven and immediately reduce the oven temperature to 400 degrees. Bake until the centers are springy and a tookpick inserted in the center comes out clean, about 20 minutes. Sprinkle the tops with sugar while hot, then cool for 5 minutes on a wire rack before serving warm with butter.

Apple Muffins

A delicious fall treat for breakfast or an after-school snack. Let children help with the muffin tins, apple grating, and sugar topping. Participation makes them eager eaters.

Makes 12 muffins

2 cups flour
½ cup plus 1 tablespoon sugar
1 teaspoon double-acting baking powder
1 teaspoon baking soda
½ teaspoon salt
1 teaspoon cinnamon

1 egg
1¼ cups buttermilk, at room temperature
4 tablespoons unsalted butter, melted
1 large or 2 small apples, peeled, cored, and finely chopped to make 1 cup

- Grease 12 muffin tins well or line with paper baking cups. Preheat the oven to 400 degrees.
- Sift together the flour, ½ cup of the sugar, baking powder, baking soda, salt, and cinnamon.
- Combine the egg, buttermilk, and melted butter and add to the dry ingredients, stirring quickly but gently with a fork until nearly combined. Fold in the chopped apples.

continued on next page

▪ Fill the muffin tins nearly full and sprinkle the tops with the remaining tablespoon of sugar. Put the muffin tins on the middle rack of the oven and immediately reduce the oven temperature to 375 degrees. Bake until the muffins are golden and a toothpick inserted in the center comes out clean, about 25 to 30 minutes. Cool 5 minutes before serving.

$\mathcal{M}$ulled Cider

182

Perhaps because we live in an area rich with native apples, cider is often our drink of choice. (We even named our golden retriever Cider.) From cold apple cider on Indian summer days, we move on to warm spiced cider. Winter and holiday gatherings wouldn't be complete without warm mulled cider, sometimes spiked with rum or brandy. On some occasions, I use the same recipe for mulled *wine,* and sweeten it to taste.

The mulling spices can be tied in cheesecloth for easy removal but I simply add them to the pot and pour the cider into a mug through a fine mesh strainer at serving time.

Serves 4 to 6

1 quart apple cider

1 cup orange juice

1 lemon, sliced

1 cinnamon stick

4 to 6 cloves

2 cardamom pods, pinched open

3 allspice berries

¼ cup sugar, or more to taste

¼ to ½ cup rum or brandy (optional)

▪ In a large saucepan, combine the cider, orange juice, lemon, and spices. Bring almost to a boil and remove the pan from the heat. Cover and let the cider sit for an hour.

▪ At serving time, reheat the cider and sweeten to taste, beginning with a few tablespoons of sugar. Remove the spices and lemon and add the rum before serving. If rum or brandy is added, more sugar may be needed than for simple mulled cider.

MUSTARD

I know collectors who have mustard cellars to rival wine cellars: domestic and imported; hot and sweet; with horseradish, peppers, peppercorns, sherry, Balsamic vinegar, wine. All are based on ground mustard seeds.

Sweet and Hot Mustard

This makes a welcome hostess or holiday gift when you include it in a decorative basket with a smoked turkey or ham and scones or a loaf of homemade bread. Try a little of it mixed with Mayonnaise (see page 174) for a fast sauce that's great with chicken sandwiches or cold shellfish.

Makes 2½ cups

1 cup (4 ounces) dry mustard	½ teaspoon salt
1 cup cider vinegar	⅛ teaspoon cayenne pepper
1 cup sugar	3 eggs

- Combine the dry mustard and the vinegar in a plastic or glass bowl and whisk until smooth. Cover and refrigerate a few hours or overnight.
- In a heavy saucepan, whisk together the sugar, salt, cayenne pepper, and eggs. Stir in the mustard mixture. Heat slowly, stirring often, until the mustard thickens and just comes to a boil. Remove the pan from the heat and stir occasionally as the mustard cools to let the heat escape. Pour into glass jars, cover, and refrigerate.

*N*oodle Pudding

This dish goes well with roast chicken, barbequed spare ribs, and pot roast—and children love it too. It is easily doubled to serve a crowd.

Serves 6

½ pound broad egg noodles

6 tablespoons butter

1 cup sour cream

1 cup small-curd cottage cheese

½ cup milk (¾ cup if using jam or marmalade)

½ cup applesauce, *or* 3 tablespoons apricot jam or orange marmalade

2 tablespoons sugar, or to taste

1 teaspoon salt

¼ teaspoon cinnamon (optional)

¼ teaspoon ground ginger (optional)

3 tablespoons unseasoned bread crumbs

- Preheat the oven to 375 degrees. Butter a shallow 2-quart baking dish.
- Cook the noodles in boiling salted water until tender, about 6 minutes.

continued on next page

Drain well and toss with 4 tablespoons of the butter. When the butter has melted, add the sour cream, cottage cheese, milk, applesauce, sugar, salt, cinnamon, and ginger. Stir well and adjust the seasoning, adding more sugar or salt to taste.

▪ Spoon the noodles into the prepared dish and sprinkle with the bread crumbs. Dot with bits of the remaining butter and bake on the middle rack of the oven until nicely browned, about 1 hour.

N

Oatmeal Bread

Oatmeal gives my favorite all-purpose bread a moist texture as well as delicious flavor. The oats can be cooked just for this bread or may come from leftover breakfast cereal. Occasionally I substitute other cooked cereals (Wheatena, Cream of Wheat, cornmeal) or leftover mashed potatoes for the oatmeal.

Makes 2 loaves

2 cups water
1 cup quick-cooking rolled oats
⅓ cup vegetable or corn oil
¼ cup brown sugar
1 tablespoon salt
1 egg, lightly beaten

¼ cup warm water
Pinch of sugar
1 ¼-ounce package (1 scant table-spoon) active dry yeast
4½ to 5 cups all-purpose or bread flour

• Bring the 2 cups of water to a boil and add the oats. Stir, cook for 1 minute, and remove from the heat. (If substituting other cereals or using leftover cereals, cook according to directions to yield 2 cups cooked cereal.) Cool 10 minutes. Stir in the oil, brown sugar, salt, and egg.

continued on next page

- Mix the warm water and pinch of sugar; add the yeast. Proof the yeast until bubbly, about 10 minutes.
- Add the yeast mixture to the cooled cereal and stir vigorously. Add 2 cups of the flour and mix well. Gradually add more flour until the dough is fairly stiff. Turn the dough out onto a floured flat surface and knead until smooth and springy, adding more flour as needed until no longer sticky.
- Generously oil a large bowl and put the dough in the bowl, turning the dough to coat all sides. Cover the bowl lightly with a towel and let the dough rise in a warm spot until double, about 1 hour.
- Thoroughly grease two 4½-by-8½-inch loaf pans with shortening. Preheat the oven to 375 degrees.
- Punch the dough down and turn out onto a lightly floured surface. Knead to eliminate any air holes. Divide the dough in half and form into 2 loaves that will fit into the prepared pans, seam side down. Cover lightly with a towel and let the dough rise until nearly doubled in size.
- Bake the bread on the middle rack of the oven until golden and the bottom of the bread sounds hollow when turned out of the pan and rapped, about 50 minutes. When done, remove the bread from the pans and cool on a wire rack. Brush the tops with a teaspoon of butter if you like. Cool completely and store in a plastic bag. Slicing is much easier when the bread has cooled completely.

Oatmeal Cookies

My mother-in-law, Pauline Glass, is famous for her "fork cookies"—buttery rich oatmeal cookies baked in a hot oven and pressed with a fork to a crispy thinness. If you can't stand the heat, add dates and walnuts to the dough and skip the fork-pressing during baking. Thick and lumpy *or* crisp and brittle, either is a great cookie.

Makes 4½ dozen cookies

½ pound unsalted butter, softened
1 cup firmly packed brown sugar
1½ cups flour
2 cups quick or old-fashioned rolled oats
¼ teaspoon salt

1 teaspoon vanilla extract
⅓ teaspoon baking soda
2 tablespoons boiling water
½ cup chopped walnuts (optional)
½ cup chopped dates (optional)

189

- Cream the butter and sugar. Add the flour, oats, salt, and vanilla, stirring to combine. Dissolve the baking soda in the water and add to the dough. Stir in the nuts and dates. Cover and chill the dough for 1 hour to make handling easier.
- Preheat the oven to 400 degrees. Lightly grease 2 heavy baking sheets.
- Form pieces of the dough with your hands into 1-inch balls; arrange the balls at least 2 inches apart on the prepared baking sheet. Flatten the cookie dough with a fork.
- Bake about 8 minutes until golden, removing the cookies from the oven a few times to flatten with a fork. To prevent the dough from tearing, keep a glass of water next to the fork and wet it before pressing each cookie down. You will get very good at this. Shut the oven door while you're flattening the cookies to prevent the oven temperature from dropping. When the cookies are golden, remove them with a spatula to a wire rack to cool.

Onion Rings

Serves 6 to 8

4 large sweet onions, peeled, cut in ¼-inch slices and separated into rings

Ice water

For the batter

1 cup flour
½ teaspoon salt
½ teaspoon baking soda
1 egg

1 cup buttermilk

Vegetable oil
Salt

- To eliminate the sharp raw taste of the onions, soak them in ice water for 30 minutes, changing the water a few times.
- To make the batter, sift the flour, salt, and baking soda into a wide bowl. Beat the egg and buttermilk together and add to the flour mixture. Stir until well mixed.
- In a heavy saucepan or deep fryer, heat 1½ inches of vegetable oil to 375 degrees. Preheat the oven to 225 degrees.
- Drain and dry the onion rings. Dip the rings in batches in the batter. Let the excess batter drip off and carefully drop the rings into the hot oil, a few at a time. Fry until golden, about 2 minutes, turning them once.
- Remove the onions with a slotted flat ladle and drain on paper towels. Salt lightly.
- Bring the oil back to 375 degrees and deep-fry the remaining onion rings in batches. Meanwhile, transfer the drained rings to a jelly-roll pan lined with multiple layers of paper towels to absorb the excess fat. Keep them warm in the preheated oven, uncovered, until all the onion rings are cooked and ready to serve.

Onion Soup

College weekends in Manhattan always included a trip to The Brasserie where the onion soup was memorable, affordable, and truly delicious! Topped with a cheese crouton, the soup was a filling lunch with a salad and glass of wine. Onion soup at home can be equally memorable.

A good homemade stock of almost any kind (beef, veal, or chicken) will make all the difference in onion soup. If you must use canned broth, dilute the saltiness with water and a little white wine before you add it to the sweet, meltingly soft sautéed onions. And don't forget the important topping: a cheesy toasted French bread crouton to soak up the juices.

Serves 6

3 tablespoons vegetable oil

3 tablespoons butter

3 large or 5 medium (2½ pounds) onions, cut in half and thinly sliced

1 teaspoon caraway seeds (optional)

¼ cup flour

8 cups heated beef or chicken stock, preferably homemade, *or* a mixture of 5 cups beef or chicken broth, 2 cups water, and 1 cup white wine

1 clove garlic, peeled and toothpicked

1 bay leaf

Bouquet garni: celery stalk, parsley stems, and sprigs of thyme tied together with string

2 tablespoons brandy or sherry (optional)

Salt and freshly ground black pepper to taste

For the croutons

6 slices French bread

1½ cups grated Gruyère or Emmenthal or Monterey Jack cheese

2 tablespoons vegetable oil

- In a large heavy pot, heat the oil and butter. Add the onions and sauté over low heat, stirring often to prevent them from coloring, about 30 minutes. Add the caraway seeds and sauté until the onions are very soft and sweet, about 10 minutes more (40 minutes in all).
- Add the flour and stir to mix well. Add the stock and stir well. Add the garlic, bay leaf, and bouquet garni. Simmer, partially covered, for 1 hour.

continued on next page

• To make the croutons, preheat the oven to 375 degrees. Arrange the bread on a baking sheet, top each bread slice with ¼ cup of the cheese, and drizzle with oil. Bake until the bread is browned and the cheese is bubbly, approximately 5 minutes.

• Remove the garlic, bay leaf, and bouquet garni from the hot soup. Add salt and pepper to taste. Add the brandy. Ladle into six soup bowls and top each with a cheese crouton.

$\mathcal{O}$ven-Crisp Potatoes

Serves 6 to 8

192

2 slices bacon, cut in 1-inch pieces, *or* 3 tablespoons vegetable oil

1 teaspoon caraway seeds

½ teaspoon paprika

6 medium (2 pounds) boiling potatoes, quartered

Salt and freshly ground black pepper to taste

Minced parsley for garnish (optional)

• Preheat the oven to 375 degrees.

• Sauté the bacon until most of the fat is rendered. Remove the bacon and reserve. Heat the caraway seeds in the bacon fat. (Alternately, heat the vegetable oil and sauté the caraway seeds in it for 1 or 2 minutes.)

• Add the paprika and potatoes to the pan and toss well to coat.

• Transfer the potatoes to a shallow baking dish and bake, turning often, until crisp on the outside and tender when tested with a toothpick on the inside, about 45 minutes.

• Season to taste with salt and pepper. Add the reserved bacon if you like. A sprinkling of minced parsley will make this more colorful.

Note: When time is short, reduce the cooking time by boiling the potatoes until half done, draining and drying them well, tossing them with oil, and baking in a 400-degree oven until crisp. Be sure to turn the potatoes often to insure even browning.

PANCAKES

Pancakes from scratch couldn't be much easier since they're made with simple, readily available ingredients that are stirred together and quickly cooked on a hot griddle. Shape the batter into teddy bear faces with raisins or blueberries for eyes and noses to make breakfast fun for small children. A pitcher of pancake batter next to the griddle makes it easy for late sleepers to make their own when the cook has moved on to other activities.

Buttermilk Pancakes

Makes 24 to 30 pancakes

2 cups flour

3 tablespoons sugar

1 teaspoon baking soda

1 teaspoon salt

4 tablespoons unsalted butter, melted,
  or vegetable oil

2 eggs

2 cups buttermilk (see note below)

¼ cup water, approximately, to thin
  the batter

Butter and maple syrup

- Heat the griddle while you make the pancake batter. When it's hot enough for cooking, water drops sprinkled on the surface should "dance," but the griddle shouldn't be smoking.
- Sift the flour, sugar, baking soda, and salt into a large bowl. Whisk the butter, eggs, and buttermilk together and add to the flour mixture, stirring lightly with a fork just until mixed. If the batter is too thick, thin with water as needed.
- Brush the griddle with oil or butter before adding the batter. Ladle about ¼ cup batter onto the hot griddle for each pancake. Turn when the underside is browned and a few holes appear on the edges of the top surface. Cook until the other side is lightly browned.
- Serve hot with butter and maple syrup.

Variations

For added flavor and texture, substitute ½ cup old-fashioned rolled oats or fine yellow cornmeal for ½ cup of the flour.

To make Peanut Butter Pancakes (serve with jelly of course!) substitute 2 tablespoons peanut butter for 2 tablespoons of the butter or oil.

To make Pumpkin Pancakes, add 1 teaspoon cinnamon and ¼ teaspoon each ginger and nutmeg to the dry ingredients and 1 cup pumpkin purée to the wet ingredients before stirring together. Reduce the buttermilk by ½ cup.

Note: If you don't have buttermilk on hand, you can substitute 1½ cups plain yogurt thinned with ½ cup water, or 2 cups milk mixed with 4 teaspoons lemon juice or vinegar for the 2 cups buttermilk. Powdered buttermilk keeps well on a shelf.

PASTAS

Pasta has been around for centuries in Italian and Chinese cuisines and has a secure place in American cooking. When time is short and ingredients are few, the answer for dinner is always prepared pasta: frozen ravioli, fresh pasta, spaghetti from a box. When pasta is tossed with butter, cream, or olive oil and topped with freshly grated Parmesan cheese and such interesting tidbits as sun-dried tomatoes, fresh herbs, anchovies, prosciutto, leftover sauces or vegetables, capers or cornichon, caviar or smoked salmon, lemon zest, garlic, smoked oysters, or cooked seafood, dinner is just minutes away.

But I also love to make pasta as a children's activity, and even take the pasta machine on vacation for rainy or cold days. At home, puréed leftover vegetables (spinach, pumpkin, carrot, roasted peppers, or garlic) and fresh herbs and spices or flavorings (thyme, dill, pepper, or lemon zest) add such flavor and interest to the pasta that it needs only butter and salt.

I usually double the pasta recipe so I have enough for a few dinners. After cranking out the dough and cutting it, the fresh pasta is ready for a minute's cooking in boiling salted water. Or dredge handfuls of pasta in flour and store it in "nests" in a covered container in the refrigerator for a day or two. The flour dredging is important to prevent the strands from sticking together.

For Egg Pasta (Makes approximately 1¼ pounds)

2½ cups flour
½ teaspoon salt
3 eggs
1 tablespoon oil

3 tablespoons water (approximately)
Pepper, snipped herbs, spices, zests (optional)

continued on next page

For Flavored Pasta (Makes approximately 1 pound)

2 cups flour
½ teaspoon salt
2 eggs
2 teaspoons oil
Water

3 tablespoons cooked, puréed vegetables, such as spinach, roasted peppers, pumpkin, beets, or pesto (approximately), *or* 2 teaspoons tomato paste

The technique for making either pasta is the same:

- Combine the flour and salt in a bowl or on a flat surface. Make a well and add the egg, oil, water and vegetable purée.
- Mix the wet ingredients with a fork and stir the flour into the center until a dough begins to form. Knead well, adding flour from the edges as needed until the dough is very smooth and no longer sticky. Consistency is the key: it must be neither too dry and crumbly nor too wet and sticky.
- Wrap the pasta dough in plastic wrap and let the dough rest at least 15 minutes.
- Roll and cut the dough according to your pasta machine instructions, keeping extra flour on the table to dust the dough if it seems sticky.

Ravioli in Cream Sauce with Prosciutto and Peas

This is our favorite prepared pasta dish; it appears once a week for dinner.

Serves 4 to 6

1½ pounds frozen or fresh cheese ravioli

4 tablespoons unsalted butter

2 cups heavy cream

1 cup freshly grated Parmesan cheese

½ 10-ounce package frozen petite peas

⅛ pound prosciutto or boiled ham, thinly sliced and julienned

Freshly ground black pepper

- Cook the ravioli in boiling salted water until it reaches the desired doneness, about 15 minutes for the frozen, less for the fresh. Drain well in a colander, return to the cooking pot, and toss with butter.
- While the ravioli are cooking, make the cream sauce by boiling the cream in a large sauté pan until it is reduced by almost half and is thickened. Add ¾ cup of the cheese and mix well.
- Add the cooked ravioli, the frozen peas, and prosciutto and stir gently. Simmer a few minutes, stirring constantly to prevent sticking.
- Spoon into a serving dish or onto a platter and top with the remaining Parmesan cheese. Grind black pepper over the top and serve while still very hot.

$\mathcal{P}$each Cobbler

Cobblers are old-fashioned summertime desserts made with little effort and great results. They're like fresh fruit pies with only a top crust of biscuits or shortcake. Use your favorite summer fruit and top it with this simple dough that bakes to a golden crust. You can substitute plums, nectarines, apples, or cherries for the peaches. Bake the cobbler in a 9-inch pie plate or baking dish and serve warm with vanilla ice cream.

Serves 6

2 tablespoons unsalted butter
2 pounds (approximately 6) fresh peaches, peeled and cut in chunks
½ cup sugar
1 tablespoon cornstarch, *or* 2 tablespoons flour

1 tablespoon lemon juice
½ teaspoon cinnamon
Pinch of salt

For the crust

¼ cup solid vegetable shortening
3 tablespoons sugar
1 egg
½ teaspoon vanilla extract
¾ cup flour
½ teaspoon double-acting baking powder

Pinch of salt
2 tablespoons milk

Vanilla ice cream

• Preheat the oven to 375 degrees. Lightly butter a 9-inch pie plate or baking dish with 1 tablespoon of the butter.
• In a bowl, combine the prepared fruit, sugar, cornstarch, lemon juice, cinnamon, and salt, stirring to mix well.
• Turn the fruit into the prepared baking dish. Dot with the remaining tablespoon of butter.
• To make the crust, beat the shortening and sugar together. Add the egg and vanilla and beat until light.

- Sift the flour, baking powder, and salt and add alternately with the milk, mixing until a dough forms.
- Drop spoonfuls of dough symmetrically over the fruit filling, covering as much surface as you can.
- Bake the cobbler on the middle rack of the oven until the crust is browned and the filling is bubbly, about 45 minutes.
- Serve slightly warm with vanilla ice cream.

$\mathcal{P}$EANUT BUTTER

I still love basic peanut butter and jelly sandwiches made with soft white bread, grape jelly, and super-chunk peanut butter. But these sandwiches aren't as simple as they seem if you consider the ingredients.

Peanut butter can be creamy or chunky, with sugar or just natural ground peanuts. Cashew and roasted almond butters are decadent substitutes if you want a gourmet nut-butter sandwich.

Jam or fruit preserves may be more to your taste than jelly, or, like my children, you may prefer honey.

The choices for the bread are wide, too. My daughter insists on banana bread or a toasted cinnamon-raisin English muffin for her peanut butter and honey sandwiches. You can skip the bread and just use a split banana to hold the peanut butter. Toothpicks will hold this slippery but delicious sandwich together. Celery stalks filled with peanut butter and topped with raisins are another children's favorite, known as "ants on a log."

For variations, I think peanut butter and bacon sandwiches are divine. From my school days, I remember grilled peanut butter and jelly sandwiches that oozed warm gooey peanut butter with every bite. With a cold glass of

continued on next page

milk, it was a child's dream. At a cocktail party I was served a surprisingly good peanut butter sandwich: natural peanut butter on fingers of kimmel-brot, topped with red onion and bacon. And, finally, there are those who insist that peanut butter and mayonnaise with lettuce is the ultimate sandwich!

$\mathcal{P}$eanut Butter

Makes 1 pint

1 pound unsalted cocktail peanuts	2 tablespoons light corn syrup
½ teaspoon salt	¼ cup peanut or vegetable oil

• Combine the peanuts, salt, and corn syrup in the bowl of a food processor. Process, adding the oil slowly through the feed tube. Stop a few times to scrape the bottom and sides. Continue to process until the peanuts have turned into a smooth butter. It may take 2 or 3 minutes.

• Transfer the peanut butter to a covered jar and store in the refrigerator.

Peanut Butter Cookies

These are great, especially with natural (unsweetened) peanut butter or roasted almond butter.

Makes about 3 dozen

4 tablespoons unsalted butter, at room temperature
¼ cup solid vegetable shortening
½ cup natural peanut butter or other nut butter, drained of any excess oil
¾ cup brown sugar
¼ cup granulated sugar
1 egg, at room temperature

1 teaspoon vanilla extract
1¼ cups flour
¾ teaspoon baking soda
¼ teaspoon salt
¼ cup rolled oats
1 cup semisweet chocolate chips (optional)

- Preheat the oven to 400 degrees.
- Cream the butter, shortening, peanut butter, and sugars until light. Add the egg and vanilla and beat until light and fluffy. On low speed, add the flour, baking soda, and salt until thoroughly mixed. Stir in the oats and chocolate chips.
- Using your hands, form pieces of the dough into 1½-inch balls and place on a heavy ungreased baking sheet. Flatten the balls slightly with a fork to make a crisscross design, dipping the fork in water occasionally to prevent sticking.
- Place the baking sheet on a rack in the upper half of the oven and immediately reduce the oven temperature to 375 degrees. Bake until very lightly colored, about 9 or 10 minutes. Cool on a wire rack.

$\mathcal{P}$ecan Pie

Before using them, be sure to taste nuts to make sure the aftertaste is pleasant and that they aren't rancid. Buy nuts in small quantities and store them in the freezer in airtight containers or heavy plastic bags. If you don't have a good local supplier, use a mail-order nut company whose business is fresh quality nuts. For pecans, one source is Sunnyland Farms, Albany, Georgia 31706.

Makes one 9-inch pie

Pastry for 1 9-inch single crust pie (see page 8)

For the filling

3 eggs
1 tablespoon flour
¾ cup light corn syrup or maple syrup
½ cup firmly packed brown sugar
2 tablespoons unsalted butter, melted
1½ teaspoons vanilla extract

¼ teaspoon salt
1½ cup pecan halves, chopped (reserve a few whole ones to decorate the top)

Vanilla ice cream or whipped cream

• Lightly grease a 9-inch pie plate. Roll out the dough on a lightly floured surface to a 13-inch circle. Transfer to the prepared pie plate and press into the bottom and sides without stretching the dough. Trim the edge, leaving a 1-inch overhang. Turn the edge under and crimp to make a decorative border. Chill the dough 30 minutes.
• Preheat the oven to 425 degrees.
• To make the filling, beat the eggs and flour together. Add the corn syrup, brown sugar, melted butter, vanilla, and salt and mix well. Stir in the chopped pecans. Pour the filling into the chilled pie shell. Arrange any reserved pecan halves decoratively around the outside edge.
• Bake the pie on the lowest rack of the oven for 10 minutes. Reduce the oven temperature to 375 degrees and continue to bake until the crust is browned and the filling is set, about 35 minutes. Cool on a wire rack and serve with vanilla ice cream or whipped cream.

Pepper-Mint Jelly

This hot-and-sweet jelly is not only our favorite match with roast or grilled lamb but a gift we like to take to friends who put it on cream cheese and serve it with crackers. It's also great on a cold turkey sandwich or stirred into Mayonnaise (see page 174) for a chicken salad. Commercial pectin helps it gel. It makes good use of your summer garden mint, or, if you make this in the winter and mint isn't available, it's just Pepper Jelly.

Makes five 8-ounce jars

4 to 6 jalapeño peppers, green and red, not seeded

½ cup packed fresh mint leaves

3 tablespoons water

4 cups sugar

1½ cups cider vinegar

3 ounces liquid pectin

5 8-ounce jelly jars with screw lids, washed and rinsed with boiling water

- Pulverize the peppers, mint, and water in a blender or food processor. Place the mixture in a large pot and add the sugar and vinegar.
- Bring to a full rolling boil, stirring to dissolve the sugar, and boil hard for 2 minutes.
- Stir in the liquid pectin. Return to a full rolling boil, one you can't stir down, for 1 minute. Remove from the heat, skim the surface, and fill the sterilized jars to within ⅛ inch of the tops.
- Wipe the jar rims clean and cover tightly with the lids. Cool on a wire rack and listen for the "ping" that let's you know there is a vacuum in the jars and the seal is tight and safe.
- Leave the jelly overnight without disturbing before labeling and storing.

Pita Bread

It's a delightful surprise to discover how easy it is to turn yeast dough into pita bread with a *hot* oven. These popular Middle Eastern pocket breads are perfect for sandwich fillings and salads.

Makes 10 breads

1 ¼-ounce envelope (1 scant table- spoon) active dry yeast
1¼ cups warm water
Pinch of sugar

3 to 3½ cups bread flour
1½ teaspoons salt
3 tablespoons vegetable or corn oil
2 tablespoons cornmeal

- In a small bowl combine the yeast, ¼ cup of the water, and the pinch of sugar. Stir and set aside to proof until bubbly, about 10 minutes.
- In another bowl, combine 3 cups of the flour and the salt. Add the remaining warm water, 2 tablespoons of the oil, and the proofed yeast. Stir to combine. Turn the dough out onto a lightly floured flat surface. Knead the dough, adding the remaining flour until the dough is smooth and no longer sticky. Add the remaining tablespoon of oil to a clean bowl; place the dough in the bowl, turning to coat all sides with the oil. Cover the bowl with a towel and let the dough rise in a warm place until doubled in size, about 1 hour.
- Lightly grease 2 heavy baking sheets and sprinkle with cornmeal.
- Punch the dough down, cover, and let it rest 30 minutes. Divide into 10 equal pieces. Form each piece into a smooth ball and roll out to a 5-inch circle. Place the circles of dough on the prepared baking sheets and cover lightly. Let the dough rise until puffy, about 30 minutes.
- Preheat the oven to 500 degrees.
- Bake one sheet at a time on the lowest rack of the oven until lightly colored and puffed, about 7 minutes. Immediately place the breads in a brown bag to cool. Bake the remaining breads and cool in the bag. The steam will soften the bread and the pockets will deflate. Cut the cooled breads in half and fill with cheese, salads, or sandwich fillings.

Pizza

The difference between a great pizza and a mediocre one is the crust. The secret to a crisp crust is high bottom heat and a well greased or oiled pan. Johanne Killeen and George Germon, owners of Al Forno and Lucky's restaurants in Providence, Rhode Island, *grill* their pizza crusts! Allow the dough to rise until puffy if you like a chewy, more breadlike texture.

After years of trial and error, here's the winning crust and baking technique. It gives homemade pizza that authentic pizzeria taste and a crust that keeps its crisp but chewy texture even under the sauce, extra cheese, and your favorite toppings.

Makes one 18-inch pizza

For the dough

1 ¼-ounce envelope active dry yeast
1 cup warm water
Pinch of sugar

3½ cups all-purpose or bread flour
1 teaspoon salt
1 tablespoon olive oil

For the toppings

1½ to 2 cups thick, homemade tomato sauce or your favorite spaghetti sauce from a jar
1 pound Mozzarella or Monterey Jack cheese, grated
½ cup grated Parmesan cheese

1 cup sliced mushrooms, peppers, onions, pepperoni, ham, or cooked sausage (optional)
2 tablespoons olive oil
Freshly ground black pepper
Oregano

- Proof the yeast in ¼ cup of the water with a pinch of sugar until it's bubbly, about 10 minutes.
- Combine 3 cups of flour and the salt in a bowl. Add the yeast, oil, and remaining water. Mix well and turn out onto a floured surface. Knead until smooth, adding flour if needed to prevent the dough from sticking.

continued on next page

- Transfer the ball of dough to a well-oiled bowl, turning to coat all sides of the dough. Cover loosely with a towel and let the dough rise in a warm place until doubled in bulk.
- Preheat the oven to 450 degrees. Thoroughly oil an 11-by-17-inch jelly-roll pan or 18-inch round pizza pan.
- When the dough has doubled, punch it down and press to a uniform ¼-inch thickness or roll it out to fit the prepared pan. Press the edges to a uniform thickness. Trim any excess. Cover loosely with a towel and let the dough rest 10 minutes. If you like a chewier, thicker crust, let the dough rise just until puffy, about 10 to 15 minutes.
- Spread the tomato sauce evenly over the dough. Bake the pizza on the bottom rack of the oven for 10 minutes.
- Remove the pizza from the oven and top with the cheeses and toppings of your choice. Drizzle the olive oil over the top and season with pepper and oregano.
- Continue to bake on the bottom rack until the cheese is bubbly, about 12 minutes more. Lift the pizza with a spatula to be sure the bottom of the crust is browned and crisp. Carefully transfer the pizza to a wooden board and slice. Serve hot.

$\mathcal{P}$lum Jam

I'm partial to plum jam on my toast for breakfast, but this versatile recipe can be made with nearly any fruit or combination of fruits. The proportion of fruit, sugar, and pectin is the critical factor. Some fruits contain more natural pectin (the gelling factor) than others, which means the consistency will vary a bit. The jam may be softer or firmer but always delicious if you use good ripe fruit. The high amount of sugar in jams and jellies acts as a preservative. If the jar seals properly and a vacuum forms, the jam can be stored in a cool, dark place. Once the jar has been opened, store it in the refrigerator.

Makes eight 8-ounce jars

2½ pounds ripe plums
¼ cup cider vinegar
7 cups sugar
3 ounces liquid pectin

8 8-ounce jars with *new* lids and bands, washed and sterilized with boiling water

- Pit and chop the plums to make about 4½ cups of fruit. If the flesh clings to the pits, cook the plums slowly in the vinegar for a few minutes until softened; then remove the pits.
- Place the chopped plums in a deep kettle. Add the vinegar and sugar and stir well.
- Place the kettle over high heat and bring to a full boil, stirring often.
- Add the liquid pectin and boil hard, stirring constantly, for 1 minute.
- Remove the kettle from the heat and skim the foam from the top of the fruit mixture.
- Ladle the jam into the hot sterilized jars immediately. Wipe the rims clean and place the lids on securely. Screw the bands on tightly and set the jars on a trivet to cool. Listen for the "ping" that lets you know the jars have sealed properly. The center of the lid should not give way when pressed.
- Cool the jars on a trivet and let them sit overnight. Label and store.

$\mathcal{P}$opcorn

I've never been tempted to buy an electric popcorn machine or the new microwave popcorn since popcorn is so easy to make in an ordinary saucepan. I usually start with corn or vegetable oil although I've used confit fat (garlic-and-thyme–flavored goose or duck fat) to make popcorn for a cocktail party. My mother sends me 5-pound bags of Orville Redenbacher's gourmet popping corn from a farm stand in Valparaiso, Indiana, *and* the magical superfine popcorn and nut salt made by Diamond Salt Co. That salt is so fine that it sticks to the popped corn without any butter, making popcorn a delicious low-calorie snack.

Makes 2 quarts popcorn

2 tablespoons vegetable or corn oil   Butter, melted, and salt to taste
¼ cup popping corn

- In a 2-quart lidded saucepan, heat the oil over medium-high heat until very hot.
- Add the popping corn and cover at once, swirling the pan constantly over the surface of the burner and letting it rest only a few seconds at a time as the corn pops. When the popcorn reaches the top of the pan and the popping slows, remove the pan from the heat and take the cover off carefully.
- Turn the popped corn into a bowl and add butter and salt, or only superfine salt, to taste.

$\mathcal{P}$opovers

Makes 6 popovers

1 cup flour	1 tablespoon unsalted butter, melted
½ teaspoon salt	2 eggs, at room temperature
1 cup milk, at room temperature	

- Preheat the oven to 450 degrees. Generously oil a popover pan or 6 deep custard cups or ramekins.
- Heat the popover pans in the oven or arrange the individual cups on a baking sheet and heat while making the batter.
- In a bowl, combine the flour, salt, milk, butter, and eggs. Whisk together just until smooth; do not overbeat.
- Remove the heated pans or cups from the oven and fill ½ to ⅔ full with the batter.
- Bake the popovers on the middle rack of the oven for 15 minutes. Without opening the oven, reduce the temperature to 350 degrees and bake until golden brown and crusty, about 20 minutes more.
- Remove the popovers from the pan or cups and poke the side of each with a knife to let some steam escape. You can return the popovers to the oven for a few more minutes to cook the insides and crisp them more. Serve very hot with butter.

$\mathcal{P}$

Poppy Seed Cake

Serves 10 to 12

1 cup buttermilk

⅓ cup poppy seeds

2½ cups flour

1 teaspoon double-acting baking
   powder

1 teaspoon baking soda

½ teaspoon salt

8 tablespoons unsalted butter, at room
   temperature

½ cup vegetable oil

1½ cups sugar

1 teaspoon vanilla

Grated zest of 1 orange

4 eggs, at room temperature

1 tablespoon sugar

1 teaspoon cinnamon

- Thoroughly grease a 10-inch bundt pan or a 9-by-13-inch cake pan and dust lightly with flour. Preheat the oven to 350 degrees.
- In a measuring cup, combine the buttermilk and poppy seeds. Stir to mix and set aside.
- Sift the flour, baking powder, baking soda, and salt together.
- Cream the butter until soft. Beat in the oil until thoroughly combined. Gradually add the 1¾ cups sugar, beating until light. Add the vanilla and orange zest. Add the eggs, one at a time, beating until light and fluffy and scraping the bowl often.
- On low speed, alternately add the dry ingredients and the buttermilk to the butter mixture until thoroughly combined and smooth.
- In a small dish, mix the sugar and cinnamon together.
- Spread half the batter in the prepared pan. Sprinkle with the cinnamon-sugar mixture without touching the sides of the pan, and then spread the remaining batter on top.
- Bake on the middle rack of the oven until the cake is springy and begins to pull away from the sides of the pan, about 1 hour in the bundt pan, 35 minutes in the cake pan. Let the bundt cake cool 15 minutes before turning it out onto a wire rack to cool completely. Cool the layer cake in the pan and frost with Cream Cheese Frosting (see page 293).

Poppy Seed Dressing

As a sweet-tart topping on a green salad with fruit, this dressing is a summertime regular. For an occasional change, I process the dressing with a handful of fresh mint leaves in place of the poppy seeds.

Makes 1½ cups

⅓ cup white vinegar

1 tablespoon finely chopped onion or shallot

⅓ cup sugar

1 teaspoon dry mustard

1 teaspoon salt

⅛ teaspoon cayenne pepper

¾ cup vegetable oil

2 tablespoons poppy seeds, *or* a handful of fresh mint leaves

- In a food processor or blender, combine the vinegar, onion, sugar, dry mustard, salt, and cayenne pepper. With the motor running, add the oil in a thin stream until the dressing is thickened and emulsified. Add the poppy seeds and process briefly.
- Store in a covered jar in the refrigerator.

POTPIES

A flavorful beef stew topped with a crust or biscuits makes a great beef potpie, but we like the chicken variety with a single top crust best. I often cook two chickens at a time to get the stock for the gravy, the cooked carrots, and enough chicken for *two* pies. The potatoes and optional baby onions cook in the same broth while you remove the meat from the cooked chicken and dice the carrots. Bound with a rich, creamy sauce, the filling chills before the crust goes on. This is easily made ahead, refrigerated, and baked at mealtime.

Chicken Potpie

Serves 8

1 4-pound chicken, cleaned

1 large onion

2 to 3 celery stalks (or use the tops of a bunch)

8 parsley stems, tied together with string

1 teaspoon salt

8 whole black peppercorns

¼ cup vegetable oil

6 to 8 cups water

3 large carrots (½ pound), peeled and cut in half

2 all-purpose potatoes (about ¾ pound), peeled, cut into ½-inch cubes, and reserved in a bowl of water

12 very small white boiling onions, peeled and an X cut in the root ends

⅓ cup frozen petite peas

For the sauce

4 tablespoons unsalted butter
5 tablespoons flour
1 cup light cream

Salt, freshly ground black pepper, and
   cayenne pepper to taste

For the top crust

1½ cups flour
½ teaspoon salt
4 tablespoons unsalted butter
¼ cup solid vegetable shortening

1 egg yolk
2 to 3 tablespoons cold water
Egg wash made of 1 egg yolk beaten
   with 2 tablespoons milk

- In a pot just large enough to hold the chicken and vegetables, combine the chicken (breast down), onion, celery, parsley, salt, pepper, and oil. Add 6 to 8 cups water, enough to just cover the chicken. Bring to a boil, cover, and simmer for 30 minutes. Add the carrots and continue to simmer for 45 minutes. Cool and remove the chicken and the carrots. Strain the cooking stock through a fine mesh strainer, skim off the fat, and return the stock to the pot.

- Skin and debone the chicken and cut the meat into large chunks. Cut the cooked carrots into ½-inch cubes. Put the chicken and carrots in a large bowl.

- To make the sauce, melt the butter in a heavy saucepan. Add the flour, whisk until smooth, and heat until bubbly. Off the heat, whisk in the cream until smooth. On the heat, add 1½ cups of the strained and skimmed stock. Bring to a boil, whisking to prevent any lumps, and cook until thickened. Add the salt, a generous grinding of pepper, and a pinch of cayenne pepper. Cool slightly and add the sauce to the bowl of chicken and carrots.

- Bring the remaining stock in the pot to a boil. Drain the reserved diced potatoes and add. Cook, uncovered, until tender, about 15 minutes. Remove the potatoes with a slotted spoon to a strainer. Add the drained potatoes to the bowl of chicken, carrots, and sauce.

- Add the onions to the remaining stock (about 3 cups) in the pot and boil, shaking the pot occasionally, until tender but not falling apart, about 30 to 35 minutes. The stock should reduce to just a few tablespoons. Add

continued on next page

water at the end if necessary to finish cooking the onions. Add the cooked onions and the reduced glaze in the bottom of the pot to the bowl of meat and vegetables. If there are more than a few tablespoons of reduced stock, reduce further to 2 tablespoons before adding to the bowl. Add the frozen peas to the bowl of filling, stir gently, and cool.

• Lightly grease a 10-by-2-inch deep pie dish or casserole. Spoon the chicken-vegetable filling into the dish. Cover with plastic wrap and refrigerate until *cold.*

• Meanwhile, make the top crust. Combine the flour and salt in a bowl or food processor. Cut in the butter and shortening until it looks like meal. Combine the yolk and water and toss in quickly with a fork until the dough holds together in a ball; or process, adding the liquid all at once and stopping before the dough forms a ball; turn the dough out on a flat surface and press into a ball. Cover the dough with plastic wrap and chill for 30 minutes.

P

~~~

214

• Preheat the oven to 450 degrees.

• Roll the dough into a 12-inch circle. Using a pastry scraper, carefully fold the dough in quarters and place the center point on the center of the chilled pie filling. Unfold and cut the edges with a scissors, leaving a ¾-inch overhang to turn under and form a decorative edge. Roll out and cut leaf decorations and rolled branches from any extra pastry scraps.

• Mix the egg wash and brush lightly over the top dough and edges. Arrange the decorative leaves on top and brush with the egg wash. Cut a few vent holes around the dough.

• Place the pie on a heavy baking sheet (to catch any overflow) on the middle rack of the oven and bake 12 minutes. Reduce the oven temperature to 350 degrees and continue to bake until the crust is golden and the filling is bubbly, about 35 minutes. Let the potpie rest 5 minutes before cutting and serving.

Pot Roast

Serves 8 to 10

4 tablespoons oil

4 to 5 pounds beef brisket, well trimmed of fat

½ teaspoon salt

Freshly ground black pepper

2 large onions, chopped

2 cloves garlic, minced

3 tablespoons flour

1 teaspoon caraway seed

2 cups beef broth *and* 1 cup water, *or* 3 cups beef stock

2 tablespoons tomato paste (optional)

- Heat the oil in a heavy pot.
- Sprinkle the beef with salt and pepper and brown well on both sides in the hot oil. Remove from the pot and set aside.
- Add the onions to the pot and sauté them over low heat for 5 minutes. Add the garlic and continue to sauté, stirring often, until the onions are soft but not colored, a few minutes more.
- Stir in the flour and caraway seeds and cook for 1 minute.
- Whisk in the broth and water (or the stock) and the tomato paste. Return the meat to the pot.
- Bring the liquid to a boil and cover with foil placed directly on the surface of the meat and the liquid. Put the cover on and reduce the heat to low.
- Simmer the pot roast until fork tender, about 2 to 2½ hours.
- Cool slightly before you remove the meat and slice thinly against the grain. Skim the fat from the juices and serve with the meat.

Note: If you make this ahead, cool and refrigerate it. The congealed fat will rise and harden at the top, making it easy to remove. Slice the meat thinly, return the sliced meat to the pot, and reheat at serving time.

$\mathcal{P}$otato Pancakes

The food processor has revolutionized the making of potato pancakes. It shreds the potatoes in no time. But whatever method you use, be sure to squeeze out the excess liquid before mixing them into the batter. Although you are careful about keeping the air from oxidizing the potatoes, the batter will eventually turn a strange gray-brown color. It's aesthetically unappealing but the batter will still make fine pancakes. Stir the potatoes before making each batch and be sure to flatten them to lacey thinness.

Serves 4

1½ pound boiling potatoes
1 small onion, peeled
1 egg
2 tablespoons flour
½ teaspoon double-acting baking
  powder

1 teaspoon salt
¼ teaspoon powdered ginger
½ to ¾ cup vegetable oil
Sour cream and applesauce

- Preheat the oven to 250 degrees.
- Scrub the potatoes well but don't peel them. Grate the potatoes and onion by hand or shred in a food processor. Squeeze out all excess liquid in a dish towel and transfer the vegetables to a mixing bowl.
- Stir in the egg and add the flour, baking powder, salt, and ginger. Stir to combine thoroughly.
- Add ¼ cup of the oil to a heavy 12-inch frying pan. Heat thoroughly. Cook 4 pancakes at a time, using a few tablespoons of the batter for each pancake. Flatten the pancakes with the back of a spoon. Cook over medium heat until well browned and crisp, about 3 to 4 minutes on each side.
- Drain the pancakes on paper towels and transfer to a paper-towel-lined baking sheet. Place the baking sheet in the oven to keep the finished pancakes warm while you cook more. Add a few more tablespoons of oil to the frying pan and continue making pancakes until the batter is used up.
- Serve hot with the sour cream and applesauce.

Note: Potato pancakes can be reheated in a hot 450-degree oven until crisp, about 5 minutes. Or they can be frozen on a baking sheet and packed in a plastic bag. Reheat in a 400-degree oven until crisp, about 10 minutes.

POTATO SALADS

Potato salads come in so many popular varieties: with a mayonnaise or boiled dressing (American); with sausage or bacon and a sweet-sour dressing (German); or with a vinaigrette dressing, olives, anchovies, and vegetables (Mediterranean). Here are two we love—All-American Red Potato Salad and Potato Salad Niçoise from southern France.

All-American Red Potato Salad

Serves 4 to 6

1½ pounds red Bliss boiling potatoes
2 tablespoons cider vinegar
Salt
Freshly ground black pepper
Sugar
2 tablespoons minced shallots, or onion (optional)

2 hard-boiled eggs, peeled and chopped
2 stalks celery, finely chopped
2 teaspoons capers (optional)
¼ cup Mayonnaise (see page 174)
¼ cup plain yogurt or sour cream
1 tablespoon coarse-grained mustard

• Put the unpeeled, scrubbed potatoes in a pot and thoroughly cover with water. Bring to a boil and cook just until tender, 15 to 20 minutes.

continued on next page

- Drain the potatoes and cut them in large chunks. Put them in a bowl and sprinkle them with vinegar, salt, pepper, and a few pinches of sugar. Toss gently and let them cool.
- Add the shallots, eggs, celery, and capers.
- Combine the Mayonnaise, yogurt, and mustard and add to the potatoes. Toss gently and refrigerate until serving time. Season to taste with salt and pepper.

*P*otato Salad Niçoise

Serves 6 to 8 with the additions

2 pounds new or other waxy boiling potatoes, scrubbed
⅓ cup red wine vinegar
1 tablespoon Dijon mustard

½ teaspoon salt
Freshly ground black pepper
½ cup olive oil
¼ cup minced shallots or red onions

Additions (optional)

3 hard-boiled eggs, peeled and sliced
3 roasted peppers or pimientos, peeled, seeded, and cut in strips
½ pound small green beans, blanched and chilled

Cherry tomatoes
1 7-ounce can tuna fish, drained, *or* skinless, boned sardines, *or* 8 anchovy fillets

- Cook the potatoes in boiling salted water just until tender and the skins begin to crack, about 15 to 20 minutes.
- Combine the vinegar, mustard, salt, and pepper in a bowl. Whisk in the oil very slowly until thickened.
- Drain the potatoes, peel them, and cut them in thick slices. In a bowl, alternately layer the potatoes with a sprinkling of shallots and some of the

vinaigrette. Cover with a plate and let the potatoes cool and absorb the vinaigrette.

- Toss the potatoes gently and transfer them to a serving platter. Surround the potatoes with any additions you like. Spoon any extra vinaigrette over the vegetables.

$\mathcal{P}$ound Cake

This cake freezes well, so you might consider making two at a time and freezing one. Serve pound cake at teatime, with sugared berries or ice cream, or just for great snacking.

Makes 1 loaf

8 tablespoons unsalted butter, at room temperature	2 eggs, at room temperature
3 ounces cream cheese, at room temperature	1½ cups flour
	1 teaspoon double-acting baking powder
1 cup sugar	½ teaspoon salt
½ teaspoon vanilla extract	¼ cup milk, at room temperature

- Thoroughly grease a 4½-by-8½-inch loaf pan with shortening; flour lightly. Preheat the oven to 350 degrees.
- Cream the butter and cream cheese in a mixing bowl. Add the sugar gradually and beat until light. Add the vanilla and eggs, one at a time, beating until fluffy and light.
- Sift the flour, baking powder, and salt. On low speed, alternately add the dry ingredients and the milk to the egg-sugar mixture, beating just until thoroughly combined.
- Spread the batter in the prepared pan and bake on the middle rack of the oven until the cake is golden, a toothpick in the center comes out clean, and the cake sounds quiet, about 1 hour. Cool 15 minutes before running a knife around the edge and turning the cake out on a wire rack to cool completely.

Pretzels

Playing with playdough and making pretzels are two rainy-day activities my children never tire of. Making and twisting pretzel dough, glazing the pretzels with an egg wash, and sprinkling them with salt or poppy or sesame seeds is as much fun as eating the pretzels. They taste best when eaten warm from the oven, but you won't have to worry about their staying around for a second day. Kids find their homemade creations irresistible.

Makes about 24 pretzels

1¼ cups warm water

1 ¼-ounce envelope (1 scant tablespoon) active dry yeast

2 teaspoons sugar

3½ to 4 cups flour

1½ teaspoons salt

2 tablespoons oil

1 egg beaten with 1 tablespoon milk for a glaze

Toppings: coarse salt, poppy, sesame, *or* caraway seeds

• Place ¼ cup of the water in a bowl and sprinkle the yeast and sugar over it. Stir to dissolve and let the yeast proof until bubbly, about 5 to 10 minutes.

• Combine 3½ cups of the flour and the salt. Add the remaining cup of water, the oil, and the proofed yeast. Stir to combine. Turn the dough out onto a lightly floured board and knead the dough until smooth and elastic, adding the remaining flour if necessary to prevent it from sticking.

• Preheat the oven to 425 degrees. Lightly grease 2 heavy baking sheets with shortening.

• Divide the dough into 24 pieces and roll each into thin strips about 10 inches long. Shape into pretzels by crossing the ends to make a loop, then flipping the ends back across the loop; or make a 6-inch rope and tie into a single knot or twist. Place on the prepared baking sheets. For chewy pretzels, cover the dough loosely with a towel and let the pretzels rest in a warm place until puffy, about 15 minutes. Bake them immediately for crunchier pretzels.

• Lightly brush the egg-milk glaze over the pretzels, trying not to let it drip down onto the baking sheet. Sprinkle each pretzel with a pinch of salt or seeds. Bake until the pretzels are lightly colored, about 15 to 20 minutes, depending on the size and thickness of the pretzels.

Pumpkin Bread

Like many of its quick-bread cousins, pumpkin bread makes wonderful tea sandwiches, lunch or brunch treats spread with softened cream cheese, or even peanut butter sandwiches. The walnuts give the spiced, golden, cakelike bread a crunch.

Makes 1 loaf

2 cups flour
1 teaspoon double-acting baking pow-
    der
1 teaspoon baking soda
½ teaspoon salt
2 teaspoons ground cinnamon
1 teaspoon powdered ginger

¼ teaspoon grated nutmeg
2 eggs, at room temperature
1½ cups sugar
½ cup vegetable oil
1 cup canned pumpkin or squash purée
½ cup coarsely chopped walnuts

P

221

- Preheat the oven to 350 degrees. Grease a 5-by-9-inch loaf pan with shortening.
- Sift together the flour, baking powder, baking soda, salt, and spices.
- In a mixing bowl, beat the eggs and add the sugar gradually, beating until light. Add the oil gradually, mixing until smooth.
- Alternately add the dry ingredients and the pumpkin to the egg mixture, beating on low speed just until thoroughly combined. Stir in the walnuts. Turn the batter into the prepared loaf pan.
- Bake the bread until the center is springy, a toothpick in the center comes out clean, and it sounds quiet, about 1 hour and 10 minutes. If the bread begins to brown too much, reduce the oven temperature to 325 degrees for the last 10 minutes.
- Cool the bread in the pan on a wire rack for 15 minutes before running a knife around the edge and turning the bread out onto a wire rack to cool completely. Wrap in foil to store.

$\mathcal{P}$umpkin Pie

Use canned or fresh pumpkin, but when buying fresh, look for the sweet cooking pumpkins, not the jack-o'-lanterns.

The high initial baking temperature sets the crust. The lower temperature cooks the filling without causing cracks.

Makes one 10-inch pie

For the crust

1¼ cups flour	3 tablespoons unsalted butter, chilled
¼ cup quick or old-fashioned rolled oats	3 tablespoons solid vegetable shortening
1 tablespoon sugar	3 to 4 tablespoons cold water
¼ teaspoon salt	

For the pumpkin filling

1½ cups canned or fresh puréed pumpkin	1 teaspoon ground cinnamon
3 eggs, at room temperature	¾ teaspoon ground ginger
¾ cup dark brown sugar, firmly packed	¼ teaspoon grated nutmeg
1 tablespoon flour	⅓ cup light corn syrup
	1 cup heavy cream

For the topping

1 cup heavy cream	2 tablespoons confectioners' sugar

- Lightly grease a 10-inch pie plate with butter or shortening.
- To make the crust, in a deep bowl or food processor, combine the flour, oats, sugar, and salt. Add the butter and shortening and either work with a pastry blender until the mixture resembles meal or process by turning the machine on and off a few times.
- Add the water gradually to the bowl and toss with a fork until the mixture nearly comes together, or add all at once through the feed tube of

the processor and process until the dough just begins to form a ball. Turn the dough out on a lightly floured flat surface and knead gently 2 or 3 times until it holds together in a mass. Flatten the dough slightly to form a disc and wrap it in plastic wrap. Refrigerate to chill well.

- Preheat the oven to 425 degrees.
- On a lightly floured surface, roll the chilled dough out to a 15-inch circle. Fold in quarters or roll up on the rolling pin and transfer to the prepared pie plate. Without stretching the dough, press it into the bottom and sides of the plate. Trim the edge, leaving a 1-inch overlap. Fold the edge under to form a thicker edge and crimp decoratively. Refrigerate while you make the pie filling.
- To make the filling, in a bowl, whisk together the pumpkin purée, eggs, and brown sugar. Add the flour and spices and mix well. Whisk in the corn syrup and cream, mixing until smooth.
- Pour the filling into the chilled pie shell. Bake on the bottom rack of the oven for 15 minutes.
- Reduce the oven temperature to 325 degrees and continue to bake until the filling is set and the center no longer looks wet, about 45 to 50 minutes more.
- Cool the pie on a wire rack. Serve the pie at room temperature or cover with plastic wrap and chill before serving.
- To make the topping, whip the cream with the sugar until it mounds. Serve the chilled pie topped with whipped cream.

P
~~~

$\mathcal{P}$umpkin Soup

Here's a favorite fall soup and Thanksgiving opener that can use winter squashes interchangeably with pumpkin. Be sure to buy a sugar pumpkin meant for cooking, or use butternut, buttercup, hubbard, or acorn squash.

Serves 6

3 tablespoons butter
1 large onion, chopped
1 large carrot, chopped
1 baking potato, peeled and chopped
1 pound pumpkin or squash, peeled and cut in chunks
1 tablespoon peeled and grated fresh gingerroot

1 tablespoon brown sugar
6 cups chicken broth
2 cups water
Salt and freshly ground pepper to taste
Grated nutmeg
1 cup light cream

- In a large heavy pot, melt the butter and sauté the onion over low heat for 5 minutes. Add the carrot, potato, pumpkin, and gingerroot. Sauté, stirring often, for 5 minutes. Add the sugar, broth, and water and bring to a simmer. Stir well, cover, and simmer until the carrot is tender, about 35 minutes.
- Purée the mixture in a blender in batches, beginning on low speed and increasing until the soup is puréed. Return the soup to the pot and season to taste with salt, pepper, and nutmeg. Stir in the cream and heat well, but don't boil.

$\mathcal{P}$unch

Makes 12 to 16 one-cup servings

1 quart cranberry juice

1 quart Lemonade (see page 166)

1 bottle red wine (optional)

½ cup orange liqueur (optional)

1 quart (or 1 liter) ginger ale

Lemon and orange slices, for garnish

▪ Stir together the cranberry juice, lemonade, wine, and orange liqueur. Chill.

▪ At serving time, pour in the ginger ale, add ice, and garnish with fruit slices.

$\mathcal{P}$

*R*aisin Bread

Raisin bread is usually a basic white bread dough with a swirl of cinnamon and raisins. This version kneads raisins into a pumpkin-cornmeal dough to make a bread perfect for ham or smoked turkey sandwiches or for toast with butter and honey.

Makes 2 loaves

¼ cup fine yellow cornmeal
¼ cup cold water
½ cup boiling water
1½ cups pumpkin (or squash) purée
¼ cup brown sugar, molasses, or honey
¼ cup vegetable oil
1 tablespoon salt
¼ teaspoon cinnamon, allspice, nutmeg, *or* mace

½ cup warm water
1¼-ounce envelope (1 scant tablespoon) active dry yeast
Pinch of sugar
4 to 5 cups flour
½ cup raisins
1 teaspoon butter for brushing on the baked bread (optional)

▪ Combine the cornmeal and cold water in a saucepan. Add the boiling water and cook, stirring, until thickened, for 1 minute. Stir in the pumpkin purée, brown sugar, oil, salt, and cinnamon. Let the mixture cool until just warm.

continued on next page

- Place the ½ cup warm water in a bowl and sprinkle the yeast and pinch of sugar over it. Allow it to proof until bubbly, about 10 minutes.
- Grease two 4½-by-8½-inch loaf pans and lightly dust them with cornmeal.
- Put 2 cups of the flour in a large bowl. Make a well and add the cornmeal mixture and the proofed yeast. Stir well to combine and begin adding the remaining flour. Turn out onto a lightly floured board and knead, adding flour as needed, and incorporating the raisins, until the dough is smooth and no longer sticky.
- Place the dough in an oiled bowl, turning to coat all sides, and cover with a towel. Let rise in a warm place until doubled in bulk, about 45 minutes to 1 hour.
- Punch the dough down, divide it in half, and roll each half into an 8-by-10-inch rectangle; roll up tightly from the short side. Place each loaf, seam side down, in a prepared pan and cover loosely with a dish cloth.
- Preheat the oven to 375 degrees.
- When the loaves have reached the tops of the pans and are nearly doubled in size, bake for 45 minutes. Turn the bread out of the pan and rap the bottom to see if it sounds hollow. If not, return the bread to the pan and bake 5 minutes more. Reduce the oven temperature to 350 degrees if the tops begin to brown too much. Turn the bread out onto a wire rack and brush with butter while still warm.

$\mathcal{R}$hubarb Pie

Rhubarb and asparagus always announce the arrival of spring in New England markets. This pie is for rhubarb-lovers like my son who used to take his piggy bank to a neighbor's house to pick rhubarb at two cents a stalk as a hint for me to make his favorite pie.

Makes one 10-inch pie

For the crust

1½ cups flour
4 tablespoons sugar
¼ teaspoon salt

4 tablespoons unsalted butter
¼ cup solid vegetable shortening
4 to 5 tablespoons orange juice

For the filling

5 cups (about 1¾ pounds) rhubarb, cut in ½-inch pieces
1¼ cups sugar
3 tablespoons quick-cooking tapioca

¼ teaspoon salt
2 tablespoons butter
1 tablespoon grated orange (or kumquat) zest

For the meringue

4 egg whites
¼ teaspoon cream of tartar

½ cup sugar

▪ To make the crust, combine the flour, 2 tablespoons of the sugar, and the salt in a bowl or food processor. Add the butter and shortening and work with a pastry blender, or turn the processor on and off until the mixture resembles meal. Add the juice slowly, tossing with a fork until the dough nearly comes together, or add all at once through the feed tube of the food processor with the motor running, and process until the dough just begins to come together.

• Turn the dough out on a lightly floured surface and knead gently a few times until it is more homogenous and forms a ball. Flatten the dough into a disc and wrap it in plastic wrap. Chill for 30 minutes.

• Lightly grease a 10-inch pie plate. Preheat the oven to 400 degrees.

• Roll out the dough on a lightly floured surface to about a 14-inch circle. Transfer the dough to the prepared pie plate and press it onto the sides and bottom without stretching the dough. Trim the edge, leaving a ¾-inch overhang. Turn the edge under, pinch, and form a decorative border. Prick the bottom with a fork and, covered, refrigerate for 30 minutes.

• Line the pie crust with foil and fill with dried beans or raw rice to weight it. (The beans or rice can be cooled, stored in a jar, and used every time you prebake a pie crust.) Bake the crust on the bottom rack of the oven until set, about 15 minutes. Carefully remove the foil and weights. Sprinkle the crust with the remaining 2 tablespoons sugar, prick the bottom with a fork, and continue to bake until browned, about 12 to 15 minutes. Cool on a rack.

230

• To make the filling, combine the rhubarb, sugar, tapioca, and salt in a large heavy saucepan. Mix thoroughly and let stand for 30 minutes, stirring occasionally.

• Bring the fruit to a boil, stirring often, and cook over medium heat until the rhubarb is softened and the juices are thickened, about 6 to 8 minutes. Remove the pan from the heat and stir in the butter and zest.

• Preheat the oven to 425 degrees.

• To make the meringue, beat the egg whites on high speed until foamy. Add the cream of tartar and beat until soft peaks form. Very slowly add all but 1 tablespoon of the sugar, beating on high speed until stiff and glossy.

• Turn the hot filling into the baked and cooled crust.

• Spread the meringue completely over the rhubarb filling, touching the crust all around to anchor it, or transfer the meringue to a pastry bag with a medium star tip. Pipe the meringue decoratively over the filling, anchoring it to the crust. Sprinkle the remaining tablespoon of sugar over the meringue.

• Bake until lightly colored, about 5 minutes. Cool completely on a wire rack away from a draft. Refrigerate and serve chilled the same day.

$\mathcal{R}$ice

There is nothing more basic and versatile than plain boiled rice.

Serves 6

1½ cups long-grain white rice   1 teaspoon salt
3 cups cold water

- In a heavy saucepan, combine the rice, water, and salt. Bring to a boil over medium-high heat, stirring to prevent sticking.
- Reduce the heat to low and place a triple thickness of paper towels over the pan to absorb the steam. Cover tightly with the pan lid and simmer 12 minutes.
- Remove the cover and the towels, being careful of the hot steam, and continue to cook 3 minutes more.
- Let the rice sit a few minutes before serving.

$\mathcal{R}$

$\mathcal{R}$ice Pilaf

Serves 8

8 tablespoons butter

¼ cup vermicelli or thin spaghetti, broken into ¾-inch pieces

2 cups raw long-grain white rice

¼ cup minced onion

4 cups boiling stock or broth

1 teaspoon salt (omit if using broth)

- Melt the butter in a heavy 2-quart saucepan over medium-low heat. Add the vermicelli and sauté until lightly colored, about 2 or 3 minutes.
- Stir in the rice and onion and sauté, stirring constantly, until the rice is very hot, the vermicelli is browned, and the onion is soft but not colored, about 4 minutes.
- Stir in the boiling water and salt. Reduce the heat to low. Place a triple layer of paper towels over the top of the pan and cover tightly.
- Simmer 20 minutes, remove the cover and the towels, and continue cooking until all the liquid has evaporated, a few minutes more. Fluff the pilaf with a fork and serve immediately.

Variations: Sauté a minced clove of garlic, a tablespoon of sesame or poppy seeds or ½ cup of chopped nuts with the rice, onion, and vermicelli. Or toss the finished pilaf with 2 tablespoons minced fresh herbs, ½ cup toasted nuts, the grated zest of a lemon, or ¼ cup minced parsley for added flavor, texture, and color.

Rice Pudding

Stovetop rice pudding, warm or cold, is an old-fashioned treat that needn't be restricted to the nursery. This tried-and-true recipe with raisins, nutmeg, and cinnamon is a treat that's hard to resist for breakfast or dessert.

Makes 8 servings

⅔ cup long grain white rice (not the converted or instant kind)

1 quart fresh milk

⅓ cup raisins (optional)

⅓ cup sugar or to taste

1 teaspoon vanilla extract

¼ teaspoon salt

⅛ teaspoon each ground nutmeg and cinnamon

1 cup heavy cream

- Combine the rice and milk in a heavy saucepan. Bring to a boil, stirring a few times. Place over a heat diffuser, lower the heat, and cook, stirring occasionally, until the milk is absorbed and the rice is very tender and thick, about 1½ hours. Add the raisins during the last 15 minutes to plump them.
- Off the heat, add the sugar, vanilla, salt, and spices. Stir to dissolve.
- Stir the cream into the rice. Return to the heat and cook the pudding over low heat, stirring, until slightly thickened, warm, and creamy. Adjust the flavorings to taste.
- Spoon the pudding into a decorative bowl or individual bowls and serve warm with a pitcher of cold milk, if you like.

Roast Chicken

Serves 4

1 3- to 4-pound chicken
Salt and pepper
White butcher string for trussing the
    chicken
2 tablespoons butter, softened
Spices or herbs (optional):
    1 clove garlic, cut in half, *or*

1 teaspoon chili powder, *or*
1 teaspoon seasoned salt, *or*
4 sprigs fresh tarragon or thyme
1 onion, cut in quarters

- Preheat the oven to 425 degrees. Place a rack in the bottom of a shallow roasting pan large enough to hold the chicken.
- Remove the giblets from the inside cavity and wash the chicken under running water. Pat it dry with paper towels. Cut the wing tips off the chicken and pull off any excess fat.
- Sprinkle the cavity with salt and pepper. Rub the skin with the garlic, chili powder, *or* seasoned salt, *or* place the tarragon sprigs in the cavity. Place the onion in the cavity.
- Truss the chicken by tying the legs together with the center of a 24-inch piece of string and crossing the string over the breast and around the wings. The legs should be together and the cavity closed, and the wings should be tied against the back of the chicken.
- Arrange the chicken, breast side down, on the rack in the roasting pan. Rub the butter over the back of the chicken.
- Roast, basting occasionally with the accumulated juices and butter, for 35 minutes. Turn the chicken breast side up and roast, basting a few times, for 15 to 20 minutes more. The chicken should be nicely browned and the juices should run clear when pricked with a fork near the thigh. A small 2-pound chicken will take a total of only 35 to 45 minutes. For high-temperature roasting, 18 minutes per pound is about right.
- Transfer the chicken to a platter and let it rest, breast-side down, for 10 minutes. Remove the string and the onion and herbs from the cavity. Cut the chicken in quarters for serving.

Russian Dressing

Russian dressing is a favorite iceberg lettuce topping, sandwich spread, and sauce for cold lobster or crabmeat. It guarantees vegetable eating when children can use it as a dip for raw carrot, cucumber, and pepper sticks. My son says that Russian dressing is like Thousand Island dressing without all the little islands of chopped pickles, onions, and olives. I sometimes add a teaspoon of horseradish to give the dressing zip or lemon juice to thin it, but basically, Russian dressing is a mix of mayonnaise and chili sauce or ketchup. Use good quality mayonnaise and chili sauce, which is a bit more spicy and textured, and less sweet than ketchup.

Makes 1½ cups

1 cup Mayonnaise (see page 174)
⅓ cup chili sauce

1 tablespoon lemon juice
1 teaspoon horseradish (optional)

- Combine the ingredients in a bowl and whisk until smooth. Cover and refrigerate until serving time.

R

RYE BREAD

Salty rye sticks and seeded marble ryes (dark and light swirled together) were part of my childhood. It was my husband who introduced me to corn rye, the dense, moist rye bread that is used to make fabulous bite-defying, thick deli sandwiches. It's the only rye bread I make now.

236

Corn-Rye Bread

1 large free-form loaf

½ cup yellow cornmeal
1 cup cold water
1 cup boiling water
2 tablespoons butter or oil
2 tablespoons brown sugar
2 teaspoons salt
¼ cup warm water

1 ¼-ounce envelope (1 scant table-spoon) active dry yeast
Pinch of sugar
1½ cups rye flour
1 tablespoon caraway seeds
2½ to 3 cups all-purpose flour

For the glaze

2 tablespoons water
¼ teaspoon cornstarch

1 teaspoon caraway seeds

- In a saucepan, whisk the cornmeal and cold water together. Stir in the boiling water and bring to a boil, whisking until thick and smooth. Off the heat, add the butter, sugar, and salt. Stir well and cool until just warm.
- Place the warm water in a small bowl or measuring cup, add the yeast and pinch of sugar and allow it to proof until bubbly, about 10 minutes.
- When the cornmeal has cooled, add the proofed yeast, rye flour, and caraway seeds. Mix thoroughly and stir vigorously. Add 1 cup of the white flour and mix to form a stiff dough. Turn the dough out on a floured surface and knead until smooth, springy, and no longer sticky, adding the remaining flour as needed.
- Oil a large bowl and add the dough, turning the dough to coat all sides with oil. Cover loosely with a clean towel and let the dough rise until doubled in bulk, about 1 hour.
- Grease a heavy baking sheet and sprinkle it with cornmeal.
- When the dough has doubled in size, punch it down and form it into an oblong or round loaf. Place the dough on the prepared baking sheet. Make a few slash marks across the top with a sharp knife. Cover loosely with the towel and let the dough rise until doubled in bulk, about 1 hour.
- Preheat the oven to 400 degrees.
- When the loaf has doubled in bulk, place it on the middle rack of the oven and bake for 10 minutes. Reduce the oven temperature to 375 degrees and continue to bake for 30 minutes more.
- While the bread is baking, make the glaze by combining the water and cornstarch in a small saucepan. Bring to a boil and heat until thickened. Brush the hot bread with the glaze and sprinkle with additional caraway seeds.
- Return the bread to the oven and bake until browned and the bread sounds hollow when you turn it over and rap the bottom with your knuckles, about 5 to 10 minutes more. Cool the bread on a wire rack and slice with a serrated knife.

R

SALMON

Cucumber-scaled poached salmon was *the* summer luncheon standard of my childhood, then *the* Fourth of July dish of New England when I married and moved to Boston. When cured with salt and dill and weighted, it's also a great appetizer for parties, thinly sliced and served on buttered rye rounds. With asparagus and new potatoes, salmon marks the welcome arrival of spring.

When buying any fish, use your nose and eyes. Fresh fish should never have a "fishy," offensive smell. The flesh should be glistening, not dull. If buying a whole fish, the eyes should be bright and bulging. A fishmonger who sells large quantities of fish or a grocery store with a fish department that gets frequent deliveries is a good place to buy quality fresh fish. But the best place is down on the docks where the fishermen are catching them or bringing them in on their boats. "The fresher the better" couldn't be truer for fish!

In cooking any fish—broiled, baked, or poached—the important thing is not to overcook it. Fishermen friends tell me if it flakes, it's too cooked. Fish should be cooked just until opaque in the center.

Poached Salmon

Poaching salmon, or any fish, means cooking it just to opaqueness in barely simmering liquid (water and white wine) that includes such flavorings as onion, celery, parsley, thyme, bay leaf, and is seasoned with salt and pepper. The poaching liquid should simmer to develop its flavor before the fish is submerged and cooked for about 10 minutes per inch of thickness (measured at the thickest point).

Aside from the cucumber "scales" as a garnish on the poached fish, an accompanying sauce can be as delicious and simple as a good homemade mayonnaise thinned with lemon juice and flavored with Dijon mustard.

Serves 8

6 cups water
1 cup dry white wine
1 small onion, sliced
1 stalk celery, cut up
Parsley stems
Sprigs of thyme
½ bay leaf

2 teaspoons salt
¼ teaspoon peppercorns
1 4- to 5-pound whole fresh salmon
1 English cucumber, thinly sliced, salted, drained, and dried
Lemon wedges
Mayonnaise (see page 174)

- In a pan or pot large enough to hold the fish, combine the water, wine, onion, celery, parsley, thyme, bay leaf, salt, and peppercorns. Bring to a boil, cover, and simmer for 15 minutes.
- Add the fish, making sure it is covered by an inch of liquid. Bring to a simmer, and cook, uncovered, until the fish is opaque in the center, about 10 minutes per inch of thickness. Test with a knife.
- Carefully remove the fish with a spatula. Cover and refrigerate until cold.
- At serving time, carefully remove the skin and pull out the backbone. Arrange the fish on a platter. Dry the cucumber slices on paper towels and arrange in an overlapping "scale" pattern over the fish. Serve with lemon wedges and mayonnaise.

Salmon Croquettes

Croquettes are an old-fashioned way of dealing with leftover fish, vegetables, cheese, and rice. The binding can be a white sauce, mashed potatoes, or bread crumbs and eggs. The croquettes are rolled in crumbs and fried. The chilling and coating, and chilling and frying steps are too much for me—too much time and too much fat. Since I love the idea of salmon croquettes as an appetizer or light lunch, I make this *baked* salmon croquette recipe that we all like. Serve topped with a spoonful of sour cream and a bit of caviar, or simply with a squeeze of lemon.

Serves 6

2 tablespoons butter, softened
1½ pounds fresh salmon, cooked and flaked to make about 3 cups
1 cup fresh bread crumbs made from 2 slices quality white bread, crusts removed
1 tablespoon minced white of scallion
1 tablespoon snipped fresh dill
Grated zest of ½ lemon

1 egg
1 cup heavy cream
½ teaspoon salt, or to taste
Freshly ground black pepper
Cayenne pepper
½ cup sour cream, and red lumpfish, whitefish, *or* salmon caviar for the top (optional)
Lemon wedges

- Preheat the oven to 350 degrees. Thoroughly grease 6 individual ramekins or custard cups with 1 tablespoon of the butter.
- Place the flaked salmon in a bowl. Add ¾ cup of the bread crumbs, the scallion, dill, lemon zest, egg, and cream. Mix gently with a fork. Season with salt, pepper, and cayenne pepper.
- Divide the mixture among the buttered cups and pack it down slightly. Top the croquettes with the remaining ¼ cup of bread crumbs. Dot with the remaining tablespoon of butter.
- Arrange the cups in a roasting pan. Pour in enough hot water to come halfway up the sides of the ramekins. Bake until fairly firm and set, about 30 minutes. Cool for 5 to 10 minutes. The croquettes can be unmolded, right side up, or served in the ramekins.
- Top each croquette with sour cream and caviar, or simply garnish with lemon.

Sangria

Summer *al fresco* meals wouldn't be complete without a pitcher of sangria, the sparkling red or white wine and citrus juice punch of Spain that has become an American picnic standard.

Serves 4

½ cup orange liqueur or brandy
2 oranges, thinly sliced
2 lemons, thinly sliced
¼ cup sugar

1 bottled dry red or white wine
½ cup orange juice
2 cups club soda (approximately)
Orange or lemon slices for garnish

- In a large pitcher, combine the orange liqueur, oranges, lemons, and sugar. Stir to dissolve the sugar, pressing on the fruit to extract some of the juice. Let the mixture stand for 30 minutes.
- Add the wine and orange juice, stir well, and let the mixture stand another 30 minutes to develop the flavors.
- At serving time, stir the sangria well and add the club soda. Serve in tall glasses with ice and garnish with an orange or lemon slice.

Scalloped Potatoes

Scalloped potatoes is a fancy name for a layered potato casserole. It's the perfect accompaniment for roasted meats, fish, or chicken. My aunt Margie insists that her recipe is just a technique—"layer the potatoes with salt, pepper, butter, cheese, and a sprinkling of flour; then pour in enough milk so you can see it." The sprinkling of flour eliminates the need to make a bechamel sauce. I cook the potatoes briefly before layering to make the baking time shorter. Scalloped potatoes need not be *au gratin*. The layers may include sautéed mushrooms, or sautéed onions, sautéed vegetables, or slices of ham. It's hard to make a mistake with this classic dish.

4 tablespoons butter

1 clove garlic, cut in half

2 pounds (approximately 5) medium boiling or all-purpose potatoes

Salt and freshly ground black pepper

Grating of nutmeg

3 tablespoons flour

6 ounces Cheddar cheese, grated to make 2 cups

2½ to 3 cups milk or half and half

¼ cup unseasoned bread crumbs

- Thoroughly grease a shallow 2-quart casserole or baking dish with 1 tablespoon of the butter. Rub the bottom and sides of the casserole with the cut sides of the garlic. Discard the garlic. Preheat the oven to 350 degrees.
- Peel the potatoes and slice about ⅛-inch thick. Cook in boiling water until just tender but *not* falling apart, about 3 minutes. Drain well and add 2 tablespoons of the butter, gently mixing until melted.
- In the prepared pan, layer ⅓ of the potatoes and sprinkle with salt, pepper, nutmeg, and 1½ tablespoons of the flour. Spread with ⅓ of the grated cheese. Add another ⅓ of the potatoes and sprinkle with salt, pepper, nutmeg, the remaining flour, and ⅓ of the grated cheese. Add the remaining potatoes, salt, pepper, nutmeg, and cheese.
- Pour the milk in until you can see it reach the top of the potatoes. Sprinkle the bread crumbs over the top and dot with the remaining tablespoon of butter.
- Bake until bubbly and golden, about 45 minutes. As the casserole cools, the liquid will set more. If you want a saucelike consistency, bake for less time; for a firmer casserole, bake longer.

Scones

Nothing is better at breakfast or for brunch than these small variations of soda bread. Use a light hand on these rich cream biscuits loaded with currants and a sprinkling of caraway seeds. For lunch or hors d'oeuvres, these make great sandwiches with sliced ham and chutney, or even with peanut butter and bacon!

Makes 15 scones

2¼ cups flour

¼ cup cornstarch

¼ cup sugar

4 teaspoons double-acting baking powder

½ teaspoon salt

Pinch of ground cardamom (optional)

6 tablespoons unsalted butter

½ cup currants

1 teaspoon caraway seeds (optional)

¾ cup light cream

2 eggs

• Preheat the oven to 450 degrees. Lightly grease a heavy baking sheet with shortening.

• Sift the flour, cornstarch, baking powder, 3 tablespoons of the sugar, the salt, and cardamom in a large bowl.

• Cut in the butter until the mixture looks like meal. Stir in the currants and caraway seeds with a fork.

• In a small bowl, mix together the cream and eggs. Slowly add all but 1 tablespoon of the mixture to the dry ingredients, tossing gently with a fork until a dough forms. Turn the dough out onto a floured surface and pat or roll it to a ¾-inch thickness. Cut out the scones with a 2½-inch round cutter or glass or empty frozen juice can.

• Arrange the scones on the prepared baking sheet and brush the tops lightly with the reserved tablespoon of the egg-cream mixture. Sprinkle the tops with the remaining tablespoon of sugar and place on the middle rack of the oven. Immediately reduce the oven temperature to 425 degrees.

• Bake until lightly colored and fairly firm, about 12 to 15 minutes. Cool on a wire rack.

Note: These freeze well in a tightly sealed plastic bag and will taste as if they were freshly baked if you put the *frozen* scones on a baking sheet and place them in a *cold* oven. Set the oven to 300 degrees. In 15 minutes, they'll be warm and ready to eat.

$\mathcal{S}$eafood Newburg

I used to think this was the ultimate in luxury and indulgence: a buttery cream sauce binding chunks of lobster and shrimp, doused with sherry, and served in a flaky puff-pastry shell. It's a dish that needn't be quite that extravagant when it's the main event of a family dinner. Lobster and shrimp can share the stage with less costly fish. The sauce can be as rich with butter and cream as your diet permits. A French bread crouton or rice can substitute for the puff-pastry shell.

Serves 4

For the cream sauce

3 tablespoons butter
3 tablespoons flour
2 cups light cream
2 teaspoons Dijon mustard
1 teaspoon Worcestershire sauce

¼ teaspoon curry powder
½ teaspoon salt
Freshly ground black pepper
Pinch of cayenne pepper
Pinch of sugar

For the seafood

3 tablespoons butter
1 tablespoon finely minced shallot
1½ pounds seafood (any combination of de-footed scallops, shelled and cleaned shrimp, chunks of firm white fish fillets, lobster or crabmeat)

2 tablespoons medium-dry sherry
2 tablespoons finely chopped parsley, for garnish
4 puff-pastry shells, French bread croutons, or rice (see page 231)

continued on next page

- To make the sauce, melt the butter in a heavy saucepan and whisk in the flour. Cook over low heat for 1 minute. Off the heat, slowly add the cream, whisking until smooth. Heat, whisking constantly, until the sauce is thickened and begins to boil. Add the mustard, Worcestershire sauce, curry powder, salt, pepper, cayenne pepper, and sugar.
- To prepare the seafood, in another pan, melt the butter and sauté the shallot, stirring frequently, until soft, about 5 minutes. Add the fish or scallops and cook until opaque, about 5 minutes. Add the cooked lobster or crabmeat and heat through. Stir in the sherry. Add the seafood to the cream sauce and stir gently. Heat well and season to taste.
- Serve the Newburg in puff-pastry shells, over toasted French bread, or on rice. Garnish with a sprinkling of parsley.

Shepherd's Pie

This is just one of a number of meat pies made with leftover or freshly ground meat. I should call this Cowboy's Pie since I usually use ground beef instead of lamb.

Serves 8

2 pounds raw lean ground beef
½ cup finely chopped onion
1 28-ounce can tomatoes in purée
1½ teaspoons salt
1 teaspoon ground cumin
1 teaspoon chili powder
¾ teaspoon paprika

1 teaspoon grated orange zest
Freshly ground black pepper
½ cup finely chopped parsley
⅓ cup dry bread crumbs
5 cups Mashed Potatoes (see page 172)
1 cup grated Colby cheddar or Monterey Jack cheese

- In a large sauté pan, sauté the beef and onions until the beef is no longer pink and the onions are soft. Drain off any accumulated fat.
- Stir in the tomatoes, breaking them up. Stir in the salt, cumin, chili powder, paprika, orange zest, and pepper. Simmer, stirring often, until the juices are thickened and most of the liquid has evaporated, about 15 minutes. Stir in the parsley and bread crumbs and season to taste.
- Preheat the oven to 375 degrees. Spread the hot mixture in a 9-by-13-inch or a 10-by-12-inch shallow baking dish.
- Transfer the mashed potatoes to a pastry bag with a large star tip and pipe puffy rosettes or a crisscross pattern over the meat. Sprinkle with the cheese.
- Bake until the cheese has melted and the potatoes begin to color, about 15 minutes. Serve immediately.

Snickerdoodle Cookies

Makes 3 dozen cookies

8 tablespoons unsalted butter, at room temperature

¾ cup sugar

1 egg

1 teaspoon vanilla extract

1½ cups flour

1 teaspoon double-acting baking powder

¼ teaspoon salt

3 tablespoons cinnamon-sugar (see p. 81)

- Thoroughly cream the butter and sugar. Add the egg and vanilla, beating until light.
- Sift the flour, baking powder, and salt together and add to the creamed mixture, beating until combined. Chill the dough for 1 hour.
- Preheat the oven to 375 degrees.
- Using your hands, shape pieces of the chilled dough into 1-inch balls. Place the cinnamon-sugar in a wide bowl. Roll the balls of dough in the cinnamon-sugar mixture. Place 2 inches apart on an ungreased heavy baking sheet.
- Place the baking sheet on the middle rack of the oven and immediately reduce the temperature to 350 degrees. Bake the cookies until the edges are very lightly colored, 8 to 10 minutes. Cool on a wire rack.

Soda Bread

Here's *my* favorite quick bread (chemically leavened with baking powder and baking soda rather than with yeast). With butter for breakfast or a slice of ham for lunch, it's unbeatably delicious.

Makes 1 large round loaf

4 cups flour

½ cup plus 2 teaspoons sugar

1½ teaspoons baking soda

1½ teaspoons double-acting baking powder

½ teaspoon salt

4 tablespoons unsalted butter

½ cup currants or chopped raisins

2 tablespoons caraway seeds

1½ cups plus 2 tablespoons buttermilk

1 egg

- Preheat the oven to 400 degrees. Lightly grease a heavy baking sheet with shortening and lightly dust it with flour.
- Sift the flour, ½ cup of the sugar, the baking soda, baking powder, and salt. Cut in the butter until the mixture resembles meal. Stir in the currants and caraway seeds.
- Combine 1½ cups of the buttermilk and the egg. Add to the dry ingredients and stir with a fork until a dough forms.
- Turn the dough out onto a lightly floured surface and knead gently a few times until you can form it into a 6-inch round. Transfer the loaf to the prepared baking sheet, flatten it slightly, and cut a ½-inch deep X across the top. Brush the top with the remaining 2 tablespoons of buttermilk and sprinkle the top with the remaining 2 teaspoons of sugar.
- Bake on the middle rack of the oven 10 minutes. Reduce the oven temperature to 375 degrees and continue baking until golden brown, about 35 to 40 minutes more. When you turn it out of the pan and tap the bottom, it should sound hollow. If it is browning too much, reduce the oven temperature to 350 degrees for the last 10 minutes. Cool the loaf completely on a wire rack before slicing thinly and serving with butter.

Sour Cream Coffee Cake

There are fights over who licks this cake's batter from the mixing bowl and spatula.

Serves 10

2 cups flour

1 teaspoon double-acting baking powder

1 teaspoon baking soda

½ teaspoon salt

8 tablespoons unsalted butter, at room temperature

1 cup granulated sugar

1½ teaspoons vanilla extract

2 eggs, at room temperature

1 cup sour cream, at room temperature

For the streusel

2 tablespoons unsalted butter

3 tablespoons flour

½ cup firmly packed brown sugar

½ cup chopped pecans or walnuts (optional)

1 teaspoon cinnamon

- Preheat the oven to 350 degrees. Thoroughly grease a 9-inch bundt pan or ring pan or a 9-by-13-inch cake pan; dust lightly with flour.
- Sift together the flour, baking powder, baking soda, and salt. Set aside.
- In a mixing bowl, beat the butter until soft, add the sugar gradually, and beat until well creamed and light. Add the vanilla and eggs, one at a time, beating until pale and very light.
- Alternately add the dry ingredients and sour cream to the butter mixture, beating on low speed until thoroughly combined.
- To make the streusel, combine all the streusel ingredients and blend together with your hands, two knives, or a pastry blender until it resembles meal.
- For the bundt pan, spread half the butter in the prepared pan. Sprinkle with half the streusel and top with the remaining batter. Sprinkle the top with the remaining streusel. For the cake pan, spread all the batter in the prepared pan and sprinkle the streusel evenly over the top.

• Bake on a rack in the upper half of the oven until the center is springy, a toothpick comes out clean, and the cake begins to pull away from the sides of the pan, about 60 minutes for the bundt cake or about 40 minutes for the layer cake. Cool the bundt cake 15 minutes before turning it out on a wire rack to cool completely. Cut in thin slices. Leave the layer cake in the pan and cut into squares when cool.

Spinach Pudding

The word pudding could sell anything—even spinach. My mother turned us all into spinach lovers with this easy dish that still rivals creamed spinach and broccoli as a winter vegetable favorite.

Serves 6

1 tablespoon butter

2 pounds fresh spinach, *or* 2 10-ounce packages frozen chopped spinach, cooked, squeezed dry, and chopped

3 ounces cream cheese, cut into chunks

2 eggs

1½ cups small-curd cottage cheese

⅓ cup freshly grated Parmesan cheese

½ teaspoon salt

Grating of nutmeg

Freshly ground black pepper

- Lightly grease a 1- or 1½-quart casserole with 1 teaspoon of the butter. Preheat the oven to 350 degrees.
- Add the cream cheese to the hot cooked spinach and stir to melt. Add the remaining ingredients, mix well, and turn into the prepared casserole.
- Dot the top with the remaining butter and bake, uncovered, until nearly set, about 30 minutes.

Split Pea Soup

I remember this winter soup well from my childhood, but I think it was the added sliced hot dogs and buttered homemade croutons that I liked best. If the traditional ham bone isn't around when I have a yearning for this soup, I use smoked sausages or hot dogs to give the soup that wonderful pork flavor. I enjoy the soup while my children vie for the hot dogs and buttered croutons. James Marshall's children's book, *George and Martha*, has done nothing for the popularity of split pea soup. Martha just didn't have this recipe!

Purée the soup if you like, or even add a little cream, but I like the texture of it as is.

3 tablespoons salted butter

1 medium onion, finely chopped

2 stalks celery, trimmed and finely chopped

1 carrot, peeled and finely chopped

1 clove garlic, peeled and minced

½ pound (1 rounded cup) green or yellow dried split peas

1 ham bone (wash off any sweet ham glaze)

8 cups water

1 large potato, peeled and cubed

¼ pound cooked smoked sausage, or 3 hot dogs, cubed or sliced, if no ham bone is available

Salt and freshly ground pepper

4 slices of bread, crusts removed and cubed

2 tablespoons butter, melted

§

• In a large, heavy pot, melt the butter and sauté the onion, celery, and carrot over low heat, stirring to prevent them from coloring, about 10 minutes. Add the garlic and sauté a few minutes more.

• Add the split peas, ham bone, and water. Stir and bring to a boil. Partially cover and simmer, stirring occasionally for 1 hour. Add the potato and continue to cook, partially covered, about 30 minutes more. If you use them, add the sausage or hot dogs at this point and simmer until heated through. Season to taste with salt and pepper.

• To make the croutons, preheat the oven to 350 degrees and lightly toast the bread cubes on a baking sheet for about 5 minutes. Drizzle with the melted butter and bake, tossing occasionally, until crisped, about 5 minutes more.

• Remove the ham bone from the soup and serve in bowls, with a bowl of croutons alongside. Add the croutons at eating time since they lose their crispness very quickly.

Sticky Buns

My children call them sticky buns, my father remembers them as *schnecken*, and they're also known as snails or pecan rolls. They're best when still warm from the oven. Rapid-rise yeast helps to make them a fast treat for weekend breakfast or brunch.

Makes 14 rolls

For the sticky glaze

4 tablespoons unsalted butter

¾ cup firmly packed brown sugar

3 tablespoons light corn syrup

1 cup coarsely chopped pecans

For the dough

¼ cup warm water

1 ¼-ounce envelope (1 scant table-spoon) active dry yeast

Pinch of sugar

¾ cup milk

¼ cup granulated sugar

4 tablespoons unsalted butter

Grated zest of 1 orange or 1 lemon

1 egg, at room temperature

1 teaspoon salt

3½ cups flour, or more as needed

For the filling

2 tablespoons unsalted butter, melted

¼ cup sugar

2 teaspoons cinnamon

⅓ cup raisins (optional)

- To make the glaze, in a saucepan combine and heat the butter, brown sugar, and corn syrup until the sugar is dissolved. Boil 1 minute. Pour into the bottom of a 9-by-13-inch baking pan or into two 8-inch cake pans. Sprinkle the pecans evenly over the glaze and set aside.
- To make the dough, combine the water, yeast, and pinch of sugar and allow to proof until bubbly, about 5 minutes. Heat the milk and add the sugar, butter, and zest. Stir to melt the butter and dissolve the sugar. When lukewarm, whisk in the egg and salt.

- Measure 3 cups of the flour into a mixing bowl. Add the cooled liquid ingredients and the proofed yeast. Mix until the dough becomes smooth. Add more flour gradually as needed; turn the dough out onto a floured surface and knead until smooth and elastic and no longer sticky. Butter a clean bowl and add the dough, turning to coat the surfaces. Cover with a towel and let the dough rise until doubled in bulk, about 1 hour.
- Punch the dough down and roll out to a 10-by-14-inch rectangle.
- To make the filling, brush the butter over the surface of the dough. Combine the sugar and cinnamon and sprinkle over the dough to the edges. Sprinkle with the raisins.
- Starting from the long side, roll the dough tightly and pinch to seal. With a sharp knife, cut the roll into 14 1-inch slices. Lay them down over the glaze and pecans, allowing some space between rolls for expansion. Cover loosely with a towel and let them rise in a warm place until they reach the top of the pan and are doubled in bulk, about 30 to 45 minutes.
- Preheat the oven to 375 degrees.
- Bake the rolls until browned and the glaze is bubbly, about 25 minutes. Turn the rolls out onto a serving platter immediately. Leave the pan over the rolls for a minute to let the glaze coat the rolls. Remove the pan and serve the rolls warm, or reheat before serving.

S

STOCK

Stock is the basis of good soups and sauces. The rich flavor and natural protein come from meaty bones, vegetables, and a long slow cooking, which can't be found in a can.

For *chicken stock*, I use strained and defatted chicken soup (see page 72), which I reduce by a third to intensify the flavor, increase the gelatinous protein, and make storage in the freezer less bulky.

Veal or Beef Stock

Veal or beef stock can be made with low-cost cuts of meat like veal breast or shanks, beef shin bones, or knuckle bones. Split calves feet are rich in natural gelatin. Ask your butcher for his suggestions and his available bones or scraps for your stock pot.

Makes 2½ quarts

5 pounds veal or beef bones (breast, shanks, shin bones)
2 carrots, cut in pieces
2 medium onions, cut in half
1 cup dry white wine
2 stalks of celery, cut up
1 large leek, washed and cut in half lengthwise

½ bunch parsley, tied with string
1 bay leaf
5 sprigs of thyme or ½ teaspoon dried
1 teaspoon salt
½ teaspoon crushed peppercorns
Approximately 3 quarts water

- Preheat the oven to 400 degrees.
- Place the meat bones, carrots, and onions in a large roasting pan. Bake until browned, turning occasionally, about 40 minutes. Transfer the browned bones, carrots, and onions to a large stock pot.
- Deglaze the roasting pan by adding the wine and reducing it by half over heat, scraping the bottom to incorporate any browned bits. Add the wine to the stock pot.
- Add the remaining ingredients to the pot with enough water to cover. Bring to a boil slowly. Partially cover and simmer about 6 hours, skimming the surface occasionally.
- Strain the stock through a fine mesh strainer, discarding the bones, meat, and vegetables. Refrigerate to solidify the fat and remove it from the surface.

Note: If you don't plan to use all the stock at once, warm it (to liquify the natural gelatin) and pour it into plastic containers for the freezer. Or, if storage is a problem, reduce the stock by half to make a super-rich concentrate that can be diluted with equal parts water when used later. Bring frozen stock to a boil before using it.

$\mathcal{S}$trawberry Jam

When pick-your-own strawberries are in season and the fruit is intensely flavored, ripe, and warm from the sun, it's time to make strawberry jam. Homemade jellies and jams provide memories of the seasons as well as delicious toppings on toast. They're a thoughtful gift that you'll be proud to give.

Makes seven 8-ounce jars

7 8-ounce canning jars with new lids
   and screw bands
2 quarts red, ripe strawberries

6 cups sugar
3 ounces liquid pectin

- Wash the canning jars and lids and rinse with boiling water. Pour boiling water in each one and over the lids.
- Prepare the strawberries by washing, hulling, and cutting them in half or quarters, depending on the size. Place in a large deep pot.
- Add the sugar and stir, breaking up the strawberries a bit. The sugar should dissolve as you mix the strawberries.
- Bring to a rolling boil over high heat, stirring often. Add the liquid pectin, stirring it into the boiling fruit mixture.
- Return the mixture to a full rolling boil and boil hard 1 minute, stirring constantly. Remove the pan from the heat and immediately skim the pink foam from the top with a metal spoon.
- Drain the canning jars and quickly ladle the hot jam to within ¼ inch of the tops. Wipe the rims clean. Quickly put the lids on securely and tighten the bands. Cool on a rack and listen for the "ping" that lets you know a vacuum has formed. The center of the lids should not give way when pressed. Cool on a trivet. Label, date, and store.

Strawberry Shortcake

Good strawberries should not only look red and delicious but they should smell great, too. Pineapples and melons are other fruits whose aroma should match their beauty when they're ripe and sweet.

Serves 6 to 8

For the shortcake biscuits

2 cups flour

1 tablespoon double-acting baking powder

¼ cup sugar

½ teaspoon salt

5 tablespoons unsalted butter

¾ cup heavy cream

For the strawberries

2 quarts ripe, red strawberries, cored and sliced

1 tablespoon lemon juice

2 tablespoons orange liqueur (optional)

¼ cup sugar or to taste

1 cup heavy cream

2 tablespoons confectioners' sugar

- Lightly grease a heavy baking sheet with shortening. Preheat the oven to 450 degrees.
- To make the biscuits, sift the flour, baking powder, sugar, and salt into a bowl. Cut in the butter until the mixture resembles meal. Stir in the cream and mix lightly with a fork until the dough begins to hold together. Turn out onto a lightly floured surface and knead gently a few times until the dough forms a mass.
- Pat the dough out to a ¾-inch thickness. Cut into 8 biscuits with a 2½-inch cutter or glass or empty frozen juice can. Arrange on the prepared baking sheet ¾ inch from each other.
- Put the baking sheet in the upper half of the oven and immediately reduce the oven temperature to 425 degrees. Bake the biscuits until very lightly colored, about 12 minutes. Cool on a wire rack.

continued on next page

▪ To prepare the strawberries, combine them with the lemon juice, liqueur, and sugar. Toss well and refrigerate no more than an hour before assembling the shortcakes.

▪ At serving time, whip the cream with the sugar until it mounds softly. For each serving, split a biscuit and arrange on a plate. Top the bottom half with a large serving spoonful of berries and some of the accumulated juice. Partially cover with the top of the biscuit and serve with whipped cream on the side.

260

$\mathcal{S}$tuffed Cabbage

Freezing and thawing the whole cabbage softens the leaves and eliminates the need to cook the leaves in boiling water before separating and filling. My mother-in-law patiently taught me her rolling technique that keeps the filling snugly inside the cabbage leaf.

Makes about 30 rolls

1 large (4-pound) green cabbage,
  frozen and thawed

For the filling

2 pounds lean ground beef
1 medium onion, grated
2 eggs
¼ cup uncooked white rice

¼ cup water
2 teaspoons salt
Freshly ground black pepper

For the sauce

2 tablespoons oil

1 onion, sliced

Center and core of the cabbage, grated or chopped

1 28-ounce can peeled and crushed tomatoes

1½ cups water

¼ cup vinegar

2 tablespoons lemon juice

½ cup brown sugar, or to taste

Salt and freshly ground pepper to taste

- Remove a few of the tough outer leaves of the cabbage and discard. Carefully peel off the remaining leaves of the cabbage, running them under water to help separate them without tearing. You will need about 30 leaves. Shave off the center vein with a sharp paring knife. Chop the center leaves and core of the cabbage.
- To make the filling, combine all the filling ingredients and mix thoroughly.
- To make the sauce, in a very large, heavy pot heat the oil and sauté the sliced onion and chopped cabbage until soft. Add the tomatoes, water, vinegar, lemon juice, and sugar. Stir together and bring to a simmer while you stuff the leaves.
- Place 1 to 3 tablespoons filling (depending on the size of the leaf) in the center of the cabbage leaf. Start at the bottom end and roll, folding one side over as you roll. Poke the open side down into the filling to secure it and hold it snuggly. Place the rolls, seam side down, in the sauce. Arrange in layers, close together.
- Cover well and simmer over very low heat for at least 2 hours. Season with salt, pepper, more sugar, or lemon juice to taste. Let the cabbage rolls cool to room temperature and refrigerate. These are best made ahead to allow the flavors to mingle. At serving time, heat well and serve with rye bread and butter.

Stuffed Mushrooms

Makes 15 large mushrooms

1 pound (about 15) large white cultivated mushrooms

4 tablespoons butter

2 tablespoons minced shallots

½ cup finely ground toasted almonds

1 tablespoon sherry

1 tablespoon heavy cream

1 teaspoon minced fresh tarragon

Salt and freshly ground black pepper

Tarragon or parsley for garnish

- Wipe the mushrooms with a damp cloth or sponge to remove any dirt; twist off the stems. Chop the stems finely and reserve the caps.
- In a sauté pan, heat 2 tablespoons of the butter and sauté the shallots until softened, stirring often to prevent them from coloring, about 5 minutes. Add the chopped mushroom stems and sauté, stirring, until most of the liquid is evaporated, about 5 minutes more.
- Off the heat add the almonds, sherry, cream, and tarragon. Season with salt and pepper to taste.
- Preheat the oven to 375 degrees.
- Melt the remaining 2 tablespoons of butter. Brush the melted butter over the mushroom caps, inside and out, placing them top down in a shallow baking dish. Sprinkle the mushrooms with salt and pepper.
- Stuff the mushrooms with the almond mixture.
- Bake on the middle rack of the oven until the caps are softened, about 20 to 25 minutes. Baste a few times with any juices that accumulate in the baking dish.
- Garnish with tarragon.

262

Stuffed Peppers

The traditional meatloaf mix baked in green peppers has given way to a bean, tomato, and bacon combination in colorful red, yellow, and purple peppers. With a salad, these could be a meal in themselves, or a great accompaniment to roast chicken.

Serves 6

1½ cups dried small white beans, *or* 2 pounds canned white beans, well drained

1 onion, peeled

Parsley stems

Bay leaf

Thyme

Salt and freshly ground pepper

6 slices smoked bacon, cut in ½-inch pieces

1 cup finely chopped onion

2 large cloves garlic, minced

1 cup peeled, seeded, and chopped

tomatoes, *or* 1 1-pound can peeled tomatoes, drained and chopped

½ cup dry white wine

¼ cup minced parsley

Salt and freshly ground black pepper

6 large red, yellow, or purple peppers, roasted and skinned (see note below)

½ cup fresh bread crumbs

4 tablespoons butter, melted (substitute 4 tablespoons olive oil if serving the peppers at room temperature)

- If using dried beans, soak them in water overnight.
- Drain the beans and place them in a saucepan with enough water to cover them by 2 inches. Add the whole onion, herbs, salt, and pepper. Bring to a boil, partially cover, and simmer until the beans are tender, adding more water if necessary, about 1 hour.
- Cook the bacon in a large heavy pan until crisp. Remove and set aside. Pour off all but 2 tablespoons bacon fat and add the chopped onion. Sauté over low heat until soft, stirring often to prevent coloring, about 5 minutes. Add the garlic and sauté, stirring, a few minutes more. Add the tomatoes and wine and simmer until the liquid is reduced by half, about 5 minutes. Stir in the parsley and the reserved bacon. Drain the beans you've cooked or the canned beans and mix in. Season with salt and pepper to taste.
- Preheat the oven to 375 degrees. Brush a shallow baking dish (just large enough to hold the peppers) with some of the melted butter.

continued on next page

- Divide the bean filling among the peppers and arrange the filled peppers in the dish. Top with the bread crumbs and drizzle with the remaining butter.
- Bake the peppers until the beans are heated through and the crumbs are golden, about 20 to 30 minutes.

Note: To roast the peppers, turn on the broiler. Wash the peppers, core them, and arrange them on their sides on a foil-lined jelly-roll pan or baking sheet. Place the pan 4 inches from the broiler element. Roast the peppers, letting the skin of the peppers blister and turning frequently so they are evenly roasted, about 10 minutes. The peppers should be fairly firm, *not* mushy. Remove the peppers and place them in a bowl when they're done. Cover to let them steam until cool enough to handle. The skin should peel off easily. Drain upside down until ready to be filled. The accumulated pepper juices from the bowl can be added to the bean mixture. The roasted peppers can be refrigerated in a covered bowl overnight before using.

Sugar Cookies

Every holiday and occasion seems to have its symbols made into cookie cutters. I've used this sugar cookie dough for innumerable school treats in the shapes of turkeys, stars, bells, hearts, birds, flowers, birthday numbers, and animals. Decorating is more than half the fun for children.

Makes about 4 dozen cookies

8 tablespoons unsalted butter, softened
1 cup sugar
1 egg, at room temperature
1 teaspoon vanilla extract
2¼ cups flour
2 teaspoons double-acting baking powder

½ teaspoon salt
¼ cup colored sugar or sprinkles for the top (optional)
1 cup confectioners' sugar combined with 2 tablespoons water and a few drops food coloring for a glaze (optional)

- Preheat the oven to 375 degrees.
- Thoroughly cream the butter and sugar. Add the egg and vanilla.
- Sift together the flour, baking powder, and salt; add the dry ingredients, ⅓ at a time, to the butter-egg mixture to make a dough.
- Divide the dough in 2 parts, wrap each in plastic wrap, and refrigerate a few hours to make handling easier.
- Roll the dough out on a lightly floured surface to a ⅛-inch thickness. Cut out cookie shapes with a cutter and place on a heavy ungreased baking sheet. Reroll the scraps to make more cookies.
- Sprinkle with colored sugar or sprinkles if you like.
- Place the baking sheet on a rack in the upper half of the oven and reduce the oven temperature to 350 degrees. Bake until barely colored, about 8 to 10 minutes. The cookies should be pale.
- Immediately remove the cookies from the baking sheet and cool on a wire rack. If you haven't sprinkled them with sugar, you can paint the cookies with the colored glaze while they're warm.

Sweet-and-Sour Meatballs

Serves 4 to 6

For the meatballs

1¼ pounds lean ground beef
3 tablespoons minced white part of scallion
1 clove garlic, minced
1 teaspoon peeled and grated fresh gingerroot

1 egg, lightly beaten
½ cup gingersnap crumbs
2 tablespoons sesame seeds
⅓ cup water
1 teaspoon salt
Freshly ground black pepper

For the sauce

1 20-ounce can pineapple chunks in unsweetened juice
1 cup chicken broth or stock
¼ cup rice wine vinegar
2 tablespoons soy sauce
2 tablespoons hoisin sauce or Ketchup (see page 155)
½ cup brown sugar

2 tablespoons cornstarch
3 tablespoons water
1 red pepper, seeded and cut in bite-size chunks
1 green pepper, seeded and cut in bite-size chunks

• Preheat the oven to 375 degrees.
• To make the meatballs, combine all the meatball ingredients and mix thoroughly. Form into 1½-inch balls (1 inch for hors d'oeuvres). Arrange on a jelly-roll pan and brown in the oven for 15 to 20 minutes, depending on the size of the meatballs, turning carefully half way through the baking time.
• To make the sauce, drain the pineapple and reserve ¾ cup of the juice.
• In a large sauté pan, combine the broth, vinegar, soy sauce, hoisin sauce, brown sugar, and the reserved pineapple juice. Heat to dissolve the sugar. Mix the cornstarch and water until dissolved and whisk into the sauce. Heat the sauce until it comes to a boil and thickens.

- Add the cooked meatballs to the pan with the drained pineapple and the peppers and simmer until heated through, about 10 minutes. Serve over rice (see page 231) for dinner or in a chafing dish with toothpicks for hors d'oeuvres.

$\mathcal{S}$weet Potato Casserole

I love simple baked sweet potatoes or yams (a little moister and more orange in color) with butter and salt. But for holiday buffets with turkey or ham, a sweet potato casserole is just the thing. Marshmallows were made for hot chocolate and S'Mores (toasted and put between graham crackers with chocolate bars), not for sweet potato toppings.

Serves 6 to 8

4 sweet potatoes or yams (about 2 pounds), quartered
4 tablespoons butter
¼ cup apricot or peach jam
¼ cup brown sugar

Grated zest and juice of one orange
1 teaspoon cinnamon
½ teaspoon salt
Freshly ground black pepper
Pinch of ground cloves

- Simmer the potatoes in boiling salted water until tender, about 15 to 20 minutes.
- Preheat the oven to 375 degrees. Lightly butter a 2-quart casserole.
- Drain the cooked potatoes and peel them. Mash the potatoes or cut them in 1-inch chunks.
- In a saucepan, combine the butter, jam, sugar, grated zest and juice, cinnamon, salt, pepper, and cloves. Stir well and bring to a boil over low heat. Stir into the mashed potatoes, or pour over the potato chunks and toss well.
- Turn the potatoes into the prepared casserole and cover. Bake on the middle rack of the oven for 15 minutes. Remove the cover and bake until the sauce is thickened, about 15 minutes more. Stir the chunks of potato a few times until nicely glazed.

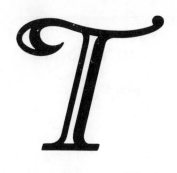

*T*apioca Pudding

6 servings

3 tablespoons quick-cooking tapioca	3 strips of orange zest (use a vegetable peeler)
6 tablespoons sugar	
¼ teaspoon salt	1 teaspoon vanilla extract
1 egg	½ cup heavy cream
2½ cups milk	Sweetened fresh berries for garnish

• In a heavy saucepan, combine the tapioca, sugar, and salt. Whisk in the egg and milk and add the orange zest. Let the mixture stand 5 minutes.

• On a heat diffuser or over hot water, bring the mixture to a boil over medium heat, stirring often until thick, about 6 to 8 minutes.

• Off the heat, remove the orange zest and stir in the vanilla. Cool 15 minutes and stir. The tapioca will thicken as it cools.

• When the tapioca is completely cool, whip the cream and fold it into the tapioca. Spoon into dessert dishes and garnish with fresh berries.

Tartar Sauce

Makes 1¼ cups

1 cup Mayonnaise (see page 174)

2 tablespoons chopped capers

2 tablespoons chopped cornichon or dill pickle

2 tablespoons chopped pimiento-stuffed green olives

1 teaspoon Dijon mustard

1 teaspoon minced shallot

2 to 3 tablespoons lime juice or vinegar

Pinch of cayenne pepper

Pinch of sugar

Salt and freshly ground black pepper

- Combine the mayonnaise, capers, pickles, olives, mustard, and shallots. Stir in enough lime juice to thin to the consistency you like. Add the cayenne pepper, sugar, salt, and pepper to taste. Cover and refrigerate until serving time.

T

Tomato Sauce

This is a year-round quick tomato sauce I use atop pasta or homemade pizzas. It calls for canned plum tomatoes that are more reliable than fresh winter tomatoes. A little tomato paste thickens and binds this sauce for an authentic long-cooked taste. The food mill smooths out the lumps.

Makes 1½ pints

1 small onion, cut in quarters
3 cloves garlic, peeled and cut in half
1 stalk celery, cut in 1-inch pieces
1 28-ounce can plum tomatoes in purée
1½ cups water
3 tablespoons tomato paste
¼ cup red wine vinegar

¼ cup olive oil
1 teaspoon fennel seeds
½ teaspoon freshly ground black pepper
Parsley stems, tied together
Salt
1 tablespoon brown sugar (optional)

• Combine all the ingredients in a large saucepan. Bring to a boil slowly and simmer, partially covered, stirring occasionally, about 45 minutes.

• Remove the parsley stems and put the mixture through a food mill (*not* a processor) for a smooth tomato sauce.

• Return the sauce to the pan and reduce further if you want a thicker sauce. Season to taste, adding the brown sugar if you like a sweeter sauce.

Note: Extra tomato paste can be stored in a plastic container in the freezer. Cut off a chunk of tomato paste as you need it.

Tomato Soup

Tomatoes are unpredictable out of season, so if they're looking pale and unripe, use canned plum tomatoes, which are processed at the peak of the season. Squeeze them to eliminate the seeds.

Serves 4

4 tablespoons butter

6 large tomatoes, peeled, seeded, and chopped, *or* 1 28-ounce can plum tomatoes, seeded

½ cup finely chopped onion

½ cup finely chopped celery

1½ tablespoons honey or brown sugar

1½ tablespoons cider vinegar

1 cinnamon stick

Pinch of ground cloves

4 tablespoons tomato paste

4 cups chicken stock, *or* 3 cups chicken broth and 1 cup water

½ cup heavy cream

Salt and freshly ground pepper to taste

⅓ cup sour cream for topping (optional)

1 tablespoon snipped fresh chives for garnish (optional)

- In a large enamel or stainless-steel pot, melt the butter and add the tomatoes, onion, celery, honey or brown sugar, vinegar, cinnamon stick, and cloves.
- Cover and simmer for 30 minutes.
- Whisk in the tomato paste and add the stock. Simmer for 15 minutes more; remove the cinnamon stick.
- In small batches, purée the soup in a blender, starting on low speed and increasing to high.
- Return the soup to the pot and add the heavy cream, heating until very hot. Season to taste with salt and pepper.
- Serve with a spoonful of sour cream and a sprinkling of snipped chives.

Tuna Fish Sandwich

I make a basic tuna salad, sometimes with a hard-boiled egg added, but always with *solid white* tuna. *Tonno*, Italian tuna, in olive oil is a treat if you can afford the calories. Tuna in water needs to be drained very well or your tuna salad will become watery.

Makes 3 sandwiches

For the salad

1 6½-ounce can solid white tuna, drained well

¾ cup finely chopped celery, or to taste

1 hard-boiled egg, peeled and chopped (optional)

1 tablespoon finely minced onion, green pepper, or pickle relish (optional)

Squeeze of fresh lemon

Freshly ground black pepper

Mayonnaise (see page 174)

6 slices quality bread or toast

Tomato (optional)

Lettuce (optional)

Salt and freshly ground black pepper to taste

▪ Combine all the salad ingredients except the mayonnaise and mix with a fork to break up the tuna. Add enough mayonnaise to bind the salad.

▪ Make the sandwiches by spreading ⅓ of the tuna salad over each of 3 slices of bread or toast to their edges. Add a slice of tomato if you like and season with salt and pepper. Top with lettuce and the remaining slices of bread. Cut in half and serve.

Variation: For tuna melts, toast 3 slices of bread or English muffin halves. Divide the tuna salad between them and sprinkle the tops generously with ¼ cup each grated Swiss, Monterey Jack, or cheddar cheese. Run under the broiler or heat in the microwave until the cheese melts and bubbles.

TURKEY

At Thanksgiving and Christmas time when thoughts turn to turkey, help is only a toll-free call away on the Turkey Hot-line 1-800-323-4848. Even if you're roasting a locally raised turkey, the home economists at Butterball will be happy to answer questions about roasting time, stuffing safety, microwave possibilities, basting, what giblets are, and how to tell when the turkey is done. If you're confused or in doubt, give them a call from 9 A.M. to 9 P.M. (EST) on weekdays, and 9 A.M. to 7 P.M. on weekends during the holidays.

To roast a whole *unstuffed* turkey, fresh or thawed, roast at 350 degrees until a meat thermometer inserted in the thigh reads 185 degrees.

Pounds	Minutes per Pound
6–8	25
8–12	23
12–16	20
16–20	18
20–24	15

For *stuffed* turkeys, roast at 325 degrees and add 5 minutes per pound for roasting time.

Bread Stuffing for the Turkey

Allow ¾ cup stuffing for each pound of turkey.

Makes 6 cups

8 tablespoons salted butter

1 small onion, peeled and finely chopped

½ cup finely chopped celery

8 cups ½-inch cubes of bread, dried out slightly in a warm oven

½ cup chicken or turkey broth

Salt and feshly ground pepper

¼ cup finely chopped parsley

Variations

1 pound cooked sausage meat

½ pound chopped and sautéed mushrooms

1 cup lightly toasted and chopped nuts

2 cups roasted, peeled, and chopped chestnuts

½ cup currants *or* 1 cup chopped dried fruits

1 teaspoon dried herbs (poultry seasoning, sage, or thyme)

1 tablespoon fresh minced herbs (sage, thyme, basil)

- In a large sauté pan, melt the butter and sauté the onion and celery, stirring until very soft but not colored, about 10 minutes.
- Add the bread cubes and toss to coat. Moisten with the chicken broth, season with salt and pepper, and stir in the parsley.
- Stir in any one of the variations. Stuff loosely in the dried cavity of the turkey and cook with the turkey, or transfer the stuffing to a shallow, buttered baking dish and bake in a 350-degree oven until heated through and the top is crusted, about 30 minutes. If the stuffing is made ahead and refrigerated in the baking dish, bake covered with foil for 15 minutes to warm before removing the foil and baking an additional 20 minutes.

Gravy for the Turkey

Giblet gravy is easily made.

Giblets from 1 turkey (skinned turkey neck, gizzard, heart, wing tips—do *not* use the liver)
1 onion, chopped
1 stalk celery, chopped
Sprigs of parsley
1 carrot, chopped

Peppercorns
1 bay leaf
Pinch of salt
4 to 5 tablespoons flour
Pan juices from roasted turkey
Salt and freshly ground pepper

- Cook the giblets in water to cover. Add the onion, celery, parsley, carrots, peppercorns, bay leaf, and pinch of salt. Simmer, partially covered, until the meat is tender, about 1 hour. Strain the stock, remove the meat from the neck, and chop finely with the gizzard and heart meat. Set aside.
- Drain all the fat and juices from the turkey roasting pan into a measuring cup. Let it settle until the fat has risen to the top. With a bulb baster, extract the usable juices at the bottom of the cup and add to the strained stock. Add water if necessary to make 3 cups of liquid. Discard all but 3 tablespoons of the fat.
- Put the 3 tablespoons of fat back into the roasting pan with the flour. Whisk together and cook over low heat for 2 minutes. Whisk in the pan juices and giblet stock. Heat until thickened. Add more water for a thinner consistency. Add the chopped giblets and neck meat and season with salt and pepper.

Turkey Casseroles

Turkey à la King or Turkey Tetrazzini are based on leftover Thanksgiving turkey. At other times of the year, I cook a chicken and transform it into Chicken à la King or Tetrazzini. Turkey casserole is a creamed dish with mushrooms and a few peas for color. When I serve it in a crownlike patty shell or on toast, I call it à la King; when I serve it on pasta (spaghetti or noodles), I call it Tetrazzini.

Serves 6

2 tablespoons butter

½ pound fresh mushrooms, sliced to yield about 3 cups

½ teaspoon salt

1 tablespoon lemon juice

4 cups cut-up cooked turkey or chicken

½ cup frozen petite peas (optional)

For the sauce

3 tablespoons butter

4½ tablespoons flour

2 cups chicken broth or stock

1 cup heavy cream

2 egg yolks

½ teaspoon salt, or to taste

¼ teaspoon paprika

Grating of nutmeg

- In a large heavy skillet, melt the butter and add the mushrooms. Sauté over medium heat, stirring often, until the mushrooms begin to give up their liquid and soften, about 3 minutes. Off the heat, add the salt and lemon juice, which will prevent them from discoloring. Transfer to a bowl, add the turkey, and reserve while you make the sauce.
- To make the sauce, in the same skillet melt the butter and whisk in the flour. Cook over low heat for 1 minute; whisk in the broth slowly. Heat until it just comes to a boil, whisking to keep it smooth.
- In a bowl, mix together the cream and egg yolks. Stir into the sauce and heat until hot, but not boiling. Season with salt, pepper, and nutmeg.
- Add the turkey, mushrooms, and peas. Stir and heat thoroughly.
- To serve, spoon into warmed patty shells or over buttered toast, or serve over buttered spaghetti or noodles.

*T*urkey Casserole Extraordinaire

Serves 10 to 12

8 tablespoons butter
1½ pounds broad egg noodles
Salt and freshly ground black pepper
Turkey Casserole (see page 277)

12 ounces Swiss or Monterey Jack cheese, grated to yield about 4 cups
Creamed spinach (see page 96)
1½ cups fresh bread crumbs

- Butter a large, deep 4-quart baking dish with 1 tablespoon of the butter. Preheat the oven to 375 degrees.
- Cook the noodles in a large pot of boiling salted water until tender. Drain well and toss with 5 tablespoons of the butter and salt and pepper to taste.
- Layer the prepared dish with ⅓ of the noodles, the creamed spinach, and half the cheese. Add another ⅓ of the noodles, the turkey casserole, and the remaining cheese. Spread the remaining noodles over the cheese and top with the bread crumbs. Dot with the remaining 2 tablespoons of butter.
- Cover lightly with foil and bake on the middle rack of the oven for 30 minutes. Remove the foil and continue to bake until lighty browned, about 15 minutes more.

Note: If you assemble this ahead and refrigerate it before baking, bring it to room temperature and bake an additional 15 minutes to heat thoroughly.

*U*pside-Down Cake

These cakes are baked atop sugared fruit and turned upside down for a dramatic presentation. They're best served warm from the oven with a bit of whipped cream.

Serves 10 to 12

6 tablespoons unsalted butter, melted
1 cup light brown sugar

1 20-ounce can pineapple slices in unsweetened juice

For the cake

8 tablespoons unsalted butter, softened
1 cup granulated sugar
2 eggs, at room temperature
Grated zest of 1 orange
2 cups flour

1 teaspoon double-acting baking powder
½ teaspoon baking soda
½ teaspoon salt

continued on next page

For the topping

¾ cup heavy cream
2 tablespoons confectioners' sugar

1 teaspoon Sambucca or anise-flavored liqueur (optional)

- Brush the bottom and sides of a 9-by-13-inch or 11-inch round springform pan with some of the melted butter. Combine the remaining butter and the brown sugar and spread on the bottom of the pan.
- Preheat the oven to 350 degrees.
- Drain the pineapple, reserving ¾ cup of the juice. Halve the slices and arrange them in a decorative pattern on the bottom of the pan. Set aside.
- To make the cake, beat the butter until soft, adding the sugar gradually, and beating until well creamed. Add the eggs, one at a time, and the zest, beating until very light.
- Sift together the flour, baking powder, baking soda, and salt.
- On low speed, alternately beat the dry ingredients and the reserved ¾ cup pineapple juice into the creamed mixture just until thoroughly combined.
- Spread the batter over the fruit carefully so you don't disturb the pattern. If using a springform pan, place on a heavy baking sheet to catch any leaks.
- Bake in the upper half of the oven until the cake is golden and begins to pull away from the sides of the pan, about 45 minutes. Let the cake stand for 5 minutes before running a knife around the edge. Cover with a serving plate and carefully invert the cake. Let the brown sugar glaze drip over the fruit and then remove the pan.
- To make the topping, whip the cream and confectioners' sugar until stiff. Stir in the liqueur.
- Serve the cake while still warm with the topping.

Vanilla Layer Cake

Here's the perfect birthday cake, even if it isn't chocolate! It's a moist, light cake with an easy, fluffy frosting. Use any extra frosting to pipe a bottom border or top edge of rosettes or stars. When making confectioners' sugar frostings to use for pastry bag writing or decorating, be sure to have the butter in the frosting softened and beat until smooth before adding the sugar. Sift the confectioners' sugar so there will be no lumps to plug up the fine tip while you're writing "Happy Birthday."

Serves 8

For the cake

1½ cups flour
¼ cup cornstarch
2½ teaspoons double-acting baking
   powder
½ teaspoon salt
½ cup vegetable oil

1 cup sugar
1 egg plus 3 egg yolks, at room temperature
2 teaspoons vanilla extract
½ cup milk, at room temperature

continued on next page

Vanilla Layer Cake (*cont.*)

For the frosting

4 tablespoons unsalted butter, softened

¼ cup solid vegetable shortening

2 cups confectioners' sugar, sifted

3 tablespoons unsweetened cocoa (optional, for a chocolate frosting)

½ teaspoon vanilla extract

Pinch of salt

1 egg white

1 tablespoon warm water if needed to thin the frosting

282

- Preheat the oven to 350 degrees. Thoroughly grease two 8-inch cake pans with shortening and lightly flour the bottoms. Turn the pans over and knock out any excess flour.

- To make the cake, sift together the flour, cornstarch, baking powder, and salt. Set aside.

- In a mixing bowl, beat the oil and sugar together. Beat in the egg and egg yolks, one at a time, until very light, scraping the bowl a few times, about 5 minutes. Beat in the vanilla.

- On low speed, alternately mix the dry ingredients and the milk into the sugar-egg mixture just until thoroughly combined. Divide the batter between the prepared pans. Push the batter up on the sides to help it rise evenly.

- Bake the cakes in the upper half of the oven until the cakes are lightly colored and begin to pull away from the sides of the pan, about 30 minutes. The middle should be springy. Cool 10 minutes before turning out onto a wire rack to cool completely. Cover loosely with a towel to prevent the cakes from drying out.

- To make the frosting, cream the butter and shortening until light.

- Add the confectioners' sugar, cocoa, vanilla, and salt. Mix on low speed until combined.

- Add the egg white and mix on medium speed until light and fluffy, scraping the bottom of the bowl occasionally, about 5 minutes. Thin with water if needed until the frosting is the consistency of mayonnaise.

- Frost the top of one layer with ¼ of the frosting; place the second layer over it and spread the sides and top of the cake with as much of the remaining frosting as is needed. Use any extra frosting to make a decorative top border with a pastry bag. Any extra frosting can be frozen in a small plastic container for another use.

Vanilla Pudding

Vanilla pudding is like a pastry cream—stirred custard with a starch as well as an egg thickener. The cornstarch or flour prevents the eggs from curdling, even when the mixture comes to a boil. It's important to heat the pudding slowly over low heat and to whisk often to prevent lumps from forming.

In substituting cornstarch for flour or flour for cornstarch in puddings, sauces, or pie fillings, remember that cornstarch has twice the thickening power of flour. In this recipe, you could substitute 6 tablespoons flour for the 3 tablespoons cornstarch.

Serves 6

3 egg yolks
½ cup sugar
3 tablespoons cornstarch
Pinch of salt
3 cups milk, at room temperature

3 tablespoons unsalted butter
1½ teaspoons vanilla extract
Sweetened fresh berries, sliced bananas, or chocolate chips for the top (optional)

• In a heavy saucepan, whisk the egg yolks and add the sugar, cornstarch, and salt. Whisk in the milk slowly, mixing until smooth. Over low heat, cook until thickened and the center tries to bubble, about 10 minutes. Whisk constantly as it thickens to prevent any lumps.

• Off the heat, stir in the butter and vanilla. Cool, stirring occasionally to let the steam escape and to prevent a skin from forming on the top. Pour into 6 dessert cups, cover well, and refrigerate.

• At serving time, top with fresh berries, bananas, or a few chocolate chips.

Variations: For *chocolate* pudding, stir 3 ounces of melted semisweet chocolate into the warm pudding. For *butterscotch* pudding, substitute ¾ cup brown sugar for the granulated sugar.

VEGETABLE SALADS

There are two vegetable salads I wouldn't do without: Julienned Vegetables Vinaigrette and a Russian vegetable and rice salad (my mother-in-law calls it Gvetch), which can be served hot or cold.

Julienned Vegetables Vinaigrette

This salad has everything: ease, color, nutrition, and drama. The vegetables can be cut, blanched, and refrigerated ahead of time. The sauce, a vinaigrette, can be made far ahead and tossed over the vegetables at the last minute. Find a pretty platter and arrange the vegetables by color or toss them all together.

Ice water will keep raw julienned vegetables crisp during storage. Consider blanching such vegetables as green beans, broccoli, carrots, cauliflower, and celery root. Blanching assures that the vegetables will retain their color. Green beans, pea pods, and broccoli turn an even brighter green if blanched. Blanching simply means dunking the vegetables (one kind at a time) in boiling water, returning the water to a boil, cooking briefly, draining, and plunging the vegetables into ice water to stop the cooking. When cooled, drain and dry on towels.

Toss the vegetables with the vinaigrette at the last minute if you want to retain the beautiful green of the vegetables. Any acid (lemon, vinegar, or wine) will turn their bright green to a dull khaki color. A last-minute sprinkling of minced parsley will make the salad bright and appealing.

Use your favorite vegetables of the season:
▪ *Peppers* need not be blanched.

- Blanch *pea pods, carrots, green beans, broccoli,* and *celery root.* Remove the strings from the pea pods, stack a few together, and julienne them. Carrots can be thinly sliced on a diagonal, a few stacked together, and julienned.
- Green beans should be small and straight with their strings removed. Broccoli should be in bite-size florets.
- Raw *jicama* and *daikon* are nice additions when peeled and julienned.
- *Cherry tomatoes* make a colorful garnish.
- To make the dressing, add an extra spoonful of mustard to the Vinaigrette (see page 288). At serving time, toss the vinaigrette with the vegetables, arrange them on a platter, and give the salad a sprinkling of salt, a good grinding of freshly ground pepper, and a sprinkling of minced parsley.

*R*ussian Vegetable Salad

Serves 10 to 12

1 onion, sliced

3 to 4 stalks celery, sliced

1 small green cabbage, cut in wedges

2 or 3 tomatoes, peeled, seeded, and chopped

1 small eggplant, cut in ½-inch cubes

2 red, yellow, or green peppers, cored and seeded and cut in 1-inch pieces

1 small zucchini or yellow squash, sliced

3 carrots, peeled and sliced

1 cup raw long-grain rice

1 cup Tomato Sauce (see page 271)

¾ cup vegetable oil

1 cup water

½ cup frozen petite peas

Salt and freshly ground pepper to taste

¼ teaspoon crushed red pepper (optional)

- Preheat the oven to 300 degrees.
- In a large roasting pan, combine the vegetables, rice, tomato sauce, oil, and water. Cover well with foil and bake, tossing the vegetables 2 or 3 times, until the rice is tender and the liquid has been absorbed, about 2 to 2½ hours. Stir in the peas and season with salt and pepper.
- Serve warm or at room temperature with crushed pepper on the side. Store covered in the refrigerator.

VEGETABLE SOUPS

Here are two delicious vegetable soups from my "tried and true" file: a hot and hearty vegetable soup similar to minestrone and a cold blender soup perfect for summer.

Hot and Hearty Vegetable Soup

My aunt, Margie Kohn, uses the Thanksgiving turkey carcass to make this soup. But I like this soup all winter long, not just after Thanksgiving. Instead of using water, chicken or beef broth will give the soup a good flavor if you don't have a turkey (or chicken) carcass. Garbanzo beans and sliced zucchini can be added. I enrich the soup with the hard ungratable ends of Parmesan cheese that have been put aside in my refrigerator. They add great flavor to the soup and are the "prizes" in their softened and chewy state. The multitude of colorful vegetables make this soup irresistible.

Serves 6 to 8

2 tablespoons vegetable oil
1 small onion, finely chopped
¾ cup chopped celery
½ cup chopped green pepper
1 clove garlic, minced
1 cup shredded green cabbage
1 small zucchini, thinly sliced
1 28-ounce can peeled tomatoes
6 cups chicken broth
2 cups water

Hard ends of Parmesan cheese, cut up
  (optional)
1 potato, peeled and diced
½ cup elbow macaroni
¼ pound fresh spinach, chopped
1 18-ounce can of garbanzo beans,
  drained
Salt, freshly ground black pepper, and
  oregano to taste
Freshly grated Parmesan cheese

■ In a large heavy pot, heat the oil and add the onion, celery, pepper, and garlic. Sauté, stirring often, until the vegetables are soft but not colored, about 5 minutes.

■ Add the cabbage, zucchini, tomatoes, broth, water, and Parmesan cheese ends. Bring to a boil. Simmer, covered, for 15 minutes.

■ Stir, add the potato and macaroni, and simmer for 15 minutes more.

■ Add the spinach and garbanzo beans. Simmer 2 more minutes to cook the spinach and heat the beans. Season with salt, pepper, and oregano. Heat and serve, topped with grated Parmesan cheese. If the soup is thicker than you like, add a little more water.

$\mathcal{C}$old Blender Vegetable Soup

The blender makes this a fast soup for summer when the temperature discourages cooking of any kind. Vary the vegetables to suit your taste.

Serves 4

2 cups chicken broth
½ English cucumber, cut in chunks
1½ cups packed fresh spinach leaves
1 scallion, white and green parts
2 tablespoons snipped fresh dill
A handful of fresh parsley leaves

1½ cups buttermilk
½ cup Mayonnaise (see page 174)
1 tablespoon white wine vinegar
½ teaspoon sugar
Salt and freshly ground pepper to taste

- Add the broth, vegetables, and herbs to the blender. Starting on low, blend the vegetables, increasing the speed until puréed. Pour into a bowl.
- Whisk the buttermilk, mayonnaise, vinegar, and sugar together. Add to the vegetable purée and mix until smooth. Cover and refrigerate a few hours. Season to taste with salt and pepper.
- Serve cold, topped with a sprig of fresh dill.

$\mathcal{V}$inaigrette

There is nothing better or simpler to make than a vinaigrette dressing for a simple green salad. The number and popularity of overly salted and artificially flavored bottled salad dressings mystify me. Make a double batch of vinaigrette in a bowl or processor, pour it into a jar, and keep it in the refrigerator for weeks. The mustard holds the oil and vinegar together to form a thickened emulsified dressing. Fresh herbs and spices or varieties of vinegar flavors and types of oil make this a versatile dressing. The proportions are always the same. For a creamier vinaigrette, add a few tablespoons of mayonnaise or sour cream. Give it a dash of Worcestershire sauce, or subtly flavor the vinaigrette with a clove of garlic while it's stored in the refrigerator.

Makes 1 cup

¼ cup vinegar
1 tablespoon Dijon mustard
¾ teaspoon salt
Freshly ground pepper
1 to 2 tablespoons Mayonnaise (see page 174) or sour cream (optional)

⅔ cup oil
1 clove garlic, peeled and skewered with a toothpick (optional)
1 to 2 tablespoons fresh minced herbs (optional)

- In a deep bowl or food processor, combine the vinegar, mustard, salt, pepper, and the mayonnaise. Whisk or process to combine.
- Add the oil very slowly, whisking constantly; or pour it through the feed tube with the motor running. The vinaigrette should be thick and emulsified. Store in a glass jar in the refrigerator, with the garlic. Stir in the minced herbs and remove the garlic just before using.

WAFFLES

The obvious difference between pancakes and waffles is that one is cooked on a hot griddle and the other in a hot waffle iron. Waffles are crisper because the fat content in the batter is higher. The rich batter and a *hot* waffle iron make greasing the iron between waffles rarely necessary.

If you can't find your mother's old, seasoned-with-love waffle iron, check a good cookware store for one that's made of heavy cast iron or aluminum.

If there are any extra waffles, cool them on a wire rack and freeze them in a plastic bag; they can be heated quickly in the toaster for early school breakfasts.

Crispy Waffles

Makes twelve 6-inch waffles

1 cup flour
1 cup quick or old-fashioned rolled oats
¼ cup yellow cornmeal
¼ cup unprocessed wheat or oat bran
2 tablespoons sugar
1 tablespoon double-acting baking powder

1 teaspoon baking soda
½ teaspoon salt
2 eggs, at room temperature
8 tablespoons unsalted butter, melted
3 cups buttermilk
Maple syrup

continued on next page

- In a bowl, combine the flour, oats, cornmeal, bran, sugar, baking powder, baking soda, and salt.
- In another bowl, whisk together the eggs, butter, and buttermilk.
- Mix the wet and dry ingredients together with a quick but gentle stirring.
- Heat the waffle iron and use about ½ cup of the batter for each waffle. Cook to a golden crispness. The waffle iron should stop steaming from the sides when the waffles are ready. Let the iron get hot again before adding more batter.
- Serve with maple syrup.

292

$\int$our Cream Waffles

Makes six 6-inch waffles

1 cup flour	½ teaspoon salt
2 tablespoons sugar	3 eggs, separated
1½ teaspoons double-acting baking powder	2 cups sour cream
1 teaspoon baking soda	Maple syrup

- Sift the flour, sugar, baking powder, baking soda, and salt.
- In another bowl, beat the egg yolks and sour cream together.
- Combine the dry ingredients with the egg yolk–sour cream mixture with a quick but gentle stirring.
- Beat the egg whites until stiff and still glossy. Fold thoroughly into the batter. Use the batter immediately.
- Heat the waffle iron and use about ½ cup batter for each waffle. Cook until crisp and golden, and the iron stops steaming from the sides. Be sure to let the iron get hot again before adding more batter.
- Serve hot with maple syrup.

Waldorf Salad

Serves 4 to 6

3 firm, tart apples (Cortlands stay white the longest), cored and cut into ¼- to ½-inch cubes

1 cup finely chopped celery

½ cup chopped walnuts

⅓ cup Mayonnaise (see page 174)

⅓ cup sour cream

1 tablespoon sugar

½ teaspoon dry mustard

Pinch of cayenne pepper

1 tablespoon minced crystallized ginger, or 1 teaspoon horseradish (optional)

▪ Combine the apples, celery, and walnuts. Mix together the mayonnaise, sour cream, sugar, mustard, cayenne pepper, and ginger. Pour the dressing over the apple mixture and stir to combine thoroughly. Cover and refrigerate.

W
∼∼∼
293

Wedding Cake Sandwich

My children think this glorified sandwich is very elegant fare for special-occasion lunches and birthday parties. When it's iced with a cream cheese frosting and decorated with a pastry bag tip, this loaf of bread, sliced horizontally in thin layers and filled with things as mundane as tuna or chicken salad, or as strange (to children) as smoked salmon slices and egg salad with capers, it is transformed into a spectacular Wedding Cake Sandwich.

Serves 6 to 8

1 1-pound unsliced loaf of quality bread

2 tablespoons unsalted butter, very soft

continued on next page

For the fillings

Egg, tuna, seafood, or chicken salads (the amount will vary depending on the number of layers and thickness you want). The fillings should not be watery or they will make the bread soggy.

Watercress or thinly sliced cucumbers, salted, drained, and dried.

For the cream cheese frosting (for a 1-pound loaf)

2 8-ounce packages cream cheese, softened

4 tablespoons unsalted butter, softened

½ cup milk

Chopped nuts or small capers for decoration

Cherry tomatoes and watercress for garnish (optional)

294

- Trim the crusts of the bread to make a level-sided square look. Cut the bread into 3 or 4 horizontal slices, depending on the number of layers and fillings you want. "Waterproof" the layers with a *thin* skimming of butter.
- Spread a different filling between each of the two or three layers of bread, ending with a layer of bread. Press the top down gently to level the "cake" and push in any fillings around the edges. Arrange on a foil-covered piece of cardboard the size of the bread layers.
- To make the frosting, beat the cream cheese and butter together until soft and fluffy. Add the liquid gradually until it reaches the consistency of mayonnaise.
- Frost the top and sides of the cake. Transfer the remaining frosting to a pastry bag with a ¼- or ⅓-inch decorative tip.
- Decorate the cake with the frosting, piping a border along the top edges or making a chevron, crisscross, or diagonal design on the top. Decorate with nuts. Refrigerate from 30 minutes to a few hours.
- Remove the "cake" from the refrigerator about 20 minutes before serving to soften the frosting. Garnish with tomatoes and watercress.

Note: For a large group, call a local bakery and specially order a pullman loaf of bread, which is more uniform in shape, longer than most loaves, and weights 1½ to 2 pounds. You may even be able to order it in whole wheat or rye if that's your preference. Make a double recipe of cream cheese frosting.

Wheat Pilaf

Wheat pilaf is our crunchy, nutritious side dish favorite that works with chicken, meat, or fish. Aunt Margie's recipe card is faded but no longer necessary since I memorized the ingredients, amounts, and technique long ago.

Serves 4 to 6

5 tablespoons butter

½ cup thin spaghetti, broken in ½-inch pieces

1 cup medium-cut bulgur (cracked wheat)

3 tablespoons finely chopped onion

2 cups boiling chicken broth or water

Salt and freshly ground black pepper to taste

- Melt the butter in a heavy saucepan. Add the spaghetti and sauté 2 minutes until it changes color and looks opaque. Add the bulgur and onion and sauté 3 more minutes, stirring often, until the onion is soft and the pasta is golden.
- Pour the boiling broth over the bulgur mixture and stir well. Reduce the heat to low and simmer 15 to 20 minutes until the liquid has been absorbed and the wheat is tender. Fluff with a fork and season to taste with salt and pepper.

Note: To make this a one-dish meal, add 1 tablespoon finely minced peeled fresh gingerroot and 2 tablespoons sesame seeds with the onion. When the liquid has nearly been absorbed, add 2 cups cooked chicken. Continue to simmer until the bulgur is cooked and the chicken is heated through. Sprinkle the top with ¼ cup thin diagonally sliced scallions.

White Bread with Cracked Wheat

Yeast bread is always fun to make with children, who never seem to tire of kneading the elastic dough. It's better than playdough since it gives you a delicious loaf of bread to eat at the end—and the aroma of baking bread that fills the house is nearly as good as the taste.

I love this moist white all-purpose bread with bulgur wheat added to provide crunch, flavor, and extra nutrition. It's as good toasted for breakfast or for sandwiches as it is warm from the oven. I'm grateful to Brinna and Frank Sands for their "good" King Arthur Flour, available in the New England area.

Makes 2 loaves

½ cup fine-cut bulgur (cracked wheat)
½ cup boiling water
Pinch of sugar
2 cups warm water
1 ¼-ounce envelope (1 scant table-spoon) active dry yeast

5 to 5½ cups all-purpose unbleached white flour
3 tablespoons brown sugar
1 tablespoon salt
½ cup nonfat dry milk powder
5 tablespoons oil

- Measure the bulgur into a small bowl. Pour the boiling water over it and cover it with a plate until cool and the water has been absorbed.
- Mix the pinch of sugar and ½ cup of the warm water. Sprinkle the yeast over the water. Let the yeast proof until bubbly, about 10 minutes, to be sure it's active.
- In another bowl, combine 3 cups of the flour, the brown sugar, salt, and dry milk powder. Add the remaining warm water, 3 tablespoons of the oil, and the proofed yeast. Combine and beat on medium speed or stir vigorously by hand for 2 minutes. Add the bulgur and 1 cup more of flour and beat for 1 minute.
- Turn the dough out onto a floured surface and gradually add more flour as you knead the dough until smooth and elastic and no longer sticky.
- Add 1 tablespoon of the oil to a clean bowl and add the dough, turning the dough to thoroughly coat the entire surface. Drape a clean dish towel over the bowl and put it in a warm place to rise until doubled in bulk, about 1 hour.

- Thoroughly grease 2 4½-by-8½-inch or 5-by-9-inch loaf pans with the remaining oil.
- Punch the dough down when it has doubled, divide it in half, and form each half into a loaf by rolling it out to a 9-by-15-inch rectangle. Roll it up tightly from the short side, pushing in the ends to fit the pans and placing each loaf, seam side down, in a prepared loaf pan. Make 3 slash marks across the top of each loaf with a sharp knife. Cover loosely with the towel and let the dough rise in a warm place until it reaches the top of the pans and has nearly doubled in bulk, about 30 minutes.
- Preheat the oven to 375 degrees.
- Bake the loaves on the middle rack of the oven until nicely browned and, when you turn the loaves out of the pans and tap the bottom, the bread sounds hollow, about 40 to 45 minutes. Turn the loaves out onto a wire rack to cool.
- When completely cool, wrap well in a plastic bag if you plan to save the bread for another time. Slicing the bread is made simple with a good serrated bread knife.

$\mathcal{Y}$OGURT DRESSINGS

Yogurt dressings, savory *or* sweet, make fast and easy summer toppings for greens or fruit salads. Put them in pitchers for a buffet salad.

Makes 1½ cups

$\mathcal{H}$erbed Yogurt Dressing

8 ounces plain yogurt
½ cup Mayonnaise (see page 174)
¼ cup finely minced fresh herbs

Fresh lime or lemon juice to thin to
desired consistency

Sweet Yogurt Dressing

8 ounces fruit yogurt
3 ounces cream cheese, softened

Fruit juice to thin to desired consistency

- Process or whisk all ingredients except juice together. Thin with juice to the desired consistency.

Yorkshire Pudding

When treating your family to roast beef, make Yorkshire pudding, the traditional accompaniment that puffs magically in the roasting pan while the meat rests before carving. Use the drippings from the beef or grease the pan well and heat it before pouring in the batter.

The principle is the same as for popovers that depend on high initial heat to create steam that makes the batter rise. The ingredients must be at room temperature before whisking together.

Serves 6

Beef drippings *or* 4 tablespoons butter
1 cup flour
½ teaspoon salt

½ cup milk, at room temperature
2 eggs, at room temperature
½ cup water

- Preheat the oven to 450 degrees. Leave a generous layer of beef fat in the 7-by-11-inch or 8-by-12-inch roasting pan, or add the butter to the same size ovenproof dish.
- Sift the flour and salt into a deep bowl.
- Add the milk and eggs to the flour and whisk together. Add the water and whisk until smooth. You can do this ahead and refrigerate the batter, covered, for 1 hour before continuing.
- Put the roasting pan or ovenproof dish in the oven for a few minutes to heat the fat or butter.
- Stir the batter and pour it into the hot pan. Bake 15 minutes. Resist the temptation to open the oven door.
- Reduce the temperature to 350 degrees and continue to bake until puffed and well browned, about 15 to 20 minutes more.
- Cut in squares and serve from the pan while hot.

Zucchini-Nut Bread

When the garden produces a too-long-forgotten 4-pound zucchini monster that no one wants to eat, I remove the seeds and grate it for zucchini breads for family and gifts and freezer.

Makes 2 loaves

2¾ cups flour
1 tablespoon cinnamon
1 teaspoon baking soda
1 teaspoon double-acting baking
   powder
½ teaspoon salt
¼ teaspoon grated nutmeg
3 eggs, at room temperature

1¾ cups sugar
1 teaspoon vanilla extract
½ cup vegetable oil
8 tablespoons unsalted butter, melted
2 cups grated zucchini
1 cup walnuts, coarsely chopped (optional)

• Thoroughly grease two 4½-by-12-inch loaf pans with shortening and lightly flour the bottom.

continued on next page

- Preheat the oven to 350 degrees.
- Sift together the flour, cinnamon, baking soda, baking powder, salt, and nutmeg.
- In a mixing bowl, beat the eggs and add the sugar gradually, mixing on medium speed until light, about 5 minutes. Add the vanilla. Combine the oil and butter and add to the egg mixture, mixing just until combined.
- Alternately add the dry ingredients and the zucchini to the creamed mixture until thoroughly combined. Stir in the nuts. Transfer to the prepared pans.
- Bake on the middle rack of the oven until a toothpick in the center comes out clean, about 1 hour. The bread will rise and then settle back into the pan. Remove the pan from the oven and place on a wire rack to cool for 15 minutes before running a knife around the edge of the bread and turning it out of the pan. Cool completely. Wrap well in foil and let the bread rest overnight to make slicing easier.

Zucchini Custard

When making this recipe, remember the custard rule about heat—neither too high nor too long—and use a water bath. Remove the custard when the *edges* are cooked and a knife inserted 2 inches from the sides comes out clean. The center will continue to cook as it cools.

Serves 6 to 8

4 to 5 medium zucchini (2 pounds), grated to make about 5 cups

1 teaspoon salt

4 tablespoons butter

1 small onion, finely chopped

1 clove garlic, peeled and minced

¼ teaspoon freshly ground black pepper

Oregano, basil, thyme, *or* cumin to taste (optional)

2 tablespoons flour

1½ cups light cream

3 eggs, lightly beaten

Salt to taste

1 cup grated Longhorn cheddar or Monterey Jack cheese (optional)

- Butter a shallow 8-inch casserole or 1½-quart baking dish.
- Grate the zucchini and toss it with the salt. Place it in a colander and let it drain for 30 minutes. Squeeze out the excess liquid.
- Preheat the oven to 350 degrees.
- Melt the butter in a large sauté pan. Sauté the onion, stirring, until soft. Add the garlic and sauté, stirring to prevent it from coloring, for a few minutes more. Add the drained zucchini and sauté until crisp-tender, stirring to prevent it from sticking. Add the pepper, seasoning, and the flour. Stir to mix well and sauté for 1 minute more.
- Cool for 5 minutes; then stir in the cream and then the eggs. Season to taste with salt and pepper.
- Spoon the mixture into the prepared dish and place it in a roasting pan or larger dish. To make the water bath for slow, even baking, pour enough hot water in the roasting pan to come halfway up the sides of the casserole. Place the pan carefully on the middle rack of the oven.
- Bake until a knife inserted 2 inches from the edge comes out clean, about 25 to 30 minutes (depending on the size of the baking dish). Remove the pan from the oven and sprinkle with the grated cheese. Let the custard settle for 10 minutes before serving.

Index

310

316